The Five Sons Of King Pandu

The Five Sons Of King Pandu

The Story of the Mahabhárata

Adapted from the English Translation of
Kisari Mohan Ganguli
by

Elizabeth Seeger

With illustrations by Gordon Laite
William R. Scott, Inc.
New York

398
Se

PRODUCTION NOTES: *Composition by The Book Press, Brattleboro, Vermont and The Composing Room, New York; paper supplied by Olympic Paper Corp.; printing by Rae Publishing Co.; binding by The Book Press.*

TO THE MEMORY OF MY FRIENDS

Dhan Gopal & Ethel Dugan Mukerji

Table of Contents

Author's Introduction

The great epic stories of the world are few and their number will probably not increase—unless, for our sins, a new flood washes mankind from the face of the planet, leaving only another Noah or a Manu to start the long course of civilization over again.

For the great epics came out of the dawn of the world, when everything was new: before man wrote or read, when intuition and experience were the only sources of his knowledge; when, amazed and stirred by the cosmic drama in the midst of which he found himself, he tried to find his part in it, his relation to the earth and its creatures, to the heavenly bodies and to his fellow men. He searched his memory to find a cause and a beginning and cast his vision far ahead to seek a purpose and an end. His findings were infinitely important to him and to all who have come after him. In order to record them, he put them into stories that caught the rhythm of the turning earth. There is no better way to remember and to make others remember than to make a story and to put it into rhythmic speech.

Because the epics were composed before writing was known or before it was widely used in the country of their origin, they were not individual works but collective; for they were told by teacher to disciple, by parent to child, by storyteller to storyteller, each generation, each unusual person adding something until the story grew, like a Gothic cathedral, including many centuries in its final form. And, like a Gothic cathedral, it gathered in its growth the history, the beliefs and customs, the economy and the arts of the times it passed through, and preserved them for us. Only a great framework can hold all these things together and keep its own shape through so much handling; the epic, therefore, is always a magnificent story.

For these and other reasons, it seems unlikely that further tales of this magnitude will be produced, and for these reasons the ones we have are particularly precious. There are none greater or more precious than the two epics of India, the *Mahabhárata* and the *Ramáyana*.

The *Mahabhárata* in its entirety is the longest of all scriptures and of all poems; for it is three times as long as the Bible and eight times as long as the *Iliad* and the *Odyssey* put together. For two or three thousand years the story that forms its nucleus has been the vehicle for the moral philosophy and for the highest spiritual teaching of Hinduism; it has acquired not only enormous elaboration in the telling, but also enormous digressions amounting to whole volumes that are purely philosophical and only tenuously connected with the original narrative. It has become the very encyclopedia of Hinduism: "The storehouse," as one scholar says, "of Indian genealogy, mythology, and antiquity."

Since history, as understood in the West, has not been congenial to the Hindu mind, it seems impossible to find out, even approximately, the time when the events of this poem may have taken place. Some Hindu scholars say 3000 B.C. and others about 1500 B.C.; Western scholars, after exhaustive research, say any time between 1700 B.C. and 700 B.C. There is no mention of the great battle in the vague historical records, although the Bháratas were known in very early times as powerful rulers of northwestern India who, indeed, gave it its early name— Bhárata-varsha. There seems to be no doubt, however, that the story is based on actual events, though they were not of the colossal proportions claimed by the poem. For one of the quaint results of its long growth is the contrast between the claim of the Bhárata kings to be "lords of the whole earth with its belt of seas" and a certain incident which proves them to be no more than tribal chieftains who raid each other's borders to steal cattle.

The poem, on the other hand, has its place in history. Professor Edward Washburn Hopkins in his book, *The Great Epic of India,* states that lays, or song cycles, about the Bháratas were current by 400 B.C., that this story, with its familiar characters, was known between 400 and 200 B.C., and that the book had attained its present form and length at some time between 200 and 400 A.D. By that time it was written in Sanskrit and was available to priests and scholars.

During those centuries and afterward, the story, its incidents and characters, became known to everyone in India and in those countries colonized or influenced by India: Ceylon, Southeast Asia, and the Indies. It was and is now told in the homes, chanted in the temples, recited under the village trees; it was carved on the walls of Angkor and in the temples of Java; it was and is now shown in the shadow plays of Burma, Siam, and the Indies, played also by living actors and danced in exquisite ceremonial dances. Indeed, it is so well known in the Indies that the Javanese began their history with these legends, believing them to be their own tradition.

The great arts of India, Indonesia, and Southeast Asia are as hard to understand, if one is ignorant of the two Hindu epics, as the arts of Europe would be if one did not know the Greek myths and the Bible. Kunti and Dráupadi are of the stature of Penelope, Antigone, and Alcestis, but one knows them better because the Indian legends are much longer and more detailed than the Greek; Bhishma and Vídura, Yudhistra and his brothers stand beside David and Solomon, Odysseus and Achilles, Arthur and Roland and Galahad. Is it not time for us to become as familiar with these great figures of Indian tradition as we are with those of our own? Is not the Aryan heritage ours also? And is it not well to know the sources of the culture of a great people who will become increasingly important in the world?

The Indian epics do not belong so much to the past as ours do, for they are alive and active in the life of India today. The grandmother or the mother tells them to the children; bands of actors and of minstrels travel about presenting them in town and village, where amateurs, too, love to enact them; priests recite the sonorous Sanskrit verses while interpreters translate them for the listeners; scholars and poets rhapsodize on solemn and festive occasions, taking one incident and improvising upon it, after the manner of the Greek rhapsodes. The Pándavas, Kunti, and Dráupadi are great examples of noble and virtuous behavior, held up to children and adults; their misfortunes still draw tears from the listener or spectator and their victory brings an ever-returning joy.

I seem to have forgotten that it is not the mighty *Mahabhárata* that I am introducing, but my own humble version of its story. Yet this volume has its place in the great tradition, for the noble tale has been in the hands of every sort of storyteller; many versions and condensations of it have been made in all the vernaculars of India and the many shorter stories included in it—those of Sakuntala, Nala and Damayanti, Savitri, for example—have been told and retold in India and abroad. That great spiritual poem, the Bhagavad Gita, which is contained in the *Mahabhárata* and yet is complete in itself, is known to all the world.

The whole of the text has been translated from the Sanskrit into several of the modern languages of India, such as Bengali, Hindi, Tamil, and Canarese, and other editions are in progress. Two complete translations into English have been made by Hindus: one—which I have used, since I am ignorant of Sanskrit—by Kisari Mohan Ganguli, published in ten volumes by Pratap Chandra Roy, from 1883–1893; and another by M. N. Dutt, published in eighteen volumes from 1895–1904; the labor of translation and publication covering, in both instances, ten years. To my knowledge, only one complete translation has been made in the West: a translation into French, made by Hippolyte Fauche in 1863. There is great need of a readable and condensed version of it by someone who is master of both Sanskrit and English and who can do justice to the beauty and nobility of the subject. It seems to me that until this is done, any version, which might make this living legend more familiar to us, is justified.

When I first read the edition so devotedly published by Pratap Chandra Roy, I was amazed and delighted to find that the story, which I was primarily seeking, ran through the vast accumulation of digression, repetition, and accretion as a clear brook might run through marsh, meadow, and forest, never losing its direction and falling at last into a great river. It never loses its logic or its continuity; after disappearing from view for two or three hundred or even more than a thousand pages, it emerges in all its purity, rises to a mighty climax, and comes to a beautiful ending.

In the same way, the characters are completely consistent throughout. They are so clearly drawn, so human, admirable, and lovable that one feels that they must either have been real people whose powerful personalities have come down to us unchanged, or that the original dramatis personae were recreated by so great a poet that no other dared to alter his conception of them. For they, like the narrative but unlike the chaotic whole, emerge pure and convincing after millenia of handling.

It is this story and these characters that I have wished to bring to the knowledge of Western readers, together with the moral philosophy of India on which the epic is built and which the characters exemplify. Following the thread of narrative through the labyrinth of text, I have chosen those incidents which seem to me essential to the story or to the understanding of one or another of the characters. This has been my only purpose in selecting, perhaps, one incident from a hundred incidents, one conversation from fifty conversations, one significant paragraph from innumerable ones. Much that is very beautiful has had to be left out so that this book might not be too long. My hope is that other people may find the same delight in it that I have found.

I believe that children are particularly attuned to epic stories, which came out of the youth of the world, and I believe that the best education for them is to relive the world's life through its folk and fairy tales and its heroic legends. Therefore, this book has been written with the utmost simplicity, so that children may enjoy it; and, for the same reason, I have avoided all unnecessary complication, knowing that the setting and circumstances and the names are already alien and may present obstacles to the reader.

The names, perhaps, present the greatest difficulty. There are many characters in this complicated tale and they must be given their names, which are not only unfamiliar but often long, with the stress in an unexpected place. The blind king who is such an important personage is called Dhritarashtra. To avoid such a long and difficult word, I have given him his family name of Kuru, which also makes clearer the constant differentiation between his sons, the Kúravas (or Kauravas), and the Pándavas, the sons of Pandu. So also the name Dhrishtajumna, which means Clear Light, has been shortened to Jumna, Light. I have been told, on excellent authority, that the contraction of Yudhishthira to Yudhistra, of Sahadeva to Sadeva, of Duryodhana to Duryodha, is allowable. The stressed syllable in such names as Dráupadi, Shákuni, Pándava, is indicated by an accent so that the stress may not be placed, as is usual in the West, on the penultimate. All unnecessary names have been omitted, even that of Drupada, king of Panchala, in order not to confuse it with Dráupadi, his daughter's name, which is derived from his. Since these changes have been made for the sake of ease and pleasure in reading, I hope that scholars, in the East or in the West, will not be offended by them.

Because my purpose has been simply to tell the story, religious doctrines that are not relevant to it have been omitted. From the Bhagavad Gita only those verses that give the necessary answer of Krishna to

Arjuna have been included, for there is no place in a condensed narrative for that great poem. The part of Krishna himself, which is believed to be a later accretion, is also not given the supreme importance that it has in India. Krishna appears as the wise and powerful friend and cousin of the Pándavas, not as an incarnation of God, as that idea might be more confusing than clarifying. The miracles attributed to him have been omitted: in the famous incident of the unclothing of Dráupadi, although she called upon Krishna, it was Dharma, God of Righteousness, who clothed her in miraculous garments; I have simplified this situation by making her call upon Dharma.

Much has been omitted, but I have not been so presumptuous as to add anything of my own, excepting one small paragraph, in the first chapter, to explain the Kshatria code of honor. This is implicit in the whole book and is well known to Indians, but it is not known to Western readers, and several important episodes might be puzzling to them if it were not made clear. It was necessary to rearrange the beginning of the story, for in the text there are three beginnings, one of which starts with the creation of the world; but I have rearranged only what is told in various parts of the book and have not added or invented anything. My part has been to select, to reduce ten large volumes to one small one, to connect intelligibly the selected episodes and to change the rather formal, stiff, and complicated style of the translator into what I hope is clear and simple English. If, in so doing, I shall have increased, in any degree, the fame of the sons of Pandu, I shall be well pleased.

ELIZABETH SEEGER
Bridgewater, Conn.
January, 1967

Characters in the Story

The five principal characters in the book are always called the Pándavas or the sons of Pandu, but, as the story reveals, Yudhistra is the son of the God of Righteousness; Bhima is the son of the Wind-God; Arjuna is the son of the God of Heaven; Nákula and Sadeva are the sons of the twin Gods of Dawn and Twilight. Legally they are Pandu's sons, by his two wives, Kunti and Madri.

Abimanyu: Son of Arjuna and Subadra

Agni: God of Fire

Arjuna: Third son of Kunti

Ashvattama: Son of Drona

Bhima: Second son of Kunti

Bhishma: Uncle of Kuru, Pandu, and Vídura

Dharma: God of Righteousness or Justice

Dráupadi: Daughter of the King of Panchala, wife of the five Pándavas

Drona: Teacher of the Pándavas and the Kúravas

Duryodha: Eldest son of Kuru and Gandhari

Dushasa: Second son of Kuru and Gandhari

Gandhari: Wife of Kuru, mother of the Kúravas, sister of Shakuni, King of Gandhara

Indra: God of Heaven

Jumna: Son of the King of Panchala, brother of Dráupadi and of Shikandin

Karna: Son of Kunti before her marriage to Pandu

Kíchaka: Commander of Virata's army

Krishna: Nephew of Kunti, cousin of the Pándavas

Kunti: Wife of King Pandu, mother of Yudhistra, Bhima, and Arjuna

Kuru: King of the Bháratas, elder brother of Pandu and Vídura

Nákula: Elder son of Pandu's second wife, Madri

xvii

Sadeva: Twin brother of Nákula, son of Madri

Sánjaya: Trusted friend and charioteer of Kuru

Shákuni: King of Gandhara, brother of Gandhari

Shalya: King of Madra, brother of Madri, uncle of the twins, Nákula and Sadeva

Shikandin: Son of the King of Panchala, brother of Dráupadi and of Jumna

Shiva: One of the highest gods, the Creator and Destroyer

Subadra: Sister of Krishna, wife of Arjuna, mother of Abimanyu

Surya: God of the Sun

Uttar: Youngest son of King Virata

Uttara: Daughter of King Virata, wife of Abimanyu

Vídura: Younger brother of Kuru and Pandu

Virata: King of the Matsyas

Vyasa: A great sage, kinsman and advisor of the Pándavas

Yudhistra: Eldest son of Kunti

Pronunciation of Proper Names

As a general rule:

a = *ah*, as in f*a*ther
e = *ay*, as in ob*e*y
i = *ee*, as in pol*i*ce
o = *o*, as in h*o*le
u = *oo*, as in r*u*le
ai = *y*, as in cr*y*
au = *ow*, as in n*ow*

The *h* should be given its full value after a consonant, as in Gand-hara, Yud-histra, etc. It may seem unnecessary and difficult to Western readers to pronounce it after a *B*, as in B-*h*ima, B-*h*ishma, etc., but it is correct to do so.

In order to avoid further difficulty, no distinction has been made between the long and the short vowels.

Indian names are often accented in a way that Western readers do not expect. It is assumed in this book that proper names are accented on the next-to-last syllable unless otherwise indicated. The exceptions have been given an accent mark on the stressed syllable. This, however, is not possible when the names begin with a vowel, since the accent mark cannot be put on a capital letter. It should be noted, therefore, that Arjuna is accented on the first syllable—*ár-juna*; Uttar and Uttara are also so accented —*út-tar, út-tara*; and the less important name of the nymphs, the Apsara—*áp-sara*—is so accented.

INDIA
OF THE
MAHABHÁRATA

GANDAMÁDANA

KAMBOJA

GANDÁRA

LAND
OF THE
FIVE RIVERS

MADRA

Kamyaka
Forest

Mt. Kailasa

Indus

KURU

Kuru
Kshetra

Hastinapura

SIND

Kándava
Forest

PANCHÁLA

H   I   M   Á   L   A   Y   A   S

MATSYA

Indraprastra

Jumna R.

KÓSHALA

ANGA

Ganges

MÁGADA

Dváraka

Nerbáda

Godavari

Krishna

KISHKINDA

CHOLA

Scale of Miles

0   100   200   300   400

PANDYA

LANKA

The Five Sons Of King Pandu

The Sons of King Pandu

They Come to Hástina

The chariot of the thousand-rayed sun was rising from the eastern hills when the five sons of King Pandu with their mother, Kunti, came to the gates of their father's city. They were brought there by the holy sages who dwelt on the Mountain of a Hundred Peaks, where the sons of King Pandu had been born and where they spent their childhood. The boys had known no home but the deep forest, and as they drew near to the city, they beheld it with wonder. Its high white walls, the arched gateways as dark as storm clouds, and the countless palaces, surrounded with flowering trees, were all touched by the first light of the sun, the maker of the day. This was Hástina, the city named after the elephant, the capital of the kingdom of the Bhárata folk.

The eldest of the sages knocked at the gate, summoning the porter, who looked with amazement at the company that stood before him. He saw the stately lady Kunti and the five boys, as beautiful as gods, who stood beside her with the bearing of young lions. Around them stood those mighty sages who had cared for them and brought them to the city. They were holy men who rarely came down from their sky-piercing mountains into the world of men. Their bodies were thin from fasting and clad only in deerskins bound round their loins; their unkempt hair fell on their bare shoulders; but an inner light shone through their thin bodies, and their flashing eyes were terrible to behold. The porter had heard tales of sages such as these. They were men who had freed their hearts of anger and fear and all desire and had gained such power of soul that they could live as long as they wished; they could travel a thousand miles in the wink of an eye and could behold the whole universe as if it were a plum on the palm of the hand. The porter bowed down before them and awaited their orders.

"Go at once to the king," said the eldest of the sages. "Tell him that we await him here."

The man ran quickly to the palace and was admitted to the audience hall, where the blind King Kuru sat, surrounded by his counselors and the elders of his family. Breathlessly the porter gave the message, describing those who sent it. The king rose at once and gave orders that the court follow him to the city gate. The ladies of the royal household came after him, one of them leading the queen, who wore over her eyes a cloth gathered into many folds, because she wished to share her husband's blindness. The young sons of the king, clad in rich robes, were led by the eldest, a proud and handsome lad. The citizens, meanwhile, had heard of those who stood at the gate, and they came forth in crowds, with their wives and children. They bowed low before the sages and waited, silent and reverent, to see what would come of this visit.

The king's uncle, Bhishma, was the eldest of the Bháratas; therefore he welcomed the holy ones, offering them water to wash their feet and honey, curds, and rice to eat, while the king and his followers saluted them. When they had refreshed themselves, the eldest sage arose and addressed all those who were assembled there, saying, "You know that your former king, Pandu, went to the forest many years ago, with his two wives, to hunt the deer. A great misfortune befell him there, for one day he killed a stag that was mating with a doe, and the dying stag put a curse upon him: that he should never beget a son. Then in great grief King Pandu gave up his kingdom to his brother, Kuru, and left the pleasures of the world and went into the deep forest; he ate only fruit and roots and rid his heart of fear and anger and desire, so that his soul might be free of sin. His two wives, Kunti and Madri, stayed with him and they traveled far together, reaching at last the Mountain of a Hundred Peaks, where they abode with us. He studied with us and served us, treading the path of virtue and wisdom.

"His line did not die out, in spite of the deer's curse. Because of his virtue and that of his two wives, the gods themselves gave him sons. This eldest child, named Yudhistra, who stands at his mother's right hand, was begotten by the God of Righteousness himself. This second one, named Bhima, who will be the strongest of men, is the Wind-God's son. This third son of Kunti, standing at her left, was born of Indra, Lord of Heaven, chief of all the gods who protect the earth; his name is Arjuna, and he will humble all those who use the bow. Look here upon these tigers among men, the twin sons of Madri, King Pandu's younger wife. They are children of the lovely Gods of Twilight and of Dawn. The older of the two is called Nákula and the younger Sadeva. These boys are our pupils; you will be well pleased with them.

"Seventeen days ago King Pandu died. His wife Madri, seeing him placed upon the funeral pyre, threw herself upon it and was burned with him, going with her lord to the realms of the blessed. Here are their ashes. Here are their children, with their mother, Kunti. Receive them with due honor, for they are to you as your sons, your brothers, and your friends."

Then the sages vanished before the very eyes of the people who, filled with wonder, returned to their homes.

The king received his brother's sons with great joy, caressing each one of them, and the queen embraced Kunti lovingly, as an elder sister welcomes a younger one after a long absence. Then the king found a blessed spot on the bank of the river Ganges for the funeral rites of Pandu. Priests came out of the city carrying the sacred fire, its smoke fragrant with incense and spices, and they poured libations upon it. The ashes of King Pandu and his wife Madri were placed upon a bier covered with rich hangings and garlands of flowers. It was carried on men's shoulders, the white canopy of state was held above it, and yak tails waved around it. All the royal household, with Kunti and her sons, followed it, weeping; hundreds of people from the city streamed after it, and gifts of fine cloth and jewels and cattle were given to them for the good of Pandu's soul. When they reached the river bank, the last ceremonies were performed and the ashes of the dead were laid upon the breast of the sacred river. The sons of King Pandu and their mother stayed there for the twelve days of mourning, sleeping on the bare ground, and many of the citizens stayed with them to mourn with them and to comfort them.

When they had been cleansed by these rites from the impurity of death, the five Pándava brothers entered their father's city. They saw for the first time—their eyes wide with wonder

—the busy streets filled with fine shops, some full of excellent foods or garlands of flowers, others overflowing with finely woven cloths, jewelled ornaments, perfumes, and goods of every sort. They passed through squares shaded by flowering trees, for it was spring; they saw countless spacious houses, groves of trees, and pools of clear water, where the citizens played and refreshed themselves.

They saw also the four castes of men. They knew well the Brahmans, the highest caste, for these were the priests who knew and taught the holy books, the Vedas, and performed all the sacrifices to the gods; many of them had lived and studied in the forest where the boys grew up. But they had never seen those of their own caste, the Kshatrias, the warriors and rulers of men, until they met their uncle, the king, and his councilors. They had not seen the merchants and workmen, the farmers and herdsmen of the Vaisya caste, nor the dark-skinned Shudras, who were the servants of all. In the city called after the elephant, the four castes lived in harmony together, each doing its own work. The people were honest and happy, for the king ruled them justly and protected all living creatures in his realm.

As the Pándava brothers went through the streets, the citizens thronged out to see them, crying out, "Welcome to the sons of Pandu! Through the gods' grace we behold them! May they live among us forever!"

Then the boys entered their father's palace, and King Kuru feasted them and gave them princely dwellings and fine attire. He made no difference between them and his own sons and they grew up with their cousins as lotuses lift their heads above the waters of a pool. They saw much of their great-uncle, Bhishma, and soon loved him dearly, as indeed everyone did who knew him. He was the uncle of Kuru and Pandu and might have been king himself, but he had vowed when he was young never to marry and never to take the throne, but to devote himself to study and meditation. He was now an old man, with snow-white hair and beard, but he had won such power of soul that the gods had granted him the boon that he would not die until he himself desired death. He was the wisest and most beloved of all the leaders of the Bháratas, and the king sought his advice in everything that he did. He taught the boys many wise things and made his teaching gay with stories of birds and beasts, of gods and kings.

They found a friend and teacher also in their uncle Vídura. He was the younger brother of Kuru and Pandu and was much loved, for he was wiser than any man except Bhishma and was also a trusted adviser of the king. He helped the Pándavas when they needed counsel, as their father might have done if he had been with them. The elders of the Bháratas were pleased with these boys, for they had been well taught by the sages. Yudhistra, the eldest, was serious and pure of heart; Bhima, broad of arm and shoulder and strong as a yearling bull, was devoted to his elder brother and his mother and would do anything for them; Arjuna, slender and dark-skinned, with curling hair, was quick and clever in all that he did, but always courteous and generous. The twins, Nákula and Sadeva, beautiful as the twin gods, their fathers, were loved for their sweet natures and their humility.

It was only with their cousins, the Kúravas, that the five brothers were not always happy. Whenever they played together, these five outdid their cousins at every game they played, for they were stronger, swifter, and more skillful. Bhima alone could beat all the Kúravas put together, for they were no match for that son of the Wind-God. He was proud of his great strength and often used it mischievously, not because he wanted to harm them, but merely to show off and to tease them. He could throw them about so easily that he often hurt them without meaning to; when they were swimming together he would seize several of them by the hair and hold them under water so long that they nearly drowned; and if they climbed a tree to pick the fruit, he would shake it with his foot, laughing, until the fruit and the fruit-pickers tumbled down together. Duryodha, the eldest son of King Kuru, was just Bhima's age, a year younger than Yudhistra, and he hated Bhima for doing these things; indeed, he hated all the Pándavas, for he was proud and jealous.

Bhima Is Poisoned

When Duryodha was born, his cries were so loud and harsh that asses brayed and jackals howled in answer, while crows and vultures, cawing and croaking, gathered round the room where he was lying. King Kuru was terrified by these evil omens and summoned Bhishma and Vídura and some learned Brahmans to ask them what these sounds might mean.

They said to him, "O lord of earth, these omens mean that your son will be the ruin of his people. Cast him out, O King! Give up this one child for the good of the world! Wise men have said that one person should be cast out for the sake of a family; a family should be cast out for the sake of a village; a village may be destroyed for the sake of the country, and the whole world abandoned for the sake of the soul." But the king had not the heart to follow their advice. Indeed, he always favored Duryodha above his other children, and the boy grew up to be vain and evil-minded.

Now, when Duryodha saw the might of Bhima, he thought to himself, "No one can equal this second son of Pandu; he is stronger than all the rest of us together. Therefore I must do away with him by treachery. When he is gone, I can imprison Yudhistra and Arjuna, and then there will be no one to trouble me." For Duryodha was afraid that when his father died, the people might prefer Yudhistra to him and demand that the son of Pandu be made king. He could not rest until he had thought of a way to kill Bhima.

After much thought he made a plan. He had a pavilion built on the bank of the Ganges and called it the Water Sports Pavilion. It was built with graceful archways and pleasant rooms, their walls painted with designs of birds and beasts; gay flags waved from its roof, and in it were all the things that were needed for water sports and for games to be played indoors. When it was finished, Duryodha invited his brothers and his cousins to go to his new pavilion for a day's pleasure on the river, and all the Kúravas and the Pándavas mounted elephants or chariots and rode out of the city to the river.

When they arrived they walked about, admiring the gardens and the lotus pools, the fountains and the groves of pleasant trees; then they entered the pavilion where Duryodha had prepared a feast for them. They sat down and played games for a while and then ate, laughing together and feeding one another with the foods they liked the best.

Now Duryodha had mixed a deadly poison with a portion of the food which he had before him. He sat next to Bhima and, pretending to be very friendly, fed him with the poisoned dish until Bhima had eaten all of it; then feeling that his evil purpose was accomplished, he was pleased and continued to make merry with his cousins. When they had eaten, they played in the water until they were tired; afterwards they rested and played games in the pavilion.

Bhima, as usual, had led them all and beaten them in their

Duryodha throws Bhima into the river.

sports, and he was the last to leave the water. When he stepped out, he felt so very tired and heavy that he lay down on the bank of the river and immediately lost his senses, for the poison was working in his body. The other boys had run into the pavilion, excepting Duryodha, who stayed behind to watch Bhima. As soon as Bhima was unconscious, he bound his hands and feet with cords and threw him into the river.

Bhima sank down through the water until he reached the realm of the Nagas, those mighty, wrathful serpents that dwell beneath the waters. The Nagas rushed at him and bit him with their poisonous fangs all over his body; but their venom destroyed the poison that was in him, and he woke up. He broke the cords that bound him and crushed the serpents under his feet. A few of them escaped and fled to their king, crying piteously, "O king of snakes, a boy sank through the water, bound and unconscious, but when we bit him he came to life and began to kill us. Pray find out who he is." And the king, with his courtiers, followed them to where Bhima stood.

Now by good fortune, one of the serpents was a friend of Kunti's father, and he knew the boy. He came forward and embraced him and presented him to the king, who was pleased with Bhima's strength and courage.

"What can we do for this young hero?" he asked his courtiers. "Shall we give him gold and jewels?"

"O lord of serpents," said Bhima's friend, "if you are pleased with him, he will have no need of wealth. Let him, rather, drink of your nectar, which will give him the strength of a thousand elephants and make him invincible in battle."

"So be it," said the king.

The Nagas took Bhima to the king's palace, where they performed the proper ceremonies while he purified himself. Then he sat down, facing the east, and drank the nectar they offered him. He drained at one breath a cup of it and then drank seven more until he could not hold another drop. The Nagas prepared a couch for him, and he lay down at his ease and slept deeply.

Meanwhile the other princes had searched the groves and gardens for Bhima, and when they could not find him, they set out for home without him, thinking that he had gone ahead of them. Duryodha, sure that Bhima was dead, made light of his absence and joked and laughed with the others. But Yudhistra, as the eldest, always felt responsible for his brothers, and as soon as he arrived, he ran to his mother, asking, "Has Bhima come home? We looked everywhere for him, but could not find him. Have you seen him, dear Mother?"

Kunti was stricken with fear. "No," she cried, "I have not seen him. O go back quickly and look for him again!"

She sent for the wise Vídura, whom she trusted. "Bhima is missing, O noble one," she said. "All the others have come back from the river and he is not among them. Duryodha hates him, and I fear that he has slain my son."

"Do not fear, blessed lady," answered Vídura. "The sages have said that all your sons will live long and happily. Bhima will surely return. Wait patiently, and do not accuse Duryodha, lest he work further mischief."

Bhima slept for a long time, and when he awoke he felt strong beyond measure. The Nagas said to him, "The nectar has given you the strength of a thousand elephants, and no one will ever be able to vanquish you in battle, O bull of the Bháratas! Bathe now in this sacred water and return home, for your mother and your brothers are anxious because of you."

So Bhima bathed, put on the white robes and flowery garlands that were given him, and ate the sweetened rice that the Nagas brought him. He saluted them and thanked them and received their blessing. Then he rose up through the water and hastened back to the city.

He went immediately to his mother's rooms, where she and his brothers awaited him. He told them all that had happened to him, and Yudhistra said, "Only Duryodha could have done this. Do not speak of it to anyone, but from this day on, let us protect one another constantly." After that they were very careful, and their uncle Vídura also watched over them and gave them wise advice.

Drona's Teaching

King Kuru saw that the young princes were spending their time idly and getting into mischief, so he began to look about for a master who could teach them the duties of their caste and all the science of warfare. For this task he sought a man of godlike strength and knowledge.

Now it happened that a Brahman named Drona had come to the kingdom of Kuru a short time before this and was living quietly in the house of a friend, with his wife and his son. He was famous throughout the three worlds for his knowledge of the Vedas and his skill in the use of the bow and of all other weapons, human and divine.

One day the Pándavas and their cousins ran out of the gate of the city and began to play ball, with much laughter and shouting. Suddenly their ball fell into a dry well. The boys did their best to get it out, but all their efforts failed. Then they saw a Brahman, lean and dark skinned, standing near them, leaning on a bow and watching them; so they went to him and crowded round him, asking for his help.

He smiled at them and said, "Shame upon you! You are Kshatrias, born of the Bhárata folk. How is it that you cannot get your ball from the bottom of that well? Promise me a good dinner, and I will bring back the ball you have lost and this ring as well." With these words he took a ring from his finger and tossed it down the well.

Then, bending down, he picked some long blades of grass and said, "I shall turn these blades by my spells into powerful weapons. I shall pierce the ball with one of them, and then pierce that blade with a second, and that one with a third, until I have formed a chain of blades that will bring the ball up from the well."

He did just what he said he would do, and the boys' eyes were round with delight and amazement. "Now, O learned one," they cried, "bring back your ring!" And the stranger, taking up his bow, pierced the ring with an arrow which returned to his hand, carrying the ring with it.

The astonished princes bowed to him with folded hands, and Yudhistra said, "We salute you, O holy one! We have never seen such skill as yours. Who are you and what can we do for you? You have asked us for a dinner, but that is only a trifle. Pray, stay with us always!"

"Go to your great-uncle, the wise Bhishma," said the Brahman. "Tell him how I look and what I have just done. That mighty one will know me."

So the boys ran to Bhishma and told him all that they had seen, and Bhishma knew at once that the Brahman must be Drona, the best teacher that could be found for them. So he sought out the stranger, who was indeed Drona, and brought him with honor to the palace. "What good fortune has brought you to Hástina, O wisest of men?" he asked.

"When I was young," answered Drona, "I studied with a great sage who taught me the science of war and the use of all weapons, human and divine. At the same time, the son of the ruler of the neighboring kingdom of Panchala came to the hermitage of my master, and for many years we lived and studied together and became great friends. He used to say to me, 'Drona, I am my father's heir and shall be king after he dies. When the kingdom is mine, I will share it with you, dear friend; my wealth and my happiness will also be yours.' When he finished his studies he went back to his own country, but I always remembered what he had said to me.

"Not long after that I married, and my wife gave birth to a boy as splendid as the sun. One day this child saw some children drinking milk and he cried for it. At this I was overcome with grief and shame, because I was not rich enough to give him milk. I tried in many ways to acquire wealth, but all my attempts failed. Then I remembered my former friend who was now king of Panchala, and thought myself blessed. I went to him and said, 'Behold the friend of your boyhood, O tiger among men!'

"But he laughed at me scornfully and cast me off as if I were a vulgar fellow. 'You are not as clever as I thought you,' he said, 'if you think yourself my friend. Time destroys all things, friendship among them. There cannot be friendship between a poor man and a rich one; a king can never be the friend of one who is not a king. However, I will give you food and shelter for a night.' I left him at once, my heart filled with anger, and vowed to revenge myself upon him. I have come to Hástina to find devoted and able pupils who will help me to fulfill my vow."

"You have come to us in a lucky hour, O learned one," said Bhishma, "for we have need of you as you have of us. String your mighty bow and teach the Bhárata princes all the science of war, and when that is done your vow shall be fulfilled."

Then Bhishma gave Drona a neat and spacious house, well

filled with food and every comfort, and Drona accepted the sons of Kuru and of Pandu as his pupils. They were initiated into the Kshatria caste of warriors and rulers of men; they studied the Vedas as well as the science of war and became skilled in all athletic sports. Among them all, Arjuna was the most devoted to the study and use of weapons; he stayed close to Drona's side and excelled all the others in skill and perseverance. Indeed, in lightness of hand he became the foremost of the princes, although they all received the same teaching.

Now Drona's own son was one of his best pupils, and he began to favor his son in the hope that he might equal or surpass Arjuna. For instance, when the boys went to fetch water, he gave his son a wide-mouthed jar and to all the others jars with narrow mouths. Therefore his son could fill his jar more quickly than the others and return to his father for some added teaching. There was a certain skill that Drona wished to teach only to his son; so he said to the cook who prepared the young princes' food, "Never give Arjuna his food in the dark; and do not let him know that I have given you this command."

Shortly afterwards, when Arjuna was eating his evening meal, a wind arose and blew out his lamp; yet he did not stop eating, for his hand went, from habit, to his mouth. He thought to himself, "If I can eat in the dark, my hand finding its way so easily to my mouth, why can I not shoot in the dark, my arrows also finding their way to the target?"

So he began to practice with his bow at night. And when Drona heard the twang of his bowstring, his heart melted toward Arjuna; he ran to him and took him in his arms, and said, "Truly, no one on earth can equal you. I shall give you such teaching that you shall surpass every man that draws a bow." And after that time Arjuna was the favorite of his master, dearer to him than his own son.

Drona taught his pupils to fight on horseback, in chariots, on the backs of elephants, and on foot. He taught them the use of the mace, the sword, the spear, and the dart, as well as the bow and arrow. He taught them to use many weapons one after another, to break or turn aside the weapon of an enemy, to fight against many men at once.

He taught them also the Kshatria code of honor: that a warrior may never refuse a challenge, even to a game; that he must fight only against his equals—that is, if he is mounted upon a chariot, he may fight only against another chariot warrior; if he is on horseback, he fights another horseman. If two warriors are engaged in single combat, no one may interfere, and both sides must accept the outcome of the fight; two or more must never fight against one. If a warrior is wounded so that he can no longer fight, his adversary must also lay down his arms and allow the friends or the charioteer of the wounded man to carry him away. Even if his adversary is thrown from his horse or his chariot and is still able to fight, he must wait until the man has mounted again and is on equal terms with him. It would be a stain upon his honor if he ever attacked a man who was unarmed or off his guard, and no army would attack a town or a camp at night when the soldiers slept.

The fame of Drona's teaching spread to all the kingdoms of the world, and kings and princes came to Hástina to learn from him. Bhima and Duryodha, who were always jealous of one another, became very skillful with the mace; Drona's son excelled in the strategy of war, the twins in the handling of the sword, and Yudhistra in the use of the chariot. But Arjuna surpassed them all, for he was skillful with every weapon, and he surpassed them also in quickness and in imagination and perseverance. His fame spread over all the earth to the edge of the sea.

One day when their education was finished, Drona wished to test them in the use of the bow. He had an artificial bird set on the top of a tree as a target; then he called them all together and said, "Take up your bows and arrows and stand here beside me, with your arrows fixed on the bowstring, aiming at the bird. When I give the order, shoot at the bird's head. I shall give each of you a turn, my children."

He first addressed Yudhistra, since that prince was the eldest. "Behold," he said, "the bird on yonder tree."

"I see it," answered Yudhistra.

But Drona spoke again to the young prince standing bow in hand. "What else do you see, O Yudhistra? Do you see the tree, or me, or your brothers?"

"I see the tree and you, my brothers and the bird," replied the eldest son of Pandu.

And Drona was vexed with him and said, "Stand aside! It is not for you to hit the target."

The master asked the same question of all the sons of Kuru, one after another, and of Bhima and the twins and the other pupils who had come to him from afar. The answer was always the same, "I see the tree and you, my comrades and the bird." They were all reproachfully told by their teacher to stand aside.

Then Drona turned smiling to Arjuna, saying, "You must hit the target; therefore turn your eyes to it with an arrow fixed on the string." Arjuna stood aiming at the bird as the master had commanded, and Drona asked him, "Do you see the bird, the tree, and me?"

"I see only the bird," answered Arjuna, "not the tree or you."

Then Drona, well pleased, said, "If you see the bird, describe it to me."

Arjuna said, "I see only the head of the bird, not its body."

At these words Drona's hair stood on end with delight. "Shoot!" he commanded, and Arjuna instantly let fly his arrow and struck off the bird's head. The master clasped him to his heart, exclaiming, "You will never be vanquished by any foe, and you will win everlasting fame."

The Tournament

The Princes Show Their Skill

When his pupils had mastered every weapon, Drona said to the king, "Your children have finished their education, O best of kings. Let them now show their skill before you in a tournament."

"You have taught them well, O wisest of Brahmans," answered the king. "Arrange the place, the time, and the manner in which the tournament shall be held, just as you desire, for everything you command shall be done. My blindness makes me envy those who will behold my children's skill in arms."

Then Drona measured out a wide and flat piece of land, clear of trees and thickets. Upon this the king's workmen prepared a splendid arena, according to the rules laid down in the Vedas. On one side they raised a pavilion, shielded from the sun by a canopy of many-colored designs, the poles covered with gold and silver and wound with jewels. Beside it was another, equally beautiful, for Queen Gandhari and the ladies of her household. All round the arena the citizens built stands with seats for themselves, and the richer people pitched high and spacious tents with gay pennants flying from their tops.

Drona chose a day on which the moon and the stars would be favorable, and on the morning of that day the king, with his ministers and his warriors, entered the arena and took his seat in the pavilion. Queen Gandhari and Kunti, with the other ladies of the palace, also took their places, and the citizens, eager to behold the spectacle, came out from the city. So impatient were they that they assembled in no time, and as they surged into the arena with the sound of many voices, the blowing of trumpets and the beating of drums, the great crowd was like a tossing ocean.

When they were all seated, Drona, in white robes, with his white locks and beard, and with garlands of white flowers around his neck, came into the arena with his son; they looked like the moon and the planet Mars in a cloudless sky. He offered sacrifices to the gods, and Brahmans celebrated the rites with sweet music.

Then those mighty warriors, his pupils, entered, carrying their bows and quivers, dressed in shining mail, their fingers protected by finely wrought gloves. Yudhistra led the way, and the others followed in the order of their ages; they saluted Drona and the king and began to show their skills. At first they mounted swift horses, and as they rode expertly at different speeds around the arena, they struck targets with arrows marked with their names. Then they called for their chariots and displayed their skill in driving and maneuvering them; after that they handed the reins to their charioteers, picked up their bows again and struck the targets while driving at full gallop. The spectators were delighted and shouted,

"Well done! Well done!" Later, on foot, they took their swords and shields, and in pairs, practiced every thrust and parry, each attack and defense, while those who looked on admired their strength and grace and calmness and their mastery of the weapon. Vídura told the blind king all that they did, and Kunti described it to the queen, whose eyes were ever covered out of love and respect for her husband.

Bhima and Duryodha, eager for a fight, came in carrying heavy maces. They swung these weapons and maneuvered for place, moving faultlessly according to the science of arms and roaring like two angry elephants fighting for a mate. As the crowd watched them, some cried, "Behold Bhima!" and others, "Behold Duryodha!" and suddenly there was an uproar as each man cheered his favorite.

Drona perceived the danger in this division and said to his son, "Go quickly and forbid those warriors to fight, lest the crowd take sides and grow angry." And when they heard the message, the two cousins lowered their weapons unwillingly and forbore the fight.

Then Drona raised his hand and spoke with a voice as deep as thunder, "Behold now Arjuna, the master of all weapons! Behold the son of Indra, the lord of heaven, who is dearer to me than my own son!" And Arjuna, dressed in golden mail, his quiver full of arrows and his bow in hand, came forward looking like a storm cloud lit by the setting sun.

The whole assembly was delighted, and shouts arose, "This is the son of the mighty Indra! Behold the third son of Pandu!"

When Kunti heard these shouts, she wept for joy, and the king asked Vídura, "What is this uproar that rises suddenly and rends the skies?"

"Arjuna has just entered the arena, O King," answered Vídura.

Arjuna creates fire and clouds.

"I have been blessed, favored, and protected," said Kuru, "by the three fires that have sprung from Kunti, who is herself the sacred fuel."

The people were silent as Arjuna displayed his skill with bow and arrow, sword, and mace. From his chariot and on foot he struck the center of every target, using his right and his left hands with equal ease, shooting his arrows so swiftly that they seemed to flow in a stream from his bow. He let five shafts at once fly from his bowstring into the mouth of a moving iron boar; he shot twenty arrows into the hollow end of a cow's horn swinging on a rope. Then he took up the heavenly weapons whose use Drona had taught him. With one he created fire and with another water, with a third he created wind and with a fourth clouds, and with still another he caused all these to vanish. The people shouted with joy when he finished; conchs were blown and instruments struck up their music.

Karna Appears

When the tournament was nearly over, and the excitement of the crowd had cooled, a sound like thunder was heard at the gate of the arena. All the people turned their eyes toward it, wondering whether a thunderstorm had arisen or whether the sound betokened an earthquake. But those of the Kshatria caste knew what the sound meant, for when one warrior challenged another, he smote the hollows of his armpits with the palms of his hands, and they could tell from this thundering noise that a mighty warrior had come unbidden to the tournament. Drona rose, surrounded by the Pándavas, like the moon crowned with five planets; and Duryodha stood facing the gate with his haughty brothers around him.

Then the challenger entered and the people fell back, making way for him. He was as tall as a palm tree and handsome as the full moon; he was clad in golden mail and wore flashing rings in his ears; he bore himself as a bull or a lion or the leader of a herd of elephants. He looked round the assembly and bowed coolly to Drona, while a murmur arose like the wind in a grove of trees, "Who is he?" "Who is this unknown hero?"

Only Kunti, her heart leaping in her bosom, knew him to be her first-born son.

When Kunti was a girl in her father's palace, she made it her duty to serve his guests. There was one Brahman, fierce and splendid to behold, who often visited her father and who was very hard to please. He said he would come at one time and then appeared at another; he asked for food and drink and then refused it, asking for something else; he often woke in the night and demanded one thing or another that was hard to find at that hour. Yet Kunti always served him sweetly and kindly, and he was pleased with her. One day he taught her a spell, saying, "With this spell you may summon any one of the gods to do your pleasure."

She woke one morning at sunrise, and as she lay in bed she pondered, "What sort of spell did the high-souled Brahman teach me? Sometime I shall try it." As she wondered thus, the sun rose and poured its beams into her room and across her bed. She was overjoyed by its beauty and decided to summon the Sun-God, Surya, the maker of the day, to her presence.

As soon as she spoke the spell, that glorious god, the seer of all things, appeared before her and said, "Behold me, gentle maiden, in response to your summons! Tell me, what shall I do for you?"

Kunti was abashed and frightened by the glory of the god

and her own impertinence; she rose and stood with joined palms and said humbly with downcast eyes, "Forgive me, O radiant one! I summoned you from curiosity, to test a spell that a Brahman taught me. A woman must always be forgiven for foolishness, O lord of day."

Surya smiled at her. "The Brahman who taught you that spell," he said, "knew that you would bear celestial children. Now you shall have from me a splendid son, born with golden mail and shining earrings, who will become the strongest warrior in the world."

Now Kunti feared that she would be shamed in the eyes of her family if she bore a child in her maidenhood; therefore she told no one what had happened except her nurse. When her son was born he was radiant as a god and wore a coat of mail and earrings. She laid him in a wicker basket caulked with wax and spread with soft cloth and a silken pillow. In the dead of night she and her nurse carried it to the river bank and there, weeping piteously, she laid it on the water.

The basket floated gently from one stream into another until it came to the Ganges River, where the wife of a charioteer was washing her garments. She saw the basket and drew it to the shore, calling to her husband the while. They opened it and were amazed to see the beautiful child and believed that the gods had sent him to them. They called him Karna, and brought him up as their own son. He studied under a great master and became a warrior skilled in the use of all weapons. Everyone believed him to be the son of the charioteer, who belonged to the Suta caste, formed by the marriage of Brahmans and Kshatrias. Kunti had sent a trusted servant to watch her son and to tell her all that happened to him as he grew up, but she never saw him or claimed him as her own.

Now, when she beheld that great warrior as he appeared at

the tournament, radiant with beauty, she knew him because of the golden mail and the earrings that he had been born with, but she still kept silent.

Karna spoke to Arjuna in a voice as deep as thunder, "O son of Indra, I shall perform feats before this gazing multitude that will surpass those of yours. You yourself will be amazed when you behold them." He asked leave of Drona, and then as he had promised, he did all that Arjuna had done, with equal grace and skill, and a murmur arose among the citizens and cries of "Well done! Well done!"

Now Duryodha had been watching him with delight. Here was a warrior equal to and perhaps greater than any of the princes, and it was clear that he had come to challenge Arjuna. Duryodha hoped that this stranger would become his friend and an ally against his cousins; therefore he went forward and embraced Karna, saying, "Welcome, O wielder of weapons! A lucky day has brought you here. Stay with us and share the kingdom of Kuru!"

"I will gladly do so," answered Karna, "for I long for your friendship. I also long for single combat with Arjuna."

"Both your desires shall be fulfilled," said Duryodha. "May you bring joy to your friends and, O consumer of foes, may you put your foot upon the heads of all your enemies!"

Arjuna was shamed by the prowess displayed by the new-comer, and his anger blazed. He went to Karna and said to him, "You shall now suffer the fate of all those who come where they are not wanted and who boast of their might, O stranger. I challenge you to single combat."

"This tournament is open to all, Arjuna, not to you alone," answered Karna. "The Kshatria respects deeds; words are the weapons of the weak. Let your arrows speak for you until you are silenced by mine."

Arjuna's brothers came to him and embraced him and prepared him for battle, while Duryodha and his brothers did the same for Karna. Kunti, seeing her two sons about to fight to the death, fell back fainting, and serving maids hastened to her, sprinkling water upon her face and rubbing her hands and feet with perfume. But Drona, beholding the two warriors with their bows strung, was mindful of the rules of single combat and said to Karna, "This third son of King Pandu and of Kunti belongs to the royal line of the Bháratas. Tell us the names of your father and mother and the kingdom to which they belong. Then the battle may begin, for the sons of kings may not fight against men of inglorious birth."

Then Karna's face looked like a lotus flower pale and torn under the pelting showers of the rainy season. He hung his head and was silent, but Duryodha said, "O master, if Arjuna may not fight one who is not of royal blood, I will give this warrior the Kingdom of Anga." Then and there he ordered servants to bring a golden seat and offerings of rice and flowers and much gold, and he summoned Brahmans to perform the rites of coronation. A royal canopy was held over Karna's head and yak tails waved around him; the Brahmans poured sacred water on his head and enthroned him as the king of Anga. While this was being done, Kunti came to her senses, and seeing her eldest son made a king, she was well pleased.

"What can I give you that can compare with the gift of a kingdom, O tiger among men?" said Karna to Duryodha. "Command me and I will do whatever you desire."

"Your friendship is all that I desire," answered the son of Kuru, and they embraced one another joyfully.

At this moment Karna's old foster father, the charioteer of the Suta caste, entered the arena, trembling and perspiring, leaning on his staff. As soon as Karna saw him, he left his throne and went to meet him; he bowed his head, still wet with the ceremonial water, before his father, who embraced him with tears of joy. Seeing this, Bhima jeered at him, saying, "O son of a charioteer, you are not worthy of death at the hands of Arjuna. Lay down your bow and take up a whip instead! You are not fit to rule the kingdom of Anga, even as a dog is not fit to eat the sacrificial food."

Karna, with quivering lips, sighed deeply and looked at the god of day, whose chariot was fast disappearing over the western hills; it seemed as if he knew his real parentage. But Duryodha rose up in wrath from among his brothers, as a mad elephant rises up from a bed of lotuses. "It ill behooves you to speak such words, O Bhima," he cried. "Might is the only virtue that a Kshatria needs; if he possesses that, no one should scorn to fight him. The birth of heroes is often hidden, like the sources of mighty rivers. Karna must be of royal birth, for a doe cannot bring forth a tiger; he deserves to rule the whole earth, not only Anga. If there is anyone here who does not like what I have done this day for Karna, let him mount his chariot and bend his bow against me!"

By this time the sun had already set, and the fight could not take place. Duryodha took Karna's hand and led him out of the arena, lighted now by countless lamps. The son of Drona went with them, for he was angered by what his father had said about Arjuna, and from this time on Karna sided with Duryodha against the Pándavas. Yudhistra and his brothers waited with Drona for the king and returned with him to the palace. As the people came away, some hailed Arjuna and some Karna as the victor of the day. The Kúravas rejoiced at having won so powerful a friend and were no longer afraid of the prowess of their cousins, while the Pándavas were troubled, and even Yudhistra believed that there was no warrior greater than Karna.

The Teacher's Fee

The time had come when Drona could ask for his teacher's fee. He called his pupils together and said to them, "You remember what I asked of you in return for these years of teaching. Capture the king of Panchala and bring him before me. He is a mighty warrior, my children; it will not be an easy battle." They all shouted for joy and prepared for the fight, fastening their weapons to their chariots and putting on their armor.

Led by Drona, they marched out to the kingdom of Panchala and attacked its capital city. Duryodha, his brothers, and Karna, all vying with one another to be first in the attack, entered the city in their chariots, followed by horsemen. Arjuna, seeing their pride, said to Drona, "We shall fight after the others have shown their prowess. The king of Panchala will not be defeated by such as these." And he, with his brothers, waited outside the walls of the town.

Meanwhile the king, hearing the clamor, came out of his palace and was at once assailed with a shower of arrows. He mounted his chariot and rushed forth against the Kúravas, pouring upon them such fierce shafts from his bow that they thought a hundred kings were fighting them. While the arrows of the king fell on all sides, conchs and drums and trumpets sounded the alarm, and the Panchala army came forth, roaring like a thousand lions, while the twang of their bowstrings sounded like thunder. The citizens also showered upon the

Bháratas all sorts of missiles; young and old rushed forth to battle, while the king careered among them like a wheel of fire, smiting Duryodha and his brothers and the mighty Karna and quenching their thirst for battle.

At last they fell back before the fury of the king and fled to the gate, where the Pándavas were waiting. Then Arjuna, begging Yudhistra not to fight, drove forward in his chariot with the twin sons of Madri guarding his wheels on either side, while Bhima, mace in hand, ran on ahead. Roaring like the ocean in a tempest, Bhima rushed toward the elephants and cavalry, while Arjuna assailed the host of the Panchalas with his arrows. Bhima drove the chariots and elephants before him as a herdsman drives countless cattle, and Arjuna, like a consuming fire, slew hundreds of the warriors.

The king of the Panchalas, seeing his army driven back, aimed all his arrows at Arjuna; but that son of Kunti cut the king's bow in two with a broad-headed arrow, broke his flagstaff, and finally pierced his horses and his charioteer with five arrows loosed at one time from his bow. Then he drove close to the king and with a great shout leapt from his chariot upon that of his foe and seized the king as an eagle seizes a mighty snake. The Panchala troops fled in all directions when they saw their king made captive.

The Pándava princes took the king of Panchala to Drona, who had been watching the battle. And Drona, seeing his enemy defeated and humbled, said to him with a faint smile, "I have conquered your kingdom and your capital city, O brave King. But you need not fear for your life; we Brahmans are always forgiving. My love for you has increased with the years, ever since we studied and played together in our master's hermitage. You told me once that none but a king could be the friend of a king; therefore I am keeping half of your realm, but as a boon, I give you back the other half. You are king of all that lies on the southern side of the Ganges, while I become king of that which lies on the north. Henceforth, O Panchala, let us be friends!"

"You have a noble heart, O Brahman, and, besides, great skill in war," the king answered. "I am not surprised at what you have done. Indeed, I desire your everlasting friendship."

After that, the king lived sorrowfully in the southern provinces of his former kingdom. He knew that he could not defeat Drona by force of arms, although they were equal in skill, for now Drona could call upon the invincible strength and ability of the Pándavas. Therefore the king began to do penance and to make sacrifices so that he might have a son who could defeat the sons of Pandu in battle. Drona remained in the capital city and ruled over the northern territory, rich in towns and cities, which the Pándavas had won for him.

One day he called Arjuna to him and said, "The master who taught me all the science of arms gave me a weapon more powerful than lightning, that can burn up the whole earth. I give it to you now; you need only summon it and it will appear to you and do your bidding. Never use it against a human foe, for, if used unworthily, it might destroy the world; but if any superhuman foe attack you, you may use it then in battle. Cherish it with care, for it has not a peer in the three worlds. And now grant me what I ask of you in return for this gift."

"O master," answered Arjuna, "I will gladly grant whatever you may ask of me."

"This is the boon that I demand of you," said Drona. "If ever I should fight against you, you must fight to your utmost against me." And Arjuna, touching his master's feet, pledged his word that he would do so.

Now that they were warriors, trained and tried, the princes
went forth to war; for it was the duty of Kshatrias to rule their
kingdoms justly and to protect them, and to strike fear into
the hearts of any enemies, lest they should feel free to attack
the borders of the kingdom or to raid the outlying villages. The
sons of King Kuru were great warriors, but the Pándavas surpassed them in battle just as they had beaten them in games
when they were boys. Nákula, the elder son of Madri, became
a great chariot warrior and an expert swordsman; his twin
brother, Sadeva, was equal to him and always fought beside
him. Sadeva also loved learning and became so wise that his
older brothers came often to him for counsel. Bhima rejoiced
in battle and defeated kings whom even Pandu, his father, had
been unable to conquer, and vassals who had not been obedient
to the Bháratas felt the power of his mace. Arjuna, with the
twins at his side, challenged all the kings of the west and made
them vassals of his uncle, King Kuru; then he turned to the
south, and its rulers, who had heard of his prowess, sent
tribute to Kuru. Arjuna returned, followed by a great train of
horses, camels, elephants and carts laden with all kinds of
wealth.

The Kúrava princes were filled with jealousy as they beheld
this booty and heard of the victories of the Pándavas; even
King Kuru's love for his nephews was poisoned, and he
could not sleep because he was jealous for his sons.

The Blazing House

The Pándavas Are Banished

King Kuru's heart burned with jealousy; he loved the sons of Pandu, but he loved his own more dearly, and especially the eldest, the evil-minded Duryodha. Therefore he sent for one of his councilors, a Brahman, expert in the art of politics.

"O learned one," said the king, "the Pándavas overshadow the earth and I fear them because of my sons. Shall I have peace or war with them? Advise me truly, I pray you, for I shall do as you bid me."

The clever Brahman answered him in words as sharp as arrows: "Listen to me, O King, and do not be angry with me when you have heard me out. A king must always be ready to destroy his enemies. He must watch their every move but hide his own purposes as a tortoise hides his body under its shell. He must win their trust and then spring upon them like a wolf. He must hold them in his hands so that when the time comes

33

he can cast them down and break them in pieces as an earthen pot is smashed against a stone. He must have no pity, but must use any means, open or secret, to rid himself of them: lies or bribery or treachery or force may all be used to destroy a foe."

"Tell me truly, O best of Brahmans," said the king, "how an enemy can be destroyed by deceit or treachery or a bribe."

"Listen, O King, to the story of a jackal who lived in the forest a long time ago. This wise jackal lived with four friends, a tiger, a mouse, a wolf, and a mongoose; and they hunted together. There was in the forest a deer that they could not catch because of its swiftness and strength. So they met together, and the jackal said, 'O tiger, you have often tried to catch this deer but all in vain, because it is young, swift and very clever. Now let the mouse eat into its feet when it lies asleep; then you will be able to catch it.'

"They did as he said: the mouse ate into the feet of the deer so that it could not run, and the tiger killed it. Then the jackal said to his companions, 'Go and wash yourselves in the river, while I watch over the deer.' And they all went down to the stream while the jackal sat there, pondering deeply what he should do.

"The tiger returned first and, seeing the jackal plunged in thought, asked him, 'Why are you so sorrowful, O clever one? Let us enjoy ourselves and eat the deer.'

"But the jackal replied, 'I cannot enjoy it, O mighty one. The mouse has just been here, boasting that it was he who killed the deer and that we should feast because of the power of his teeth. I cannot eat what a mouse has slain.'

" 'My pride is also wounded,' answered the tiger. 'After this I will kill my own food.' And he went away.

"The mouse came next and the jackal said to him, 'The mongoose has been here and says that the carcass of this deer is poisoned by the tiger's claws. He also said that he would eat you instead; therefore be warned!' The mouse was frightened by these words and ran into his hole.

"Then the wolf came and the jackal said to him, 'The king of beasts, who slew this deer, is angry with you; he has gone to get his wife and will be back in a short time. I am telling you this so that you may save yourself.' The wolf, though he was hungry, ran away with his tail between his legs, making himself as small as possible.

"Last of all, the mongoose returned. 'Behold,' said the jackal, 'I have defeated all the others and they have run away. Fight with me now and, if you win, eat all that you desire.'

" 'If the tiger, the wolf, and the clever mouse have all been put to flight by you,' replied the mongoose, 'I do not care to fight you.' And with these words he took himself off. Then the jackal, well pleased with the success of his plans, ate the meat by himself.

"If kings act in this way, deceiving the strong and frightening the weak, they can be happy. O King, if your son, friend, or brother, if even your teacher becomes your enemy, slay him without mercy! The sons of Pandu are stronger than your sons. Therefore protect yourself from them; free yourself and your sons from any fear of them!"

When the Brahman had given this evil advice, he returned to his home, leaving the king sad and thoughtful.

Duryodha was also vexed in spirit, as he saw Bhima surpass everyone in strength and as he heard Arjuna praised as the best of all bowmen. He and his brothers, with Karna, tried in various ways to bring about the death of the Pándavas; but those heroes were watchful and with the help of their uncle, Vídura, they avoided the traps set for them and did not let anyone know that they perceived them.

At this time the citizens of Hástina were talking about the sons of Pandu in the streets and in the market places and whenever they met in public gatherings. They praised Yudhistra for his kindness and his honesty and said openly that he should rule the kingdom. "King Kuru," they said, "did not become our king in his youth because he was born blind; his younger brother Pandu reigned over us. Why then should he be our king now that Pandu's son is grown? Let us put Yudhistra upon the throne, for he is young, wise, truthful, and kind. He will always care for the old king and his sons and share with them the wealth of the kingdom."

Duryodha was told about these words of the citizens and his anger blazed. He plotted with his brother Dushasa and with Karna, and these evil-minded men decided that the king must exile the Pándavas to some distant place, so that they would be out of the way and the people would forget them. He went to the king and said to him, "O Father, I hear that the people are saying evil and dangerous things about us. They wish the eldest son of Pandu to be king and to set him above both you and me. If Yudhistra reigns, his son will reign after him and the kingdom will descend in Pandu's line, while we, O lord of earth, will be despised by all men. I beg of you to exile the sons of Pandu to Varanávata. We can find some good reason to send them there, and then we shall no longer have to fear them. O King, let us never suffer poverty and shame; let us not depend on others for our food!"

King Kuru thought for a moment and then answered, "My brother Pandu was always dutiful to his family and most kind to me, for he gave everything to me, even the kingdom. His son is as good as he was and is beloved by the people. How can we exile him from his father's kingdom? The ministers and soldiers of the state, their sons and grandsons, were all cherished and supported by Pandu. Will they not slay us, my son, with all our friends and kinsmen, if we injure Yudhistra?"

"All that you say is true, my Father," Duryodha replied, "but we must protect ourselves from the danger that looms above our heads. We can win over the people with wealth and honors; the treasury and the ministers of state are still under our control. Therefore, banish the Pándavas now, making some reasonable excuse for their leaving. Then make me your heir, equal to yourself in power, and we shall have nothing to fear."

"That very thought has been in my mind," his father said, "but I have not spoken of it because of its wickedness. Neither Bhishma nor Vídura, nor yet Drona, will ever agree to the exile of the Pándavas. In their eyes, dear son, we and the Pándavas are equal; those wise ones make no difference between us."

"Bhishma cares for us both and will therefore be neutral," answered his son. "The son of Drona is on my side and where the son is, the father will be also. Vídura secretly favors our enemies but he alone can do nothing. Besides, all of them depend on us for their living. Therefore exile the Pándavas without fear and without delay, my Father! If you do this, you will rid me of the grief that burns me like a blazing fire, that robs me of sleep and has pierced my heart like an iron dart."

The king could never gainsay this favorite son, and he agreed to the evil plan. Duryodha, with his brothers and Karna, began to win the people over to his side with gifts of wealth and honors. He spoke of the things that he would do when he became king and in subtle ways spoke evil of the sons of Pandu. When he thought that the time had come to set the trap, he told some courtiers who were his friends to praise the town of Varanávata as a pleasant place to live in. They obeyed him, and one day when the court was assembled, they spoke much about the town, saying how charming it was and adding, "The festival of Shiva, the creator of the worlds, is being held there now, and we have heard that the procession is most beautiful and the festival the gayest imaginable."

The Pándavas questioned them about the place, and the king, seeing that they were curious, said to them, "I have often heard that Varanávata is the pleasantest town in the world. If you wish to see it, my children, and to enjoy the festival of Shiva, go there with your friends and followers. Enjoy yourselves like gods; take pearls and jewels to give to the Brahmans and musicians and actors assembled there, and stay as long as you desire."

Now Yudhistra and his brothers kept their eyes and their ears alert, for they knew that they were in constant danger. They and their uncle Vídura had heard rumors of what was being planned against them, and they knew that the king's words did not mean that they should go to Varanávata for a pleasant holiday, but that they were to stay there in exile. They had no wealth, for they were dependent on the king, and if he were against them they were powerless; they had no friends or allies outside the kingdom that could help them. Therefore Yudhistra bowed before his uncle and said, "So be it!" Then he turned to all the others assembled there—Bhishma and Vídura and Drona, the councilors and Brahmans of the court—and said slowly, "We shall go to Varanávata, as the king commands us. Give us your blessing, that we may not be touched by sin."

And the elders all blessed them, saying, "May all the elements protect you along the way, you sons of Pandu, and may not the slightest evil befall you!"

Duryodha was overjoyed when he saw his plan so easily

carried out. He called a courtier of his, who was a builder of palaces, and said to him secretly, holding his right hand, "O friend, this world so full of wealth and pleasure is now mine, but I will share it with you if you do as I bid you. Go this very day to Varanávata in a chariot drawn by swift mules. Build there a palace rich in materials and furniture and guard it from prying eyes. In building it use hemp and resin and all other inflammable material that you can find. Mix earth with oil and fat for plaster and cover the walls with varnish from the lac tree. Leave, in places where they will not be seen, shavings of wood soaked in oil and lac so that no one, even if he looks closely, may see that the house is dangerous. When it is finished, invite the sons of Pandu to live in it, and when you are sure that they are sleeping there without suspecting anything, then set fire to the house, starting it at the outer door. The Pándavas must be burned to death and the people must think that the fire was an accident."

The builder said, "So be it!" He drove swiftly to Varanávata and began at once the building of the house.

The House Is Burned

Meanwhile the sons of Pandu and their mother, Kunti, prepared for their journey and then took leave of the king and of the elders of their family, sorrowfully touching the feet of Bhishma and Vídura and of Drona, their master. They saluted reverently the older men of the king's court and embraced those who were of their own age; they bowed before the queen and her ladies, and the children ran to them to say farewell.

Many of the citizens followed the chariots of those tigers among men, and Vídura went with them to the city's gate. The citizens said to one another, "Fie upon King Kuru! He does not honor virtue and justice. The royal sage, Pandu, cared for us as if we were his children, but now that he has gone to heaven, the king cannot abide these princes, Pandu's sons. Let us all leave this city and follow Yudhistra wherever he goes."

But Yudhistra, though he was full of sorrow, said to them, "The king is a father to us, our spiritual guide and our leader. We must do with trusting hearts whatever he bids us do. Give us your blessing now and return to your homes. When we need your help, then, truly, we shall ask you for it."

The citizens blessed the Pándavas and slowly returned homeward, praising those heroes and remembering all their good deeds. Then Vídura spoke to Yudhistra, for he was able to read the heart by outward signs and he had guessed Duryodha's evil designs by watching his face. He knew the language of the forest people, which Yudhistra also spoke, and he used that language now so that Yudhistra alone would understand him. "He who knows his enemy's plans may escape them," he said. "That which burns straw and wood cannot harm one who makes his dwelling like the jackal's, with outlets under the ground. He who wanders about in the forest finds many paths and can guide his steps by the stars. Be watchful, and remember that he who controls his five senses will never be overcome by his enemies."

"I understand," Yudhistra answered.

When Vídura had bidden them farewell and gone back with the other citizens to Hástina, Kunti said to her son, "I could not understand what Vídura said to you, because there were so many people about and he did not speak clearly. Pray tell us what he said, if it is right for us to know."

"The virtuous Vídura said to me," answered her son, "that the house that is being prepared for us in Varanávata is built of inflammable materials and will be set afire. He told me how to escape from it, and he also said that those who control their five senses can rule the whole world. I told him that I understood him."

They arrived in Varanávata after many days of travel along the sacred river Ganges. The citizens thronged out to meet them, blessing them and crying, "*Jaya!* Victory!" The Pándavas presented themselves first of all to the Brahmans; then they visited the rulers of the city and the leading men of every caste, even the Shudras. The builder came to them and led them to a house that had been made ready for them; he placed food and drink before them and made them very comfortable, and they lived happily in that town, enjoying the festival of Shiva.

When they had been there for ten days and nights, the builder invited them to see the mansion that he had made for them; he called it "The Blessed House," but in truth it was accursed. Those tigers among men entered it and looked about. Yudhistra smelled the fat and the lac and said to Bhima, "O slayer of foes, this house is indeed meant to be burned; our enemies, with the help of trusted workmen, have built it so. The wretched builder is staying here in order to burn us to death as soon as he sees that we trust him."

"Would it not be better to stay where we are living now?" Bhima asked.

"It seems to me that we should live here and pretend to be contented, while we prepare to escape," answered his elder brother. "Duryodha intends to put us to death and will follow us wherever we go. We have no power or favor with the king, while Duryodha has both; we have no armies or allies, while he has both; we have no wealth, while he has in his hands a full treasury. It is better, therefore, to allow him to think that he has killed us and then we can live in peace. And now let us follow the kind Vídura's advice; let us explore the forest paths and dig holes as the jackal does."

Shortly after this, a man came secretly to the Pándavas and said to them, "I am a miner, whom Vídura has sent to serve you. He told me that the builder plans to set fire to your house on the fourteenth night of this month, for this is the dark fortnight of the moon. When you left, O son of Pandu, Vídura spoke to you in the forest tongue and you answered him in the same way. I tell you this as proof that I truly come from him."

"Now I know that you are a true and trusted friend of Vídura," replied Yudhistra, "and therefore our friend, too. Save us from this danger, I pray you, in such a way that Duryodha will not know that we have escaped."

During the nights the miner dug a deep underground passage leading from the house into the forest. The entrance of it was in the center of the house, on a level with the floor, so he covered it with planks and a costly rug during the day, for fear of Duryodha's man, who kept a constant watch at the door. The Pándavas slept with their weapons beside them, and during the day, they went from forest to forest, finding out all the trails and where each one led. Thus they lived, on their guard, and deceived their enemy, who thought them trusting and contented. The people of Varanávata knew nothing of what was in their minds; indeed no one knew, except that excellent miner.

The treacherous builder was delighted when he saw how cheerfully the Pándavas and their mother lived in their house; and when Yudhistra, who watched him carefully, noticed his pleasure, he called his brothers to him and said, "I believe the time has come for our escape."

There was another festival at this time, at which much alms

The Pándavas escape from the blazing house.

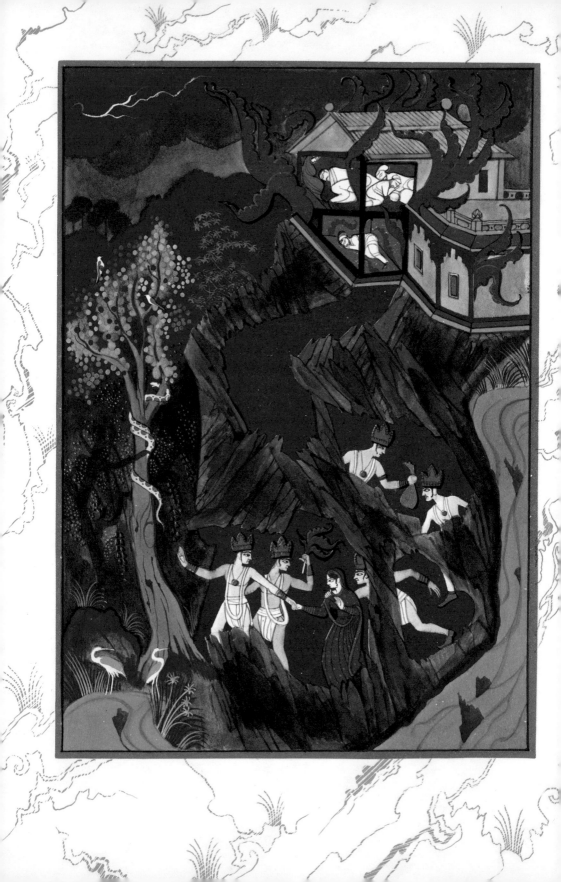

was given. The Pándavas invited many Brahmans to their house, while Kunti asked many ladies. They all enjoyed themselves, eating and drinking their fill, and then the guests took their leave and returned to their homes. Now it happened that a woman of low caste, with her five sons, saw the lights and heard music and entered the house unnoticed, hoping to find food and drink. She and her sons all took so much wine that they became drunk; they lay down where they were and slept as if they were dead. The builder also drank too much that night and slept within the house; but Kunti and her sons were wide awake.

At midnight a storm arose and a strong wind blew. Bhima got up, lighted a torch and set fire to the house just where Duryodha's friend, the builder, lay sleeping; then he set fire to the door and ran the torch along the walls. When the house was blazing on all sides, the Pándavas entered the underground passage, leading their mother. They went swiftly through it, came out into the night and fled to the forest, unseen by anyone.

The blaze and crackle of the fire awakened the townspeople. They ran to the house and saw the flames, fed by the lac and oil, leaping into the sky. They watched it until morning, for there was nothing they could do to stop it. When it had burned itself out, they went forward to beat out the last embers, and they could smell the materials of which the house had been built. "O shame upon the king's heart, which is so partial to his sons!" they said to one another. "He has burned to death the heroic sons of Pandu as if they were his enemies." They looked among the ashes and found the bodies of the strange woman and her five sons who had come unbidden to the feast and had slept there. The citizens believed that these were the bodies of Kunti and the five Pándavas, and they bewailed with sorrowful hearts the fate of these sinless ones, saying, "Now let us send word to King Kuru, 'Your dearest desire has been fulfilled: you have burned to death the sons of Pandu.' " And they sent messengers at once to Hástina.

When the king heard the evil news he wept with great sorrow, for he had not desired the death of his brother's children and knew nothing of the wicked plans of his eldest son. "King Pandu, my noble brother, has died a second time in the deaths of his heroic sons and their mother," he said. "Let priests and courtiers go quickly to Varanávata to perform the funeral ceremonies and let everything be done for the welfare of the souls of the dead."

All the people sorrowed deeply and wailed aloud, some crying, "O Yudhistra, prince of the Bháratas!" others, "Alas Bhima! Alas Arjuna!" and again, "O Kunti; O, the twins!" Duryodha and his friends hid their joy and congratulated one another in secret, and Vídura did not grieve, for he knew the truth.

The Escape

Meanwhile the five brothers and their mother followed the forest paths until they reached the river Ganges. They had not thought that they could cross it, but they found there a boatman who had been sent to them by Vídura and who had been waiting for them. He made himself known to Yudhistra just as the miner had done, by reminding him that Vídura had spoken to him in the forest language when he left Hástina; so the brothers trusted him, and he brought them safely across the great river in his boat. They sent a message by him to Vídura and he returned whence he had come. Then they continued on their way southward, along the bank of the river, finding their way by the stars. Soon they came to a deep forest, where even the sky was hidden; they heard the cries of night birds and of those animals that seek their prey in the dark. They were tired and hungry and heavy with sleep, but Yudhistra said to Bhima, "We know now that Duryodha means to kill us; we cannot rest until we are out of his reach. But how can we go further? Even we who are strong are exhausted, and our mother cannot take another step. O Bhima, you are the strongest and the swiftest of us. Help us to go on!"

Then Bhima took his mother on his shoulder, and his brothers clung to him and followed in his wake as he made a way through the forest for them all; for his father, the Wind-God, had given him the speed of storm, and the nectar of the Nagas had given him strength that could never tire. The trees and their branches trembled before him as he broke through them, treading down all that stood in his way, even as the leader of a herd of elephants passes through the forest, trampling down mighty trees if they stand in his path.

Even when the dawn came they went on, stopping now and then to eat the fruits and roots that the woods provided and to drink the water of the rushing brooks. In the afternoon, when they were overcome with sleep and weariness, they came upon a beautiful banyan tree with wide-spreading branches, and there at last they found rest and shelter. As they sat there, Kunti said, "I am the mother of the five sons of Pandu and am with them now, yet I suffer from thirst."

Bhima's heart melted with pity at these words. "Rest here while I go in search of water," he said. "There must be a pool nearby, for I hear the sweet cries of waterfowl." He followed the cries of the birds, and they led him at last to a lake. There he bathed and quenched his thirst; then, mindful of his mother, he soaked his upper garment and held it in his hands, for he had no other way of carrying the water. But when he retraced his steps to the banyan tree, he found his mother and his brothers lying fast asleep on the ground. As he looked at them his heart was filled with sorrow. He sighed like a snake as he thought to himself, "O how sad it is that our mother, who is beautiful as a lotus flower, delicate and tender, fit only to lie on the softest bed, is sleeping now on the bare ground! How sad it is that Yudhistra, who deserves to rule the three worlds, sleeps on the bare ground; that Arjuna, dark-hued as the clouds, unequaled among men, and the twins, beautiful as the Gods of Dawn and Twilight, are sleeping here on the bare ground!

"How happy is the man who has good and loving kinsmen! Even one who has no family at all is better off than we are, who have been forced into exile by our uncle and our cousins and have just escaped a fiery death! Where are we to go now? O you wicked sons of Kuru, you are alive only because Yudhistra has not yet told me to take your lives; else this very day I should send you to the realm of Yama, king of the Dead, you and your friend Karna. But what can I do, you sinful ones, when the eldest son of Pandu is not yet angry with you?" His fury blazed up again, like a half-extinguished fire; he pressed his hands together, sighing deeply. Then, beholding again those who slept so trustingly, he thought, "Since they are all asleep, I will stay awake. When they awake, they can quench their thirst." And he sat there all night watching over his mother and his brothers.

When they rose refreshed in the morning, Yudhistra said, "There must be a town not far from this forest. Let us now leave the woods, for we must be beyond the reach of Duryodha's malice."

As they left the forest, they saw striding toward them the

mighty sage Vyasa, who was a kinsman of theirs, and therefore watched over them with special care. They saluted him reverently and stood before him with joined palms.

"You bulls of the Bháratas," he said to them, "I knew beforehand that you would suffer this misfortune at the hands of Kuru's wicked son. Do not grieve at what has befallen you; it will all turn to your good fortune. Listen to me! Not far off, ahead of you, is a delightful town where no evil can overtake you. Live there, disguised as Brahmans. I will return when you have need of me."

He comforted them thus and led them into the town and to the house of a Brahman who received them kindly and let them lodge with him. Then the holy Vyasa returned to the regions whence he had come.

The Pándavas dressed themselves in deerskins and let their hair fall on their shoulders after the manner of Brahmans who dwell in the forests and beg for their food. They went to the neighboring villages with begging bowls in their hands, and they saw in their wanderings lakes and mountains, rivers and forests. They studied the Vedas and the science of government and of virtue, and they were beloved by the people of that region, for they were pure in deed, kind, and sweet of speech. When they came back each night from their begging, they placed before Kunti all that they had received and she divided it between them, each one taking the part allotted to him. She gave to four of her sons and herself half of the food; and to the mighty Bhima alone she gave the other half, because he needed it to feed his great strength, on which they all depended. In this way the heroic sons of Pandu lived in that town, unknown to anyone.

The Bridal Choice

The Winning of the Princess

When the Pándavas had dwelt for some time in that place, a wise and holy Brahman came to the house of their host, who was hospitable to strangers and gave him lodging there. The Pándavas begged the Brahman to tell them about his travels and his experiences, and he spoke to them of various countries, shrines, and sacred rivers, of kings and provinces and cities. When he had finished his stories, he told them that a great festival was about to take place in the kingdom of Panchala. At this festival the king's daughter, the beautiful Princess Dráupadi, was to choose her husband from among all the kings and princes who would come to win her hand; it was to be her *swayámvara,* her bridal choice.

Now the king of Panchala was the very one who had wronged Drona; it was he whom the Pándavas had defeated in battle and brought captive to their master. Therefore, they asked the Brahman to tell them about this king, and he, not knowing who they were, told them all about the king's quarrel with Drona and how he had to give up half his kingdom to his former friend.

"The king never forgot for a single moment how he had been shamed," said the Brahman. "He began to waste away, thinking only of how he might obtain a son who could defeat Drona in battle. He wandered from place to place, seeking some Brahman who, through his knowledge of sacrifice, might induce the gods to give him such a son. At last he found one. The king, with a delighted heart, prepared the sacrifice and had it performed with splendid ceremonies, for he was willing to give all his wealth in order to have what he most desired. And in truth, because of that sacrifice, he obtained twin children, a son and a daughter. The son is strong, beautiful as a god and terrible to behold; he was named Jumna, and the people of Panchala were mad with joy at his birth. Drona himself took the boy into his house and taught him the use of every weapon.

"The daughter, Dráupadi, is exceedingly beautiful. Her eyes are dark and large as lotus leaves, and her hair is black and curling; her waist is slender and her bosom deep; her body is as fragrant as a blue lotus flower. Indeed, she has no equal in beauty on earth. It is she who will choose her husband at the festival that is to be given in the kingdom of Panchala. Kings and princes from many lands, and mighty warriors, young, handsome, and famous, will come to it, eager to win her hand. Actors and dancers, athletes and tumblers, bards and musicians will be there to entertain the guests. The festivities will be like those in the halls of heaven."

When the sons of Kunti heard these words, it seemed as if their hearts had been pierced with arrows. They lost all their peace of mind and became listless and absent-minded. Their mother, watching them, said to Yudhistra, "We have lived for many months in the house of this kind Brahman and have passed our time very pleasantly here. I have seen much of the lovely gardens, the woods, and the rivers of this kingdom, but I have never been to Panchala. If you, too, would like to see it, let us go there forthwith, my son."

Now Yudhistra and his brothers were longing to go to Panchala, so they thanked the Brahman in whose house they had dwelt and set forth on their journey with joyful hearts, their mother walking before them. They traveled slowly, lingering in pleasant places that they found on their way. When they arrived at the royal city of Panchala, they found lodging in the house of a potter, and no one recognized those heroes as they dwelt there in the guise of Brahmans.

The Festival

The king of Panchala, ever since he had fought against Arjuna, had wished that his daughter might marry that son of Pandu, but he had never spoken of this desire to anyone excepting his son. He had heard that all the Pándavas had been burned to death in the blazing house, but he could not believe that they had been so easily tricked. Other warriors who knew the Pándavas thought the same thing, and rumors arose that the sons of Kunti still lived.

Therefore, for his daughter's *swayámvara,* the king had a bow made that was so strong that no man but Arjuna could bend it; and he set a revolving wheel on a tall pole and above that a golden fish. This was to be the target, and he thought that no one but the third son of Pandu could hit such a mark. Then he proclaimed the *swayámvara,* saying "He who can

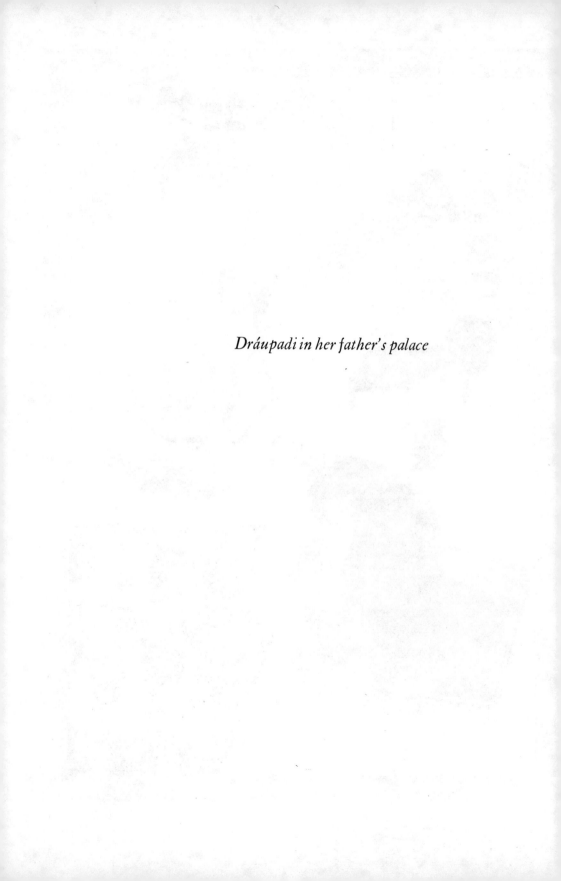

Dráupadi in her father's palace

string this bow and with these five bright arrows hit the
golden fish between the whirling spokes of the wheel may
win my daughter for his bride, for she will choose her husband
from among those who achieve this feat."

He sent this proclamation to neighboring and to distant
kingdoms, and soon princes and warriors and kings with their
retinues came from all sides into Panchala. Great sages and
Brahmans came from many lands to behold the festival.
Duryodha and his brothers and Karna came with the others,
and all were received with honor.

A level plain northeast of the city had been chosen for the
arena, which was enclosed on all sides with high walls pierced
with arched doorways. On one side was a pavilion shaded
by canopies of bright colors and designs and adorned with
flowers; there the king and the spectators would sit to see the
contest. Around the other sides mansions were built, white and
spotless as the necks of swans or the cloud-kissing peaks of
Mount Kailasa. Their doors were wide and the steps easy to
mount; the floors were covered with costly carpets, and all the
rooms were fragrant with the scent of sandalwood and aloes.
In these mansions dwelt the suitors who had come to win the
hand of Dráupadi.

When the day of the festival dawned, the citizens and
countryfolk, roaring like the ocean, poured into the enclosure
and took their places round it. The Pándavas entered unnoticed
and sat among the Brahmans. Then the king and all his guests
took their seats in the canopied pavilion, in the order of their
ages and their honors; clad in their finest garments and
adorned with jewels, they looked like the gods themselves.
Each day, for fifteen days, actors and dancers, musicians and
acrobats delighted the hearts of the spectators; each day the
king bestowed gifts and largesse on all and feasted them.

On the sixteenth day, when the gaiety was at its height, the Princess Dráupadi entered the pavilion, led by her twin brother, Jumna. She was richly dressed in silken robes and decked with jewels; she carried in her hands a golden dish with offerings to the gods and a garland of flowers to place around the neck of him whom she would choose as her husband. A holy Brahman lit the sacrificial fire and poured with due rites the libation upon it, uttering blessings as he did so. Then he stopped the musical instruments and the resounding trumpets, and commanded silence.

When the vast crowd was perfectly still, Jumna—that splendid son who had been born to avenge his father—took his sister's hand and spoke in a voice as deep as thunder: "Hear, you assembled kings and warriors! This is the bow, these are the arrows, and there is the target. The bow must be bent and strung, and with these five arrows the target must be struck between the spokes of the whirling wheel. Any man who is nobly born may attempt this feat, and my sister Dráupadi will choose her husband from among those who achieve it."

Then he turned to his sister and told her the lineage and the noble deeds of those assembled lords of earth.

"Duryodha and Dushasa and more of the mighty sons of Kuru, with Karna, the Suta's son, have come to win you for their bride, my sister. Shákuni and his three brothers, sons of the king of Gandhara; the noble Ashvattáma, Drona's son; King Virata and his two sons; that mighty charioteer, the king of Madra; the son of Sindhu's king; the king of Mágadha; Krishna of the Yadu folk, with his brother; and many other Kshatrias of world-wide fame have come, O blessed one, for you. They will vie with one another to hit the mark, and you shall place the bridal garland around the neck of him whom you choose for your husband."

The kings and warriors arose and lifted high their weapons, each thinking himself the mightiest and the most skillful in arms. They were like Himalayan elephants in the mating season, each filled with pride in his beauty and his prowess; each one thought, "Dráupadi shall be mine!" For the hearts of all of them had been pierced by the arrows of the God of Love as they gazed upon the beauty of that maiden. The sons of Kunti and the twin sons of Madri were struck by the same shafts as they looked wide-eyed upon the princess of Panchala.

Then all who desired her as their bride went down into the arena; they bit their nether lips with wrath and looked with jealousy even at their best friends. They began, one by one, to try their strength upon the great bow, but not one of them could bend it. When some of them tried, with swelling muscles, they were tossed on the ground as the bow sprang back from their hands, and they lay there helpless. The powerful king of Madra was thrown to his knees as he tried in vain to bend it, and the proud ruler of Mágadha was also flung down, whereupon he rose and left the arena in a rage. Duryodha and his brothers fared no better.

After many had tried and failed, Karna came forward. He raised the bow and strung it with ease; then he aimed at the mark. The Pándavas beheld that son of Surya with the bow drawn to a circle, and they thought that the day was lost; but Dráupadi cried out, "I will not choose a Suta for my lord!" And Karna, casting an upward glance at the sun, his father, laughed with vexation, flung the bow aside and strode away.

When all the warriors had given up the attempt among the jeering cries of the crowd, Arjuna rose from among the Brahmans who were seated in the assembly. He was clad in deerskin and his hair fell on his shoulders, but he walked like a lion across the arena, while murmurs arose from all sides as

people wondered who this Brahman might be who dared to
try what kings and warriors had failed to do. He stood for a
moment before the bow, his head bowed and his palms joined
as he prayed to Shiva, the giver of boons. Then he lifted the
bow, strung it in the wink of an eye and shot each of the five
arrows between the turning spokes of the wheel, so quickly
that they seemed to be but one, and the golden fish fell to the
ground.

Then a great uproar arose, for those who had failed cried
out in grief and anger; the crowd cheered the winner, musicians struck their instruments, and bards and heralds chanted
the praise of the unknown hero. The king looked at Arjuna
and was filled with joy; Dráupadi, rejoicing also, rose from
her seat and placed the bridal wreath about his neck.

But the kings and warriors who had come to win her looked
at one another furiously. "The king is making fools of us,"
they cried. "He scorns his own caste and gives his daughter
to a Brahman!" "He planted the tree and is now about to cut
it down just when it is ready to bear fruit!" "A Brahman may
not take part in the *swayámvara* of a Kshatria maiden!" "Let
us slay this king who thus insults all kings!"

So saying, they took up their weapons and rushed toward
the king to slay him. But he called upon Arjuna, who drew
the great bow to a circle and stood beside the king, facing the
oncoming warriors. And Bhima, with the strength of thunder,
uprooted a young tree, tore off its leaves and stood beside his
brother, looking like Yama himself, the mace-bearing king of
the dead. Yudhistra did not wish to be recognized at this
time and left the arena with the twin sons of Madri, to wait
for his brothers outside the gate.

Now Krishna, the wisest of men, a cousin of the Pándavas,
was standing with his brother, watching all that happened.

"That hero whose tread is like the lion's, who bent the mighty bow, is no other than Arjuna, the son of Kunti," he said. "It is he, if I am Krishna. And that other, who uprooted the tree, is Bhima, for no one in the world except him could do such a thing. That youth with eyes like lotus leaves, who walks like a lion but is humble withal, is the eldest son of Pandu; he left the amphitheater with two handsome youths who, I suspect, are the twin sons of Madri. I have heard it said that the Pándavas and their mother escaped from the blazing house."

Then Krishna spoke gently to the angry warriors, saying, "This maiden has been fairly won by the Brahman; let there be no quarrel about her choice." At his words they laid down their arms and returned to their dwellings, wondering much at what had come to pass. And all who had come to the *swayámvara* went away, thinking that the Brahmans had won a great victory, since one of them had won so lovely a maiden.

Bhima and Arjuna made their way with difficulty out of the crowd, and the princess of Panchala, in her bridal array, followed Arjuna, catching hold of his deerskin garment.

In the Potter's House

Now the sons of Kunti, each day after they had watched the festival, had been going on their usual rounds to beg their food and had brought it back to their mother. She did not know that this was the last day of the *swayámvara* and wondered why they should return so late. As she was thinking about them in the stillness of the late afternoon, her sons came back to the house, bringing Dráupadi with them, and Yudhistra said to her in jest, "Behold the alms we have received today!"

And Kunti, who was inside the house and did not see them,

answered as she always did, "Share it among you and enjoy it together!"

Then she turned and beheld the princess and knew at once, from her beauty and her bridal garments, who she must be. "O, what have I said?" she cried. She took the maiden's hand and said to Yudhistra, "When you presented this maiden to me as the alms that you had received, I spoke before I saw her. Tell me now how my words may be true and yet bring no harm to the princess of Panchala!"

Yudhistra thought for a moment and then said to Arjuna, "It was you who won Dráupadi, O best of bowmen. Therefore it is right for you to wed her. Now light the sacred fire and take her hand with all the holy rites."

But Arjuna replied, "Do not command me to do what is wrong, O king of men! You are the eldest of us and must therefore be the first to marry, then Bhima and then myself; after me Nákula and last of all Sadeva, who is the youngest. Bhima and I, the twins and this maiden are all obedient to you. Therefore think carefully and do what will be right in the eyes of the king of Panchala and of his daughter. We shall all obey you."

His brothers listened to these words, so full of love and respect, and they all looked at Dráupadi and she at them; they searched their hearts for an answer to this question. But truly, they could think of nothing but that maiden, for her beauty was greater than that of any other woman, and the God of Love had conquered all of them. Yudhistra, when he looked upon his younger brothers, understood what was passing in their hearts and feared that there might be a division between them. "The blessed Dráupadi shall be the wife of all of us," he said, "even as our mother has decreed." And the others heard these words of their eldest brother with great joy.

At this moment Krishna, who had recognized the Pándavas in the amphitheater, came to the potter's house. He touched the feet of Yudhistra saying, "I am Krishna, the son of Kunti's brother." Then he touched the feet of Kunti and embraced the younger brothers, and they welcomed him with delight.

"How did you find us, O Krishna," asked Yudhistra, "living as we do, in disguise?"

Krishna laughed. "O king of men," he said, "fire cannot be hidden, even when it is covered. Who but the Pándavas could have shown such might as you displayed today at the *swayámvara*? By good fortune you escaped from the blazing house; by good fortune the wicked sons of Kuru have not succeeded in their mischievous plots. May you be blessed with wealth and joy; may your good fortune increase like a fire that grows and spreads over the ground! Now let me return to my tent, lest the other monarchs find your dwelling place."

When Krishna had departed, the Pándavas went out to beg their food, and when they returned, they gave it to their mother. She said to Dráupadi, "First set aside a portion of this food for the gods and give it to Brahmans and to those who are hungry. Then, O lovely one, divide the rest into two equal portions; give one half to Bhima, for this youth, who is strong as a king of elephants, must eat much; divide the other half into six parts, four for these youths, one for me, and one for yourself." The princess did cheerfully all that she was told and they ate the food that she had prepared.

Then Sadeva, because he was the youngest, made a bed of grass upon the ground, and those heroes spread thereon their deerskins and lay down to sleep, with their heads toward the south. And Kunti lay down along the line of their heads, while Dráupadi lay along the line of their feet, as though she were their nether pillow. And the princess, although she lay along the line of their feet, on a bed of grass, grieved not in her heart nor thought unkindly of those brothers. They began to talk together, and their talk was all about heavenly weapons, about chariots and elephants and armies and kingdoms, for each of them was worthy to rule the world.

And all that they said was heard by Jumna, the brother of Dráupadi, who lay hidden in the potter's house.

The Weddings

Jumna wished to know who had won his sister's hand and had followed the Pándavas out of the arena to their lodging, where he hid himself and so heard all that was said. As soon as morning came, he hastened to tell his father what he had learned and found the king sad and anxious about his beloved daughter. "O, where is Dráupadi?" he cried when he saw his son. "Who took her away? They were not Brahmans, of that I am sure. Has anyone of mean descent, has any tax-paying Vaisya won my daughter and so placed his left foot upon my head? O son, has that wreath of flowers been flung away upon a grave? Or are the noble sons of Pandu yet alive? Was it Arjuna who struck the mark?"

"O Father," answered Jumna, "I followed those heroes and my sister to a poor abode on the edge of the city. There sat a lady like a flame of fire who, I suppose, is their mother, for when they entered they touched her feet, and Dráupadi did likewise. After they had begged for their food and eaten it, they laid themselves down to sleep, Dráupadi lying along the line of their feet as their nether pillow; and before they slept they talked in voices as deep as those of storm clouds. O Father, no Vaisya or Brahman or Shudra could talk as those heroes did! I believe that they are Kshatrias, for they spoke

only of weapons and of kingdoms. It seems that our hope has
been fulfilled, for when I saw him who hit the mark and that
other who uprooted the tree, and when I heard their talk, I
felt sure that these were the sons of Pandu living in disguise."

The king was greatly cheered by his son's words. He sent
messengers at once to the potter's house to say, "The king is
preparing his daughter's wedding in the palace. The wedding
feast is ready for the bridegroom and his company, and the
king begs him to come and partake of it after the morning
worship. Do not delay! These chariots adorned with golden
lotuses and drawn by fine steeds are worthy of kings and will
bring you to the palace." The Pándavas performed their morning worship; then they placed Kunti and Dráupadi on one of
the chariots, mounted the others themselves and were driven
swiftly to the royal palace.

Meanwhile the king, in order to make sure of the caste to
which his son-in-law belonged, made a collection of the gifts
that would please men of all the castes. He had placed in the
courtyard of the palace fruits, cattle, seeds, plows, and other
farming tools; bright rugs, finely woven fabrics and cunning
jewelry. There were also coats of mail, swords and scimitars
of fine temper, chariots and horses, bows and well-feathered
arrows.

When the bridegroom's party arrived, Kunti went with
Dráupadi into the inner rooms of the palace where the ladies of
the royal household were amazed at her stately beauty and
saluted her with joyful hearts. And when those five mighty
warriors, dressed in deerskin but walking like lions, entered
the palace, the king and his son, his ministers, and all his
court were exceedingly glad. They offered the brothers handsome seats with carven stools to rest their feet upon, and they
noticed that their guests showed no awkwardness or fear in

taking those costly seats, one after another, in the order of their ages. Skillful cooks and servants brought them food worthy of the gods, on gold and silver plates, and the sons of Pandu dined and were well pleased.

When the feast was over, the king showed them the gifts that he had prepared. The Pándavas, passing by everything else, looked keenly at all the weapons of war, taking them in their hands and testing their weight and edge and temper, walking round the chariots, while Nákula lingered among the horses, for he loved them and had a special knowledge of them. As the king watched them, he knew that they must be of royal blood; yet he still spoke to Yudhistra as if he were a Brahman. "Tell us truly, O chastisers of foes, are you Brahmans or Kshatrias or are you gods who in disguise are roaming the earth and have sought my daughter's hand? I must prepare her wedding according to the caste to which you belong."

"Let joy fill your heart, O King," said Yudhistra. "Know me to be the eldest son of Pandu and these, who won your daughter among that concourse of princes, to be Bhima and Arjuna. These are the twins, Nákula and Sadeva. We are Kshatrias, and your daughter will be carried from one royal house into another one, as a lotus is carried from one lake to another."

At these words Dráupadi's father raised his eyes in ecstasy and for some moments could not speak for joy. Then he answered Yudhistra in fitting words and asked him about the escape from the blazing house and all that had happened to them since that time. He blamed their uncle Kuru for his heartlessness and vowed that he would restore Yudhistra to his ancestral throne. And then he said, "And now let Prince Arjuna take my daughter's hand on this blessed day, and we shall perform the marriage rites around the sacred fire."

"That may not be, O king of men," answered Yudhistra, "for I am the eldest of us all and must marry before Arjuna."

"Then, if it please you," said the king, "take my daughter's hand in marriage."

But Yudhistra said, "Your daughter, O lord of earth, shall be the wife of all of us, for so my mother has decreed. Bhima is also unmarried and he is next to me in age. It is true that Arjuna has won this jewel, your daughter, but we have always shared among us anything that we may win. O best of kings, we cannot change our ways. Let Dráupadi become our wedded wife, taking our hands in turn around the sacred fire."

The king was troubled by these words. "One man may have many wives," he said, "but I have never heard that one woman may have many husbands. Yet you are true and know the path of virtue; you can never do a sinful thing that is not in accord with the Vedas."

"The path of virtue is not always clear," answered Yudhistra. "But I know that my heart has never turned to what is wrong, and when my mother told us to share this jewel together, my heart agreed with what she said. Therefore let us obey without fear or scruple."

The king said, "Let us all—your mother, myself, my son and you five brothers—talk together about this matter and decide what shall be done."

Kunti came from the inner apartments and told the king how it had happened that she had said to her sons that they must all marry Dráupadi; she also said that it seemed to her no sin, for she knew that they were all of one heart and mind. While they were talking together, the sage Vyasa, who watched over the Pándavas, came among them and they all rose and saluted him with reverence and asked for his counsel concerning this marriage.

"It is true," Vyasa said, "that such a marriage is looked upon nowadays as wrong, but it was not always so. This proposal of Yudhistra's is without sin because it was ordained of old by Shiva himself, the god of gods, the giver of boons. I will tell you how it came to pass. A noble sage lived long ago in a hermitage with his daughter, who was beautiful and chaste; but no husband came to woo her. She sorrowed over this, and therefore fasted and trained her mind and body in order to please the lord Shiva and to obtain a boon from him. At last the mighty god was pleased and appeared before her, saying, 'Ask whatever you desire, O blessed maiden, for I am Shiva and will grant your wish.'

"In her joy the maiden said again and again, 'O give me a husband graced with every virtue!'

"And the god replied to her, 'You shall have five husbands from among the Bhárata princes.'

" 'O lord of boons,' she said, 'I want only one husband!'

" 'Maiden,' the god replied, 'you have said fully five times, "O give me a husband"; therefore in some future life of yours it shall be even as you have asked.'

"O lord of men, your daughter of celestial beauty is that maid reborn; Dráupadi is destined to be the wife of five husbands. Therefore let these heroes take her hand in turn, with happy hearts, and let the marriage rites be performed."

When Vyasa had thus given his consent, the king and his son joyfully prepared the wedding. Their friends and kinsmen, the ministers of state, many Brahmans and citizens came to witness it. The king brought forth his daughter richly clad, her headdress, her arms and neck and ankles bright with jewels. Then those princes of the Bháratas, adorned with jewels and clad in costly robes scented with sandalwood, entered the hall one after another in the order of their ages, led by a priest of flamelike splendor who lit the sacred fire and poured libations upon it. He first called Yudhistra, and married him and Dráupadi who, hand in hand, walked round the sacred fire.

Day after day, one after the other, those mighty warriors, those princes dressed in splendid robes, took the hand of that most beautiful of women and were united to her in marriage. When the weddings were over, the king gave the Pándavas a hundred chariots set with rows of ringing bells and golden standards, each chariot drawn by four horses with golden bridles; a hundred elephants with marks of good fortune painted on their temples and faces, like a hundred mountains with golden peaks; a hundred serving girls in lovely robes and wreathed with flowers; and to each one of the brothers he gave much wealth, rich robes, and jewels.

Now that the Pándavas were his sons-in-law, the king of Panchala no longer feared anyone on earth; indeed he was no longer afraid even of the gods. And the five brothers, with Dráupadi as their wife, passed their days in joy and happiness, like so many gods, in the kingdom of Panchala.

The Kingdom of Indra Prastha

The Reconciliation

The kings who had come to the *swayámvara* soon heard that the beautiful Dráupadi had been wedded to the sons of Kunti. They wondered much, for they had heard that Kunti and all her sons had been burned to death. Everyone believed that Duryodha had planned that cruel plot and that his father had agreed to it; they remembered it now and said to one another, "O shame on Bhishma! O shame on Kuru of the Bhárata realm!"

Duryodha heard the news of the wedding as he was returning with his brothers and his friends to Hástina. Grief and despair filled his heart. He was his father's heir, equal to him in power; indeed, he thought himself greater than any other king. Now the mighty sons of Kunti had appeared again allied with the King of Panchala and his kinsmen, who were all powerful warriors with great armies. Dushasa, his brother, said to him softly, "Fate rules all things and our efforts are useless. Fie upon our plans, brother; fie upon the builder for his carelessness! For the Pándavas are still alive!" Talking thus with one another, they entered Hástina with cheerless hearts.

When Vídura, the wise uncle of the Pándavas, heard that they had won Dráupadi, and that the sons of Kuru were returning with their pride humbled, he was filled with joy. "Good fortune attends the Bháratas, O King!" he said to Kuru.

"What good fortune, O Vídura, what good fortune?" asked the king in great glee, for he supposed that Duryodha had been chosen by Dráupadi. He had had many fine gifts made for the bride and had planned that she and his son should be brought with great pomp to his city. Then Vídura told him that the Pándavas had won the princess, that they were alive and prospering and were allied now with the king of Panchala and his kinsmen and friends, all of whom led great armies.

"Those children are as dear to me as they were to Pandu," said Kuru shamelessly. "Nay, more so! Now I love them even more, for they are prosperous and have rich and powerful friends. Who would not be glad to have the king of Panchala as his ally?"

"May you never think otherwise, O King," said Vídura drily and left him.

The moment Vídura had gone, Duryodha and Karna entered; they had heard all that had been said. "We cannot speak any evil in the presence of Vídura," Duryodha began, "but now that we are alone with you, my Father, we shall speak as we please. Why do you praise the Pándavas? Do you look upon their good fortune as if it were your own? We should do everything we can to weaken and destroy them; the time has come for us to take counsel together, lest they swallow us up with all our kingdom and our children."

"I will do whatever you advise," replied Kuru. "I did not want Vídura to know, by the slightest word, what was in my mind. Tell me, my son, what plan you have hit upon, and give me your counsel also, Karna."

Duryodha said, so hastily that the words tumbled together out of his mouth, "O Father, let us send trusted spies to stir up trouble between the sons of Kunti and the sons of Madri, making them jealous of one another. Let them speak evil to Dráupadi about her lords, or to them about her; this should be easy, since she is married to them all. O King, let some clever spies bring about the death of Bhima, for Bhima is the strongest of them all and without him they would no longer try to regain their kingdom. Or invite them hither to a friendly feast, so that we may surround and slay them. Or let us tempt the king of Panchala and his ministers with gifts of great wealth to abandon the Pándavas and to ally himself with us. O Father, do any of these things that seems best to you. Time passes! It is better to deal with our enemies before they become firmly settled in Panchala."

"All your plans will fail, brave prince," said Karna. "You have tried before, in various ways, to kill the sons of Pandu and you have always failed. It is impossible to make them quarrel with one another, nor can you turn Dráupadi against them, no matter how clever your spies. She chose them when they were poor and unknown; will she abandon them now when they are rich and famous? The king of Panchala is honest and virtuous; even if we offer him our whole kingdom he will not betray the Pándavas. They cannot be defeated in any such ways as these.

"This is my advice, O bull among men! Attack and smite them now until they are all destroyed! Their friends and allies, their numberless chariots and horses and elephants are not yet mustered together; therefore strike them now! Put forth your power, O King, before Krishna of the Yadus comes with his host to restore the sons of Kunti to their kingdom! Let us grind Panchala to dust and the Pándavas with it! Vanquish them by your might and then rule the wide earth in peace!"

King Kuru applauded these words of Karna's. "O son of a Suta, you are very wise and are also mighty in arms," he said. "This speech suits you well. Let Bhishma, Drona, Vídura and you two take counsel together and plan whatever may be best for us." And the king called those venerable ministers to him and told them what was afoot.

"O King," said Bhishma, "I cannot give my consent to any quarrel with the Pándavas. As you are to me, so are Kunti's sons. This is my advice: make a treaty with those heroes and give them half the kingdom. Duryodha, you look upon this realm as your ancestral heritage, for you have always lived here and your father rules it; but the sons of Pandu also look upon it as theirs with an equal right, for their father ruled here before yours did, and Yudhistra is older than you. We are fortunate that they did not perish in the blazing house; from the time when I heard that they had been burned to death, I have been ashamed to face any living creature. The Pándavas are good and are devoted to one another; as long as they live, the wielder of the thunderbolt himself cannot keep them from their share of their father's kingdom. If you wish to act righteously, if you wish to please me, if you seek the welfare of us all, give half of it to them and live in peace."

After Bhishma had spoken, Drona said, "O Sire, I am of the same mind as the noble Bhishma; let half the kingdom be given to the Pándavas. This is the way of virtue. Send some messenger of pleasant speech to the king of Panchala, carrying costly gifts for the bride and the bridegrooms, and for the king and his son. Let him tell that monarch that you will be proud to be allied with him in friendship and let him tell the sons of Pandu that both you and Duryodha are exceedingly glad about their good fortune. Let him invite the sons of Pandu to return to Hástina, and let your sons go out with a noble company to meet them. Thus you should behave toward the Pándavas who are to you as your own children."

Vídura, of course, agreed to this counsel, and King Kuru, who ever wavered between good and evil, said at last, "Bhishma, Drona, and Vídura have said what is true and wise. Hasten, O Vídura; bring hither the Pándavas with their mother and their bride and treat them with love and honor."

Vídura went joyfully to the kingdom of Panchala and gave its monarch the messages that Drona had advised; he embraced his nephews lovingly and they in turn touched his feet, greeting him with words of love and praise. He gave to Kunti and to Dráupadi, to the king and his son the precious gifts that Kuru had sent to them. Then he brought the Pándavas, with their mother and their bride, to the city named after the elephant, and Kuru sent out the leaders of the Bháratas to welcome them, with Drona at their head. The whole city was crowded with the gay throng of citizens who came out to behold them, and the five princes, dear to the hearts of the people, heard their shouts of praise and welcome as they drove in their chariots through the streets.

When at last they came to the palace, they worshiped the feet of the king and those of the noble Bhishma, greeted their cousins and asked after the welfare of everyone present. Then they entered the apartments that had been prepared for them. After they had rested and enjoyed themselves for a few days, the king summoned them to his court, where he sat with the elders of the Bháratas.

"Listen, O son of Kunti and let your brothers listen to what I say," said Kuru to Yudhistra. "In order that no difference may arise ever again between you and your cousins, let us divide the kingdom equally between us. Take Kándava Prastha and all its territory for your own; build your city there where no harm can befall you, for you will be protected by Arjuna as the gods are protected by the wielder of the thunderbolt. Dwell there in peace, king of half the Bhárata realm!"

Those tigers among men agreed joyfully to what he said, and soon after, content with half the realm, they set out from Hástina and went to Kándava Prastha.

Now Kándava Prastha was no better than a desert. Nevertheless, those heroes of unfading splendor made it a second heaven. They chose, with the help of the sage Vyasa, a sacred and favorable region and measured out a piece of land for their city, asking the blessings of the gods upon their work. A fine city soon rose, surrounded by a moat as wide as a river and by high walls as white as clouds. It was protected by gateways arched like thunderclouds, well furnished with weapons of defense, and so strong that the missiles of foes could not even scratch them. The streets were all wide and carefully laid out so that there was no fear of accidents. In a delightful part of the city the palace of the Pándavas arose, filled with every kind of wealth, like the mansion of Kúvera, the God of Wealth. Gardens were laid out all around it, planted with beautiful trees whose branches bent down with the weight of fruits and blossoms and were thronged with singing birds. There were pleasure houses, charming groves, lakes full to the brim with crystal waters, pools fragrant with lotuses and lilies where swans and ducks abounded.

When it was finished, many Brahmans came to that city to dwell there in peace; many merchants came in the hope of earning wealth under the protection of a just king; and artisans, skilled in all the arts, came to that town and took up their abode there. It came to be called Indra Prastha, or Indra's Place.

Thus, because of the wise counsel of Bhishma and Drona, the Pándavas dwelt in Indra Prastha, their joy increasing from day to day in that kingdom peopled by honest and happy men. For Yudhistra cared for the welfare of all his people and worked for the good of all without making any difference between them. He made Bhima his chief minister, and that son of the Wind-God watched over all the kingdom and told his elder brother all that needed to be done. Arjuna protected the people from all enemies that might do them harm, and the wise Sadeva, the son of Madri, judged any quarrel or grievance that was brought before the king. His twin, Nákula, always devoted and helpful to his brothers, did whatever was demanded of him. Soon, therefore, there were no quarrels or fear of any kind, and the people gave their whole attention to their occupations. Trade and farming and cattle-raising flourished and the rains were always abundant. Yudhistra became known as the king who had no enemies.

The Pándavas were well aware that even brothers who were devoted to one another might quarrel because of a woman whom they loved; therefore, they made a rule among themselves in regard to Dráupadi, the beloved wife of them all. This was the rule that they made: if any one of them came to Dráupadi's room and saw one of his brothers sitting there with her, he must not enter the room or the place where they were sitting, but go his way and leave them to themselves. They kept this rule, and no quarrel ever arose between them. Dráupadi bore to her five husbands five sons, all of whom became great warriors. They were very fond of one another, they studied the Vedas, and they learned from Arjuna the use of all weapons, human and divine.

Arjuna also married Subadra, the sister of Krishna, and she bore him a son whom they named Abimanyu because he was fearless and high-spirited. He was as handsome as the moon, long-armed and broad-chested, with eyes like a bull's; he grew up like the moon in the lighted fortnight and was the favorite of his uncle Krishna. He was equal to his father in lightness of hand and swiftness of movement, in his knowledge of the Vedas and the duties of his caste. The Pándavas were filled with joy as they beheld these six godlike children growing up before them and becoming great warriors.

The Burning of the Kándava Forest

Now Krishna and Arjuna were inseparable friends; indeed, it seemed that they had only one heart and one mind between them, and Krishna came often to Indra Prastha.

One summer day they went to the banks of the river Jumna with a company of friends for a day of sport. In a pleasant place surrounded by tall trees, they all took their pleasure, some in the water and some in the woods. Some sang and danced together; some sat about laughing and jesting, while others went apart to talk seriously. After dining on delicious foods and wines, Krishna and Arjuna sought a cool spot in the woods not far from where the others laughed and played; there they sat down and talked about heroic deeds of the past and other things such as warriors enjoy.

While they were there, a Brahman came toward them. He looked as tall as a tree; his color was like molten gold, and his beard was yellow. His hair was unkempt and he was clad in rags, yet he seemed to blaze with splendor like the morning sun. The two heroes rose and saluted him, awaiting his commands.

The Brahman said, "You who are now so near the forest of Kándava are the two greatest warriors on earth. I am a greedy Brahman who needs much food. O Krishna and Arjuna, I beg of you to give me all I want to eat!"

"Tell us what food you desire, O holy one," they answered, "and we shall do our best to give it to you."

"I do not desire ordinary food," said the Brahman. "Know that I am Agni, the God of Fire. I must have the sort of food that suits me. I wish to devour the forest of Kándava, but it is protected by Indra because a friend of his lives in it. When Indra sees me blaze forth there, he pours down so much water upon me from the skies that I am never able to devour the forest, although I have tried to do so seven times. Now I come to you who know all weapons, human and divine. I pray you, keep those showers from falling and keep any creature from escaping when I begin to consume that forest, for this is the food that I desire."

"O exalted one," Arjuna said, "I have several heavenly weapons with which I can fight even the wielder of the thunderbolt. But I have no bow that will bear the strength of my arms, and my hands are so quick that I must have a supply of arrows that can never be used up. My chariot is not strong enough to carry the load of arrows that I wish to keep at hand. I need one that is splendid as the sun and whose wheels roar like thunder. Krishna, too, has no weapons suited to his power. We will do all that we can to prevent Indra from pouring down his showers, but it behooves you, O lord of fire, to give us worthy weapons."

Then the smoke-bannered God of Fire called upon Varuna, whose home is in the waters, and said to him, "Give me quickly the bow and the quiver and the ape-bannered chariot that were made by the architect of heaven, for Arjuna has need of them! Bring me also, for Krishna, a mace and a fiery discus!"

And Varuna brought to Arjuna that jewel of a bow known as Gandíva, beautiful to behold and equal to a thousand bows. He gave him also two quivers whose arrows could never be used up, and a chariot yoked with horses white as silver or as fleecy clouds, decked in golden harness and fleet as the wind. Its flagstaff bore a banner with the figure of a heavenly ape, which glared fiercely out as if to destroy all that it beheld; there were lesser flags with figures of animals whose roars and yells could cause the enemy to faint. The god gave to Krishna a mace and a fiery discus which became his favorite weapon. It could slay both men and gods; its roar was like thunder and it returned to his hand after he had thrown it in battle.

Arjuna walked around that excellent chariot, took up that splendid bow and was filled with joy. "Now blaze forth as you please, O exalted one," he said, "on every side of the great forest, for now we can withstand the gods themselves!"

Then the mighty God of Fire took his own form; he summoned the Wind-God to be his charioteer and went to the Kándava forest and surrounded it with seven flames. The trees caught fire with a roar like thunder and the burning forest looked like that king of mountains, Meru, when its snows are lighted by the rays of the setting sun. Krishna and Arjuna placed themselves on opposite sides of the wood to prevent any creature or demon from escaping. They drove around the great forest so fast that the creatures could find no place between the chariots through which they could flee. Arjuna, with his arrows, drove them back into the flames, where Agni consumed them, while the discus of Krishna, hurled by him again and again, came back into his hand after slaying countless demons.

The mighty flames leaped up into the sky until the gods themselves were troubled. They went to Indra and said to him, "O lord of heaven, why does Agni rage so below us? Has the time come for the world to be destroyed?"

Indra, the god of a thousand eyes, also beheld what Agni was doing and set out to protect the forest where his friend lived. He covered the sky with masses of clouds which began to pour their rain on Kándava, but the heat of the fire was so great that the rain dried up before it fell. Then Indra, growing angry, ordered the winds to trouble all the oceans, and they drew together heavier masses of clouds charged with torrents of rain and roaring with thunder. The flames fought against the downpour, and the forest, filled with smoke and flashes of lightning, was terrible to behold.

Arjuna hurled at the clouds a heavenly weapon that Drona had taught him to use. The torrents of rain dried up and the lightning that played among the clouds flickered and vanished. In a moment the sky was clear; a cool breeze blew and the disk of the sun could be seen again. Agni blazed forth with his flames and filled the heavens with his roaring.

Then Indra rode forth on his white elephant and ordered the leaders of his hosts and the mighty storm gods to smite down those two heroes. But Arjuna and Krishna waited calmly and fearlessly, their weapons in their hands, and when the celestial host came down, they attacked the very gods with their fiery arrows and discus and drove them back again and again. And Indra, seeing their prowess in battle, was well pleased with them, for he knew Arjuna to be his son. To test the skill of that hero, he sent down a shower of stones, but Arjuna, with his swift arrows, turned them aside. He sent a

The burning of the Kándava forest

heavier shower of stones, and Arjuna, with a thousand arrows, broke the stones into dust that the wind whirled away.

The gods saw that they could not protect the forest from the might of Krishna and Arjuna, so they retreated and returned to their places in heaven. Indra, too, perceived that his friend was not in the forest on that day, so he, too, withdrew and returned to his abode. He was pleased to behold the power of his son, and he praised the two friends.

Those heroes set up a great shout and were filled with gladness as they saw that they had won, and Agni, with blazing eyes, flaming tongue, and wide-open mouth, devoured the whole of that mighty wood. His hunger was satisfied, and he was greatly pleased.

While Krishna was slaying every creature that tried to escape from the fire, it happened that a demon named Maya rushed forth, with Agni hot on his heels. Krishna raised his weapon to smite him down. When Maya saw the uplifted discus and Agni pursuing him from behind, he shrieked, "O Arjuna, save me!" And when Arjuna heard the terror in his voice, his heart was moved with pity and he cried, "I will! Do not be afraid!" The merciful voice of Arjuna gave the demon his life, for when Krishna heard it, he lowered his discus, and Agni swept aside and left him alone.

When the fire was over, those three, Krishna, Arjuna, and Maya, sat down on the bank of a river to rest. The demon worshiped Arjuna and spoke to him humbly, with joined palms and sweet words, saying, "O son of Kunti, you have saved me from death. Tell me what I can do for you."

"Your gratitude is enough, O mighty one," Arjuna answered. "You are free to go wherever you please. May you be blessed and may you always be kind and well disposed toward me, as I am toward you."

"You have spoken worthily, O exalted one," Maya replied. "Yet I still wish to do something for you. I am the chief architect of the demons, and I should like to build a beautiful palace for you."

"O friend," Arjuna said, "you look upon me as one who saved your life; therefore I cannot ask any favor of you. But if you will do something for Krishna, I shall be fully repaid."

Maya agreed to this request, and Krishna, after thinking for a moment, said to him, "Build an assembly hall for Yudhistra, O Maya, if you are in truth so great an architect! Build such a palace that no one in the world of men can equal it; let heavenly, demonic and human design be mingled there!"

The Assembly Hall

Maya rejoiced at these words and forthwith built for Yudhistra a peerless palace, renowned throughout the three worlds. It rose, upheld by columns of gold, like a mass of new clouds lighted by the sun; it was made of excellent materials, with golden walls and archways, adorned with varied paintings, and was so brilliant that it seemed to be on fire. Within it he built a pool bordered with marble and set with pearls; a flight of crystal steps led from the marble edge into the water, where lotuses and other water flowers blossomed, while fishes and turtles of golden hue played in its clear depth. All around the palace were planted tall, ever-blossoming trees, giving cool shade; the breezes, entering the wide halls, carried with them the fragrance of the trees outside and of the lotuses within. Maya built this great palace as an assembly hall for King Yudhistra, and after fourteen months of work, announced to him that it was finished.

Yudhistra entered the assembly hall after he had feasted

many Brahmans and given them new robes and fresh garlands. He worshiped the gods there with music and fragrant incense. Then athletes and mimes, wrestlers and bards entertained the son of Kunti with their skills, and he and his brothers enjoyed themselves in that hall as the gods do in heaven. Kings and warriors came to visit him there, and learned sages talked about sacred things, gladdening his heart with their wisdom. Even the singers and musicians of the gods, the Gandharvas and the Apsaras, waited upon the son of Pandu, delighting him and all who gathered there with their heavenly melodies.

One day when the five brothers were seated there, the holy Vyasa, that sage who was their friend and adviser, came to see them. They arose and saluted him, bowing humbly before him; they gave him a seat of honor and worshiped him with offerings of food and gifts, and begged him to enlighten them with his wisdom.

"O child," he said to Yudhistra, "do you divide your days wisely between the three aims of life—duty, wealth, and pleasure? Do you know how much time to give to each? Does your mind take pleasure in duty? Is the wealth you earn wisely spent? Are you enjoying the pleasure of life? Have you banished the six evils, O king of men—sleep, idleness, fear, anger, weakness of mind, and procrastination?

"Do you wake in the small hours of the night and think of what you should do and what you should not do the next day? Do you rise from bed at the proper time, dress yourself suitably and show yourself to the people, with your ministers? Is your kingdom protected by ministers learned in the Vedas, who keep their counsel close? Even a single minister whose passions are under control, who has wisdom and judgment, can bring prosperity to a kingdom. I ask you, therefore, have you even one such minister?

"Is your priest humble, pure of blood and renown, without jealousy or greed? Is your astrologer skilled in reading faces and in reading the omens? Can he turn aside the disturbances of nature? Is the commander of your forces brave, intelligent, able, and devoted to you? Do you give your soldiers their proper food and pay at the appointed time; do you support the wives and children of the men who give their lives for you?

"O foremost of victorious kings, do the officers of your government, who are paid from the taxes levied upon the people, take only their just due? Are merchants from distant lands treated with kindness and honesty? Are the thieves who rob your people pursued by your police over the smooth and the rough parts of your kingdom? When your officers catch a thief with the booty in his hands, do they ever set him free and keep the booty themselves? I hope that they never decide unjustly a case between the rich and the poor because the rich have bribed them.

"Are the four professions—farming, cattle-raising, trading, and money-lending—managed by honest men? The happiness of your people depends on these, O oppressor of foes. Are the farmers contented? Do they lack neither food nor seed? Are dams and lakes placed at the right distances so that the farms need not depend on the showers of heaven?

"O king, do you behave with perfect justice to those who deserve punishment and to those that deserve honor? Are you as just to those whom you dislike as you are to those who are dear to you? Do you bow down to your superiors, to the aged, the gods, the sages, the Brahmans, and to the tall banyan trees in the villages that are so useful to the people? O sinless one, do you cause grief or anger in anyone's heart? Do you, like a father, cherish the blind, the dumb, the lame, the deformed, the friendless, and the homeless? Can all men come into your presence without fear? Have you faith in the religion taught in the Vedas, and do you follow in the footsteps of the wise kings who have gone before you?"

Yudhistra worshiped him and replied, "O holy one, the counsel that you have given me through your questions is right and just and according to the religion of the Vedas, which I have been taught from my childhood. I follow it as faithfully as I can, and I wish to walk in the path laid down by my ancestors. I shall try to do all that you have told me to do, for your wisdom has increased my faith."

Later, when the king was seated beside the sage, Yudhistra said, "You roam over the three worlds with the speed of thought and you see everything. Tell me, O sinless one, have you ever beheld an assembly hall like this of mine, or one more beautiful?"

"O child, O king," answered Vyasa, smiling, "I have never seen or heard of an assembly hall like this of yours, among men. But I have seen the halls of the gods and will tell you about the assembly hall of Indra, if you care to listen to me."

Yudhistra and his brothers and the Brahmans seated around them entreated the sage, saying, "Describe it to us, O exalted one!" "How long and wide is it and of what materials is it made?" "Who waits upon the wielder of the thunderbolt in his hall?"

"I cannot describe the shape or the size of that hall or say, 'it is thus and so', for I have never seen anything like it, to compare it to," answered the sage. "It seems to be made of brilliant jewels of many kinds. It is not supported by any columns, for it rests in heaven and looks like the white peaks of thunderclouds, shaming the very sun with its splendor. It moves at Indra's will and may in a moment take a different form that words cannot describe. It is filled with music and is fragrant with heavenly perfumes; it is neither cool nor hot, and in it there is neither hunger nor thirst, neither grief nor weakness of age, no weariness or sorrow.

"Sages purified by holy deeds, bright as flames, their sins washed quite away, worship Indra in his hall, and King Haris Chandra is also present there, from the world of men. All the gods and the Gandharvas and the Apsaras attend the Lord of Heaven. The lightning, O son of Pandu, the rain-charged clouds and the winds, the planets and the stars come there; and the great mountains, rich in jewels, wait in that hall, talking sweetly together. These and numberless others come and go, worshiping Indra. That glorious hall, O tiger among men, has no equal among the gods as yours has no equal among men."

"You have told us of only one king, the noble Haris Chandra, who is present in the hall of Indra," Yudhistra said. "What deeds did he do, what high vows were kept by him that made him worthy to dwell with the Lord of Heaven?"

"Haris Chandra was a powerful king who brought the whole earth with its seven islands under his sway," answered Vyasa. "When he had conquered it with all its mountains, forests, and rivers, he performed the great Sacrifice of Coronation which is called the Rajasuya. For this reason Haris Chandra shone more brightly than thousands of other kings; for know, O bull of the Bháratas, that a monarch who performs that sacrifice may enter with joy into the company of Indra. It is not an easy sacrifice to perform, for he who offers it must, like Haris Chandra, have conquered the whole earth. Other kings may resist him and there may be a war that will destroy all Kshatrias and even the world itself. Vast wealth must also be given away to Brahmans and to all who ask.

"I have a message for you, O son of Kunti, from your father Pandu, for I have also visited the hall of Yama, Lord of Death, where I saw your father among countless other kings. He knew that I was coming hither, and he bowed to me and said, 'Tell my son Yudhistra, O holy one, that he can conquer the whole earth, since his brothers are all devoted and obedient to him. When he has done this, he should perform the grand Sacrifice of Coronation, called the Rajasuya. He is my son, and if he performs that sacrifice, I may, like Haris Chandra, dwell in the mansion of Indra for countless joyous years.'

"Therefore, O son of Pandu, fulfill your father's desire and you, too, with your brothers will dwell in the realm of Indra."

When he had said this, Vyasa went away, leaving in the minds of the Pándavas the thought of the great sacrifice.

The Coronation Sacrifice

Yudhistra Is Made Lord of the Earth

Yudhistra sighed deeply as he thought about the great sacrifice and his father's message to him, for it seemed to be a vast and dangerous undertaking. He wondered whether it would bring good to his people, for there might be danger of war, and he wondered if he were worthy to be lord of all the earth. He summoned his brothers and his councilors and asked them again and again to advise him, and they always answered him, "We believe that you are worthy to rule the whole world and that the time has come for you to offer this sacrifice."

Nevertheless, to make sure, he sent for Krishna, whom he believed to be the wisest of men. Krishna came quickly from the city of Dváraka, for he loved to be with his cousins the Pándavas. When Yudhistra had told all that troubled him, Krishna said, "Your brothers and your councilors have spoken well, O son of Kunti. You are worthy to perform the sacrifice

82

and should obey your father's command. But let me tell you, O first of kings, that you will not be able to do it as long as the king of Mágadha is alive. He is proud and mighty and already considers himself lord of the earth; many kings have submitted to him from fear, and he has conquered many more and holds them imprisoned in a mountain cave. When he has as many captives as he desires, he means to sacrifice them to Shiva, as if they were so many animals, for he has made fierce vows to that great god and so gained his power. If you kill this king and set those others free, you will be acclaimed by all as lord of earth."

"I have heard of him and of his wickedness," replied Yudhistra. "Is it possible to overcome one who is so powerful? Alas, this purpose seems to me very difficult to achieve."

Then Bhima spoke. "Sometimes cleverness as well as might is needed to vanquish an enemy. Krishna can provide a plan, I have the strength, and victory always follows Arjuna. We three alone can compass the death of the king of Mágadha."

"Give me Bhima and Arjuna," said Krishna, "and we shall accomplish your purpose."

"Bhima and Arjuna are my two eyes," said Yudhistra sadly, "and you are my mind. What shall I do without my eyes and my mind?"

Nevertheless he blessed them, and the three, Krishna, Bhima, and Arjuna, set out on foot towards the east, dressed as Brahmans who are under a strict vow. They traveled for many weeks, crossing kingdoms and provinces, rivers and hills, until they reached Mágadha, a land rich in cattle and grain, in rivers and trees. They entered the capital city, unarmed and unnoticed, passing along the principal street, which was bordered with shops filled with every sort of delightful wares. They took garlands from the flower-vendors and went on to the king's palace, where, without asking permission, they boldly entered his hall of audience.

The king rose and welcomed them, for he honored all Brahmans, and asked what they wished of him. Bhima and Arjuna were silent, and Krishna spoke for all three:

"These two are keeping a strict vow of silence and therefore cannot speak. At midnight their vow is finished, and they will speak with you then, O King."

They were shown to the sacrificial apartments; their feet were washed and they were given food and drink. At midnight the king came to them, for if a Brahman asks for an audience, at no matter what hour, it must be granted.

"It is well known," the king said to them, "that Brahmans who are under a vow do not deck themselves with flowers. Who are you, then, who come here with garlands round your necks and your arms scarred by the bowstring? You have the look of Kshatrias. Why do you come here in disguise?"

"O King of Mágadha," answered Krishna, "We have come at the behest of a great king to set free the kings and warriors whom you are holding captive. Indeed we are not Brahmans. I am Krishna of the Yadu folk, and these two are sons of Pandu. We challenge you to fight! Either set free all your prisoners or go tonight to the realm of Yama, King of the Dead!"

"All of my captives have been defeated fairly by me in war," said the king, "and I mean to offer them as sacrifices to Shiva. Do you think I shall free them now out of fear of you? I am ready to do battle, either with armies in the field, or here, alone, against one, or two, or against all three of you!"

"Which one of us do you choose to fight against, O King?"

The king turned to Bhima and said, "O Bhima, I will fight against you! It is best to fight against the strongest, whether one wins or loses."

Bhima fights the King of Mágadha.

Then he took off his crown and bound up his hair and led the two brothers and Krishna to the courtyard of the palace. There he and Bhima, those tigers among men, with their bare arms their only weapons, grasped and wrestled with one another, roaring like thunderclouds, standing for a moment to breathe and to clap their armpits, then seizing one another again and throwing one another this way and that. They fought for hours until the dawn came, and the citizens, hearing the noise, crowded into the courtyard and stood there in amazement. At last the king began to tire, and Bhima, feeling his opponent's weakness, lifted him high in the air with his mighty arms and whirled him round his head, and when he flung him down on the ground, the king was dead.

Then Krishna summoned the king's ministers and ordered the royal chariot. He and the two Pándavas rode out to the mountain cave where the captives were held and ordered them set free. Kings and warriors bowed down before him, offering their homage, but he said to them, "The just king, Yudhistra, of the Bhárata race, wishes to perform the Coronation Sacrifice. Acknowledge him as your lord, for it was he who sent us here to free you. Thus you can help him to carry out his wish."

Krishna set the son of the king of Mágadha on the throne of his father, and he and Bhima and Arjuna went home, driven in fine chariots and laden with gifts of jewels and fine gold. They were followed by the warriors whom they had freed and who wished to pay their homage to King Yudhistra.

Then the four brothers of Yudhistra went forth at the head of their armies, each in a different direction, asking the rulers of every kingdom to accept the sway of the eldest son of Pandu, and to come to the celebration of his sacrifice.

The youngest one, Sadeva, the son of Madri, went toward the south, and there many rulers paid homage and tribute to

Yudhistra, who was famous over all the earth. But there was one king who stood out against the son of Madri because he was always sure of victory in battle.

This king had a very beautiful daughter, who took especial care of the sacrificial fires; indeed, it seemed as if the flame would not blaze brightly unless that maiden urged it with her gentle breath. And, in truth, the God of Fire, Agni, had fallen in love with her and wooed her in the guise of a Brahman. Her father found them together and was very angry, but when the god revealed himself, the king gladly gave his daughter to Agni to be his wife. After that, if the kingdom was attacked, Agni protected it with his flames and every enemy was driven away.

When the king refused to pay homage to Yudhistra, Sadeva attacked the city. Suddenly his soldiers were surrounded by flames and they stopped, terrified, and dared not advance a step. But Sadeva stood unmoved at the head of his army, joined the palms of his hands, and said, "I bow before you, O Agni, you whose footsteps smoke, who purify all things. I am here because I wish to help my brother, the just King Yudhistra, perform a great sacrifice. It is strange that you, who are the heart of all sacrifice, should stand in the way of this one, which will be to your glory. I beg of you, O exalted one, to help me to fulfill my purpose."

Then Agni drew back his flames and said, "You shall have your wish, O son of Madri. I was testing your courage. I shall protect this city as long as this king or his descendants rule over it; but you need not fight, for at my behest he will do what you ask of him."

And truly the king came forth, as Agni told him to, and welcomed Sadeva and offered both homage and tribute to Yudhistra.

Sadeva, with his host, marched down beyond the Nerbada River, past the famous caves of Kishkinda, and exacted tribute from the monkey kings that dwelt in the southern forests. When he reached the seacoast, he sent messengers to the just king of Lanka, who willingly accepted the sway of the son of Pandu and sent gifts of pearls and jewels.

Nákula, his twin, conquered all the countries of the west, and there he visited the family of Krishna and the kingdom of Madra, ruled by his uncle Shalya, Madri's brother, who from affection gladly accepted the overlordship of Yudhistra. He subdued the fierce barbarians who dwelt on the seacoast and the wild tribes of the hills, and then retraced his steps to his own city, bringing with him so much treasure that it was hard for a thousand camels to carry it on their backs.

The Ceremony

The great treasury of Yudhistra was so full of wealth that it could not have been emptied even in a hundred years. His friends and ministers, each separately and all together, said to him, "The time has come, O exalted one, for the ceremony. Prepare it without loss of time!"

Yudhistra summoned the wise Vyasa to help him, and then he and his brothers began to collect all the things that were necessary for the occasion, as well as food and many pleasant things to delight the hearts of the Brahmans, for many priests and sages were gathering in Indra Prastha for the celebration of this great sacrifice. The sinless Vyasa was the chief priest, and he appointed other exalted Brahmans to perform the different parts of the ceremony and to chant the Vedic hymns. All of them blessed the enclosure where the sacred festival would take place and directed builders and artists to raise halls and

pavilions that were spacious and fragrant like the temples of
the gods.

When these were finished and ready, Yudhistra said to
Sadeva, "Send out swift messengers now to invite all the
Brahmans in the land, and all the Kshatrias and Vaisyas and
Shudras who care to come, to my sacrifice!" Speedily then
those messengers invited everyone and brought with them
many guests, both friends and strangers, when they returned.
The king sent Nákula to Hástina to invite Bhishma and Kuru,
Drona and Vídura, and those among his cousins who felt
kindly toward him. The elders of the Bháratas came with joyful hearts, with Brahmans walking before them. The sons of
Kuru, with Duryodha at their head; the son of Drona with
Karna; the king of Gandhara who was brother to Kuru's
queen; the king of Madra and the king of Panchala with his
sons; all came to the sacrifice of the son of Pandu. And
hundreds of other kings and Kshatrias came with joyous hearts
from many countries to pay homage to Yudhistra, bringing
with them gifts of great wealth.

Yudhistra worshiped Bhishma and the other elders of the
Bháratas and said to them and to his cousins, "Give me your
help in performing this great rite. The treasure that is here is
yours as well as mine." He asked each one of them to take
charge of some task, and Bhishma directed them all. Dushasa
gave out the food, and Drona's son took care of the Brahmans;
Drona himself took charge of the jewels and gold, the pearls,
and other gems, and gave fitting gifts to the guests; Vídura
made the payments; and Duryodha received the tribute
brought by all the kings. Krishna, at his own request, washed
the feet of the Brahmans.

Then Yudhistra began the Sacrifice of Coronation with six
fires, giving many presents to the Brahmans and pleasing

everyone with gifts of jewels and every kind of wealth, abundance of rice and pleasant and fragrant foods. The gods were pleased with the worship offered by the great sages, by the chanted hymns and the libations poured upon the fires; indeed all the castes of men were pleased with that sacrifice and filled with joy.

On the last day the sages and the king entered the inner enclosure, where Yudhistra was sprinkled with holy water and crowned lord of the whole earth. There the other kings waited upon the son of Pandu, holding his weapons and his armor, his shoes and headgear and garlands, while Bhima and Arjuna fanned him and the twins stood at his sides. Thus that sacrifice, performed in a favorable season, blessed by sages and Brahmans, rich in wealth, food, and gifts, was in due time completed.

The kings and warriors began to take their leave of Yudhistra. "By good fortune you have become king over all kings, O virtuous one!" they said. "You have also gained honor among the gods. O lord of earth, cherish your subjects with ceaseless care and patience; be the refuge and support of all men, as the rain clouds are to all creatures, as a large tree with spreading branches is to the birds!"

When they had departed, and the Brahmans, duly worshiped and laden with gifts, and all the other guests had gone their way, the sons of Pandu returned to their own palace. No one was left in the assembly hall but Duryodha and his uncle Shákuni, the king of Gandhara, the brother of Kuru's queen. They slowly examined every part of it and found in it many beauties that they had never seen before, and Duryodha's heart burned with jealousy.

He had often lingered in that hall, for he longed to have one like it or one still more beautiful. One day he came upon a crystal floor and thought it was a pool of water; therefore he drew up his clothes, and when he saw his mistake he was very much ashamed. Another time he thought that a clear pool of water was another crystal floor and fell into it with all his clothes on. Bhima saw him and laughed uproariously. Some servants also saw him and could scarcely hide their laughter as they brought him dry and handsome garments, but Duryodha could not bear to be laughed at and would not look at them. Shortly afterwards he tried to walk through a closed crystal door and struck his brow against it and stood there with his head swimming. The twins saw this happen and came to him and held him up, saying kindly, "This way, O King; the door is open now."

But Bhima was also there and laughed again, saying mockingly, "Here is the door, O son of Kuru! This is the way."

Duryodha's Jealousy

At last Duryodha took leave of the Pándavas and returned to Hástina, thinking sorrowfully about all that he had seen and suffered. On the way home his heart was so heavy and his mind so full of grief that he answered not a word when his uncle spoke to him. "Why are you sighing so deeply?" Shákuni asked.

"O Uncle," Duryodha replied, "when I beheld the wealth of the sons of Pandu and that assembly hall of theirs and saw their servants laughing at me, my heart flamed with jealousy. I am drying up like a shallow pool in summer. I shall throw myself into the fire or swallow poison or drown myself, for I cannot bear to live. Behold, the sons of Kuru are withering away while the sons of Pandu are growing greater day by day! O Uncle, tell me how I can overcome them!"

Shákuni thought for a moment and then said, "No one can ever overcome in battle the five sons of Pandu, with the king of Panchala and his sons. But I know how Yudhistra himself may be vanquished by you. He is very fond of gambling but he is not skillful with the dice. He cannot refuse a challenge, because he is a Kshatria. Now I am an adept at dice; there is no one equal to me on earth, nay, not even in the three worlds. Therefore, challenge him to play at dice and I will win his kingdom and all his wealth for you, O bull among men. Tell this to your father and get his consent, and I will fulfill all your desires."

"Tell him yourself, O son of Súvala," Duryodha replied, "for I cannot do so."

As soon as they arrived in Hástina, they went to King Kuru and found him seated on his throne. Shákuni said to him, "O great King, your eldest son has lost his color and has become thin and sad. Can you not find out the grief that preys upon his heart?"

"What is your sorrow, my son?" asked the king. "This vast wealth of mine is all yours; your brothers and all your family do everything to please you; you wear fine clothes and eat the best of food. Why do you grieve as if you were poor and alone, O proud one?"

"I enjoy nothing, though I eat fine food and am richly clothed, for I am the prey of fierce jealousy," answered Duryodha. "Ever since I beheld the blazing wealth of the son of Kunti, I have become pale, thin, and sad. I tell you, I must be strong, since I am still alive after seeing the whole earth under the sway of Yudhistra. The Himalayas, the ocean, the shores of all the seas, the mountains with all their jewels do not hold as much wealth as fills the mansion of Yudhistra. O King, since I was the eldest of his cousins, he asked me to receive the tribute brought by all the kings. No man has ever seen before the wealth that was brought to that sacrifice. My hands were so tired receiving it that those who brought it had to wait until I was able to take up the task again.

"O Father, listen to the tale of that wealth! The people of Valhika gave him as tribute a thousand asses, large and black-necked, that run a hundred miles in a day. The kings of the west each gave a thousand elephants, dark as rocks, decked with golden girdles and fine blankets; they are exceedingly patient and of the very best breed, with tusks like plowshares. The kings of the eastern countries presented finely woven carpets, armor inlaid with jewels and gold and ivory, thousands of chariots of different shape and fine design, adorned with gold, covered with tiger skins and drawn by well-trained horses. O lord of earth, those kings also brought heaps upon heaps of jewels and gems for the son of Kunti.

"The king of Kamboja gave countless skins of the best kind, three hundred horses with noses like parrots; and a like number of camels and she-asses, all fatted with the olive. The kings of Chola and Pandya brought numberless golden jars filled with fragrant sandalwood juice from the hills of Malaya and loads of sandal and aloe wood and many jewels of great brilliance and fine cloths woven with gold. The king of Singala gave those best of sea-born gems, the lapis lazuli, heaps of pearls, and hundreds of covers for elephants. Other kings of the earth brought thousands of cows, with as many copper vessels for milking them, to be given away by Yudhistra to the Brahmans, and they presented him with thousands of serving men with their wives. Besides all this, I cannot tell you the numbers of jewels, horses, elephants, and camels that were brought to the son of Pandu.

"Even the barbarous tribes that dwell on the seacoasts, in the woodlands, or in countries on the other side of the ocean waited at the gate with gifts of asses and goats, camels and honey, blankets and skins, for there was too great a crowd to be contained within the city. The mountain tribes brought soft, black brushes and others white as moonbeams; the cruel huntsmen who live on the northern slopes of the Himalayas brought heaps of precious skins and jars of gold that is raised from the earth by ants and hence called ant-gold. Men came from the eastern, western, and the southern seas. O Father, none but birds ever go to the northern ocean, yet the Pándavas have spread their dominion even there, for I heard conchs blow that were brought from that ocean, and the sound of them made my hair stand on end. When I looked upon my foes as they received these excellent gifts, I wished for death.

"All these men, of every caste, of numberless tribes, coming from every land, made the city of the Pándavas seem the center of the earth. In Indra Prastha thousands of Brahmans are supported by Yudhistra and eat rich foods on golden plates within his palace. Thousands of elephants and cavalry, charioteers and horses, and countless foot soldiers are fed there daily, and not a man of any caste lacks food or drink or clothing. Dráupadi herself, before she eats, sees that everyone, even the dwarfs and the deformed, have had their food.

"I cannot be at peace, O chief of the Bháratas, after I have beheld all this. I am pale and thin and plunged in grief because of the riches of the Pándavas."

Then Shákuni said, "O foremost of victorious kings, I can snatch this wealth from Yudhistra and give it all to you. I am skilled at dice and have a special knowledge of the game. Betting is my bow, the dice are my arrows, and the dice board is my chariot. If I challenge the son of Kunti to play, he cannot refuse, since he is a Kshatria, and I will defeat him at every throw, either by fair means or foul. I promise to win all that wealth of his, and then Duryodha can enjoy it."

"O Father," said Duryodha quickly, "if Shákuni is able to win all the wealth of the Pándavas, allow him to do so!"

"I always follow the advice of the wise Vídura," answered Kuru. "He will tell us what is right for both sides, and what we should do."

"If you consult Vídura," Duryodha said, "he will not allow you to do it, and if you do not do it, O King, I shall certainly kill myself. When I am dead, you can enjoy your kingdom with Vídura. What need have you of me?"

At these words, the weak-minded Kuru, always partial to his son, called his servants and said, "Tell the builders to put up a spacious palace with a hundred doors and a thousand columns. It must be set with jewels and covered with many-colored carpets. Let me know when it is finished."

When it was finished, he summoned Vídura and said to him, "Go at once to Indra Prastha and bring Yudhistra and his brothers here with you. Invite him to come hither to behold this handsome assembly hall of mine and to play a friendly game of dice within it."

"I do not approve of this command, O King," Vídura said. "I fear that it will bring about the death of all your family. A quarrel may arise between your sons and the Pándavas during this gambling match and disaster will surely follow."

The king replied, "O Vídura, if the gods are merciful to us, no quarrel will arise. When you and I, Drona and Bhishma, are at hand, what evil thing can happen? Say no more! The whole universe moves at the will of its Creator; it is not free. Therefore go and bring the invincible son of Kunti hither."

And Vídura, believing that his family was doomed, set out sorrowfully for the city of the wise sons of Pandu.

The Gambling Match

Shákuni's Foul Play

When Vídura arrived at Indra Prastha, he entered the palace and came before Yudhistra. The king saluted him lovingly, and seated his uncle beside him. "Your mind seems troubled, O Vídura," he said. "Tell me, do you come here in peace and happiness? Are the sons of Kuru reverent to their old father? Are the people obedient to his rule?"

"The king, with his sons, is well and happy," answered Vídura. "He reigns like Indra himself; his sons are all obedient to him, and he has no grief. However, he is not content with this, but wishes more wealth and power. He has sent me to invite you and your brothers to Hástina, to behold his newly built assembly hall, and to see whether it is equal to your own. When you are there, he will ask you to sit down to a friendly game of dice, and then you will see the cheats and gamblers that he has brought there to win your kingdom from you. He has sent me hither for this very purpose, O King, because Duryodha is jealous of your wealth and power."

"If we sit down to a match at dice, we may quarrel," said Yudhistra. "Who, then, can wish to gamble? What shall we do, O learned one? We always obey your counsel."

"Gambling is the root of misery," answered Vídura. "I tried to stop the king from doing this, but he would not listen to me. Do as you think best."

"What other gamblers and cheaters will be there, besides the sons of Kuru?" Yudhistra asked. "Tell us, my uncle, against whom shall we have to play, staking all that we possess?"

"Shákuni, the king of Gandhara, will be there," answered Vídura. "He is expert at dice, a desperate gambler."

"It seems then," said Yudhistra, "that there will be foul play. The whole universe, however, moves at the will of its Maker; it is not free. I have no desire to gamble, and I shall not do so unless Shákuni challenges me in the assembly hall; but if he does, I cannot refuse."

Yudhistra ordered his attendants to prepare for the journey without delay, and the next morning he set out for the city of Kuru, riding upon his splendid chariot and attired in royal robes. His brothers went with him, each in his chariot, and they were followed by Dráupadi and Subadra, Arjuna's wife, with their children and their servants. When they arrived in Hástina, Yudhistra entered the palace and saluted Bhishma and Drona and his uncle Vídura; he went to Duryodha and greeted him and his brothers and Karna, as well as Shákuni and other kings of neighboring realms who had been invited to behold the match. Then he and his brothers went to the apartments of the old king, who welcomed them joyfully, caressing each one of them, while Dráupadi and Subadra went to the inner apartments to be with the queen.

The Pándavas rose at dawn the next morning, wakened by sweet music, and after their daily worship they entered the assembly hall, greeting those who were already there for the gambling.

Then Shákuni, king of Gandhara, said to Yudhistra, "The assembly is full, O King; we have all been waiting for you. Now let us fix the stakes, and let the game begin without delay."

"Gambling is a sinful thing," said Yudhistra. "There is no virtue in it and no bravery. The game of honest men is to make war without crookedness or cunning, for even enemies should not be vanquished unfairly. We use our wealth for good purposes, O Shákuni, and give it to the Brahmans. Do not win it from us by fixing desperate stakes or in dishonest ways!"

"Men take part in any sort of contest because they wish to win," Shákuni answered. "Whether it is a contest of arms or a contest of learning or a game, the purpose is victory, O King. So also a man skilled in dice plays with another who is not so skilled, because he wishes to win. The purpose may not be a high one, but it is not dishonest. If you think that I shall not play fairly or if you are afraid, then do not play!"

"I cannot refuse a challenge, O King," said Yudhistra. "With whom in this assembly am I to play? Who can stake as much as I?"

Then Duryodha spoke, "I shall supply jewels and every kind of wealth for my uncle Shákuni, who is playing for me."

"Gambling with the hands of another person seems to me to be against the rules of play, as you, O learned one, must know," said Yudhistra. "However, if you are bent upon it, let us begin!"

When the match began, the kings and Kshatrias who were present took their seats in the assembly, with Kuru at their head, while Bhishma and Drona and the high-souled Vídura sat behind them with heavy hearts. The mansion looked splendid with these assembled kings, like heaven itself with a conclave of the gods.

Yudhistra said to Duryodha, "O King, this excellent diadem of pearls set in gold is my stake; what is yours?"

"I have many jewels, but I am not vain of them," Duryodha replied. "I stake them all against your wreath. Win them if you can."

Yudhistra cast the dice, and then Shákuni, well skilled in play, took them up and cast them deceitfully, but so cunningly that few perceived it. He said to Yudhistra, "Lo, I have won!"

"You have won this stake of me by unfair means," Yudhistra answered, "but do not be proud, Shákuni! Let us stake thousands upon thousands! I have many beautiful jars full of jewels in my treasury, inexhaustible gold and much silver. This wealth, O King, I will stake against what I have lost."

They played, and again Shákuni, casting the dice unfairly, said to the eldest son of Pandu, King Yudhistra of unfading glory, "Lo, I have won!"

"I have thousands of serving girls," Yudhistra said, "adorned with garlands and rich robes, with golden bracelets on their arms and wrists, and jewels round their necks. They are well skilled in the four-and-sixty arts, especially in dancing and singing; they serve the gods, Brahmans, and kings at my command. This wealth is my stake, O King!"

They threw the dice, and Shákuni cried out, "Lo, I have won!"

"I have, O son of Súvala," Yudhistra said, "thousands of elephants with golden girdles, decked with ornaments, with fine white tusks as long and thick as plowshares. They are worthy of carrying kings on their backs; they can bear every kind of noise on the field of battle, and each possesses eight female elephants. This wealth, O King, I will stake with you."

When Yudhistra had spoken thus they played, and Shákuni laughed, saying, "Lo, I have won it!"

"I have as many chariots as I have elephants," said Yudhistra, "all furnished with golden poles and flagstaffs, all drawn by well-trained horses and manned by warriors. I have also sixty thousand broad-chested warriors who eat rice and drink milk. This is the wealth, O King, that I stake."

They cast the dice, and the wretched Shákuni, who had cheated again, said, "Lo, I have won it!"

While this gambling that was bringing ruin upon Yudhistra was going on, Vídura spoke to Kuru, "O great King, listen to what I say, though my words may be bitter to you, as medicine is to one who is ill unto death! When this sinful Duryodha was born and began to bray like an ass, it was known to all that he would bring death to the Bháratas. Know, O King, that he will be the ruin of you all! Men who collect honey in the mountains and climb to dangerous heights in quest of it do not see that they are about to fall, for they think only of the sweetness that they seek. Duryodha is maddened by the play at dice and does not see that if he makes enemies of these great warriors he will surely die. O King, give up Duryodha and make the Pándavas your heirs! Exchange this crow, your son, for these peacocks, the Pándavas! Exchange this jackal for these tigers! O King, do not ruin the sons of Pandu for their wealth! What will you gain by winning it from them? Win the Pándavas themselves, and they will be more to you than all their kingdom!"

Duryodha heard these words and said, "O Vídura, you always boast of the fame of our enemies and belittle the sons of Kuru. We know you, O traitor; we know whom you really love. We have cherished you like a serpent in our laps; like a cat, you scratch those who feed you. Go from us, then, and live with them! Why should we give shelter to the friends of our foes?"

"O King," said Vídura, turning to his brother Kuru, "what do you think of one who abandons his minister for giving him good advice? Henceforth, if you wish to hear sweet words about everything you do, ask women and idiots and cripples for their counsel! A man who speaks the truth when it is bitter and one who listens to it are both rare."

Shákuni said, "You have lost much of your wealth, Yudhistra. Tell me, have you anything that we have not won, O son of Kunti?"

"I have numberless cattle and horses, O son of Súvala," replied Yudhistra, "milk cows with calves, goats and sheep in the country that extends to the eastern bank of the Indus. I will stake this wealth, O King."

They cast the dice, and Shákuni said to him, "Lo, I have won!"

"I have my city," Yudhistra said, "my land, the wealth of everyone who dwells therein, except the Brahmans, and all those people, excepting the Brahmans. My kingdom still remains to me and I will stake it against all that I have lost."

They threw the dice, and Shákuni, playing skillfully and crookedly, said to him, "Lo, I have won!"

Then Yudhistra was carried away by the madness of the game and said, "This son of Madri, Nákula of mighty arms and neck like a lion's, is now my one stake. He is my wealth."

And Shákuni cast the dice and said, "Lo, I have won him! O King Yudhistra, prince Nákula is dear to you and he now belongs to us to do with as we please. Whom will you stake against him?"

"This Sadeva," answered Yudhistra, "administers justice and is renowned for his learning. He does not deserve to be staked at play, yet even such a dear thing as this will I stake against all that I have lost."

They threw the dice, and Shákuni said, "Lo, I have won! O King, the sons of Madri, both dear to you, have been won by me, but Bhima and Arjuna remain to you."

"O wretch," cried Yudhistra, "it is sinful of you to divide us, who are all of one heart!"

"A man who is drunk falls into a pit and lies there unable to rise," Shákuni said. "You know, O bull of the Bháratas, that gamblers, when they are excited by the play, do things that they would never dream of doing at any other time."

"Arjuna," said Yudhistra, "is like a boat that carries us from one shore of the sea of battle to the other shore. He is ever victorious over his foes, the hero above all other heroes in the world. He does not deserve to be staked, but he is all that I have and I will play with him!"

When he had spoken thus and played, Shákuni cast the dice and said, "Lo, I have won him! This foremost of all wielders of the bow, this son of Pandu who uses both his hands with equal skill, now belongs to us. Play now with what remains to you, even with Bhima, your dear brother, as your stake, O son of Kunti!"

"O King," Yudhistra said, "he does not deserve to be staked at play, but I will stake Bhima, that prince who is our leader, the foremost in fight, the high-souled one with the lion's neck and arched eyebrows, who cannot put up with an insult, who has no equal in arms or in the wielding of the mace."

And, as they played, Shákuni cast the dice deceitfully and said, "Lo, I have won him! You have lost, O son of Kunti, your wealth, your horses and elephants, your kingdom and your brothers. Tell us if there is anything that you have not lost, that you can still stake in order to regain them all."

"I alone, the eldest of my brothers and dear to them, have not been lost," said Yudhistra. "If you win me, I shall do whatever the loser must do."

The Insult to Dráupadi

Shákuni, having cast the dice, said, "Lo, I have won! It is wrong of you, O King, to have lost yourself, for there is still one thing most dear to you that you have not staked. Stake Dráupadi, the princess of Panchala, and with her win all that you have lost."

"I will now play with Dráupadi as my stake," Yudhistra replied. "She is a woman whom a man might dream of as a wife, for her heart is tender, she is beautiful and virtuous and sweet of speech. Her waist is as slender as a wasp's; her hair is long and curling, her lips are red, and her eyes are like the leaves of the autumn lotus. O King, the slender-waisted Dráupadi is now my stake!"

When Yudhistra had spoken, the older people in the assembly said, "Shame! Shame!"; and the kings who were present were grieved at heart. Bhishma and Drona wiped the sweat from their brows, and Vídura sat with his head between his hands like one bereft of reason. But King Kuru could not hide his joy and asked again and again, "Has the stake been won? Has the stake been won?" Karna and Dushasa laughed aloud, while many wept.

Shákuni, proud of his success and in a flurry of excitement, kept saying, "There is still one stake—there is still one stake—" Then, playing with skillful hands, he cried, "Lo, I have won!" and picked up the dice.

"Come, Vídura," cried Duryodha, "bring hither Dráupadi, the beloved wife of the sons of Pandu! Let her sweep the rooms and dwell among our serving-women!"

"O wretch!" Vídura answered, "do you not know that you are tying yourself fast with cords? Do you not understand that you are hanging on the edge of a precipice, that you are like a deer that provokes tigers to rage? In my judgment, Dráupadi has not been won, since she was staked by the king after he had lost himself and was no longer his own master."

Drunk with pride, Duryodha said, "Fie upon Vídura!" He ordered a servant, a Suta's son, "Go, and bring Dráupadi hither! You need not heed the words of Vídura nor fear the sons of Pandu."

The servant ran to the apartments of the Pándavas, entering there as a dog enters a lion's den. He found Dráupadi and said, "Yudhistra, maddened by dice, has lost you to Duryodha, O Queen. Come now, and I will put you to some menial task."

"How can you speak thus?" cried Dráupadi. "What king has ever gambled, staking his wife? He must have been mad indeed if he could find no other stake."

"He staked you, O Queen, when he had nothing else to lose," said the servant. "He lost first his brothers, then himself and lastly you."

"O son of the Suta caste," said Dráupadi, "go and ask that gambler which he lost first, himself or me. Then come and take me with you."

The messenger went back into the assembly and said to Yudhistra, "Dráupadi asks you, 'Whose lord were you at the time when you lost me in play? Did you lose yourself first or me?'" But Yudhistra sat there like one who had lost his mind and said not a word.

Then Duryodha looked triumphantly at Yudhistra and said

to the messenger, "Tell the princess of Panchala to come hither and put her question to him herself. Bring her hither at once!"

The servant was afraid to face the anger of Dráupadi and asked, "What shall I say to the princess of Panchala?"

Duryodha turned impatiently to his brother, "Dushasa, this stupid fellow is afraid of Dráupadi. Go yourself and bring her here!" At his brother's command, Dushasa rose with blood-red eyes and strode into the apartments of the Pándavas.

"Come, come, Dráupadi, princess of Panchala," he said, "you have been won at dice by us. Put aside your modesty, come and behold Duryodha and accept the sons of Kuru as your lords!"

Dráupadi rose up in horror, covered her face with her hands and ran to the rooms where the ladies of Kuru's household were sitting. Dushasa, roaring with rage, ran after her and seized her by her long, curling locks, those locks that had been sprinkled with holy water at the Rajasuya sacrifice, and dragged her, trembling like a tree in a storm, into the assembly.

Helpless, with bent body, she cried faintly, "O wretch, it is not fitting to take me before the assembly, for I am not properly dressed and have but one garment on."

But Dushasa, dragging her forcibly, answered, "It does not matter whether you have one garment or none. You have been won by us; you are our slave and must live among our serving-women."

Dráupadi's hair was loosed and her garment half torn off; she burned with shame and anger and cried out, "O wretch! O cruel one! Do not drag me! Do not uncover me in the presence of the elders! The sons of Pandu are bound now by honor, but they will never forgive you for this, even if Indra were your ally! O shame! Does no one here rebuke you? Surely the Bháratas have forgotten their honor as Kshatrias; surely Drona and Bhishma have lost their virtue and so have the high-souled Vídura and the king. How else could they look on silently at this great crime?"

Thus did the slender-waisted Dráupadi cry out in her distress in that assembly. She glanced at her husbands who sat, furious but helpless, since they now belonged to the Kúravas; and her glance shamed and angered them still further, for it hurt them more than the loss of all their kingdom and their wealth. But Dushasa and Karna laughed aloud, and Shákuni applauded all that Dushasa did. Everyone except these three and Duryodha was filled with sorrow.

Bhishma beheld Dráupadi thus shamed in the assembly and said to her, "O blessed one, the way of virtue is sometimes hard to find. I cannot answer the question that you have asked. The son of Kunti played willingly and staked you in the game, for wives belong to their husbands. Yudhistra will give up a world of wealth, but he will never give up honor. I cannot decide whether you were won or not."

Then Vikarna, one of Kuru's sons, rose and said, "You Kshatrias, answer now the question that the blessed daughter of Panchala has asked, and declare which side each of you upholds." But none would answer him, because they feared Duryodha.

Vikarna wrung his hands, sighing, and said, "You kings of the earth and you Bháratas, I shall say what seems to me just and right, whether you answer or not. It is said that hunting, drinking, and gambling are the vices of kings. This son of Pandu has been carried away by the vice of gambling and made Dráupadi a stake, but he did so after he had already lost himself. Therefore, I do not think that she was lost."

An uproar arose in the assembly at these words, for many agreed with them. But Karna rose, beside himself with anger, and said, "O younger brother of Duryodha, you speak like a

fool, while your elders are silent because they all believe that
Dráupadi was justly won. How can you think that she was not
won, when here in this assembly Yudhistra staked all that he
had? Is Dráupadi not a part of the possessions of her lord? If
anyone thinks it is improper to bring her here attired in one
garment, are her robes not ours also? Dushasa, take their robes
from the Pándavas and take her garment from Dráupadi!"

When the Pándavas heard these words, they took off their
upper garments and threw them down, while Dushasa seized
Dráupadi's robe and began to pull it off. Then Dráupadi, still
radiant in her beauty, covered her face and cried aloud, "O
Dharma, lord of justice, protector of the virtuous, save me who
am suffering here in the presence of the Bháratas!" And
Dharma, the God of Righteousness, heard her and covered her
with beautiful garments of many colors. Dushasa pulled one
after another from her body, but another always appeared,
covering her, until many robes of different colors were heaped
up in that assembly hall, and Dushasa, tired and ashamed, sat
down.

The kings that were in that hall cried, "Shame!" and
Bhima, wringing his hands with rage, swore a mighty oath in
the midst of them all. "Hear these words of mine, you
Kshatrias of the world! I shall tear open in battle the breast of
this wretch, this wicked scoundrel, and drink his lifeblood!
May I never follow the path of my ancestors if I fail to keep
this word!" This terrible vow appalled those who heard it;
many of them applauded him and blamed the son of Kuru.

But Karna said to Dushasa, "Take away this serving-woman,
Dráupadi, to the inner apartments!"

"Wait a little, O wicked-minded Dushasa, worst of men!"
Dráupadi cried. She knelt upon the ground, weeping piteously,
and spoke to all who were assembled there. "Alas, I have been

Dráupadi is clothed by the God of Righteousness.

seen only once before, at my *swayámvara,* by the kings who were gathered there, but never since that time. The sun itself never beheld me in my palace, and now I am dragged into this hall and shamed before the gaze of the crowd! Alas, the sons of Pandu would not suffer even the winds to touch me, and now my hair has been seized by this wretch and I have been dragged hither! Alas, these elders of the Bháratas allow their daughter to be so ill-treated before their very eyes! I can bear it no longer. You kings, I am the wedded wife of the just king Yudhistra, and I come from the same caste to which he and you belong. Tell me now, whether I am a serving-woman or not, whether I am won or unwon at dice. I will accept your answer, whatever it may be."

The kings sitting there uttered not a word, for good or ill. Duryodha beheld this and smiled a little and said to Dráupadi, "O daughter of Panchala, let your husbands decide this matter for themselves. If Bhima and Arjuna, Nákula and Sadeva, will declare that Yudhistra is not their lord, if he himself declares that he is not your lord, you shall be free from slavery."

There was a hum of many voices and when they were still, Bhima arose and said, "The high-souled Yudhistra is our eldest brother and the lord even of our lives. If he considers himself won, then we are all won. If it were not so, no man who touches the earth with his feet would have escaped from me with his life after he had laid his hand on the hair of the princess of Panchala."

Then Karna said to Dráupadi, "O beautiful one, Bhima has spoken: you are now a slave. Go into the inner apartments and serve the king's family. The sons of Kuru are now your masters; choose another husband from among them, one who will not make you a slave by gambling."

Bhima sat, breathing hard, barely able to control his fury

at these words, while Duryodha, in order to encourage Karna and to insult Bhima, drew up his robe and slapped his bare thigh before the eyes of Dráupadi.

Bhima saw this and said with blazing eyes to the son of Kuru, "May I never enter those regions where my ancestors dwell if I do not break that thigh of yours in the great battle!"

Duryodha paid no heed to him and said, "I am still willing to abide by the words of Arjuna and the twins. Let them say that Yudhistra is not their lord, and Dráupadi shall be freed."

"The noble son of Kunti, the just king Yudhistra, surely was our master before he lost himself," answered Arjuna. "But after he had lost himself, whose master could he be?"

Just then a jackal howled loudly in the sacrificial room of the king's palace; asses brayed in response, and terrible birds added their cries. Vídura, who understood all omens, went to the king, and Gandhari, who also knew the meaning of these sounds, came from the inner apartments to warn him. Both told the king that great danger hung over him and all his race. He was filled with fear and listened to their counsel. He said to his son, "O wicked-minded Duryodha! Behold, ruin has already come upon you for insulting these bulls among the Bháratas and their wedded wife, Dráupadi!" Then he called Dráupadi to him and comforted her, saying, "Ask any boon of me, O lovely one! You are chaste and virtuous, the best of all my daughters-in-law."

"If you wish to grant me a boon, O foremost of kings," she answered, kneeling before him, "let the just and dutiful king Yudhistra be freed from his bond. Do not let my child, his son, be called the child of a slave!"

"It shall be as you wish, O blessed one," said Kuru. "Now ask for another boon, for my heart is inclined to grant you a second one."

"I ask, O King, that Bhima and Arjuna and the twins, with their chariots and their weapons, be given their freedom," replied Dráupadi.

"They are free, my daughter," the king declared. "Ask now a third boon, for you deserve more than two."

"O first of kings, O noble one," Dráupadi said, "one who is greedy loses all virtue. I do not deserve a third boon and dare not ask for more. My husbands, when they are freed from bondage, will be able to achieve whatever more they need."

Then Bhima rose and stretched his mighty arms. "Shall I here and now," he said, "slay all our enemies, O Yudhistra, or shall I destroy them from the roots outside this palace? Allow me to slay them now, so that you may rule the whole earth without a rival!" And the mighty-armed hero began to burn with the fire of his fury until sparks and smoke came out of his ears and nostrils, and his face was as terrible to behold as that of Yama, the God of Death.

But Arjuna, with pleading eyes, soothed his elder brother, and Yudhistra forbade him, embracing him and saying, "Do not be so angry! Let there be silence and peace!" After he had calmed Bhima, he approached King Kuru with his hands joined.

"O King," he said, "you are our father and we are obedient to you. Counsel us now, as a father does his sons."

"I bless you, O righteous one," replied Kuru. "Go in peace and safety and rule your kingdom with all its wealth. And take to heart, my child, this advice of an old man. You know the difficult path of virtue; you are wise and also humble, and you honor those who are old. Therefore follow the counsels of peace. Do not remember the harshness of Duryodha, but look upon me who am old and blind and look upon Gandhari and remember only what is good. Return to Indra Prastha.

Let there be brotherly love between you and your cousins and
let your heart be ever fixed on virtue."

Thus blessed by his uncle, Yudhistra took his leave of everyone with the greatest courtesy. Then he and his brothers, with
Dráupadi and Subadra and their children, mounted their
chariots and set out for Indra Prastha.

Exile to the Forest

When the Pándavas had gone, Dushasa hurried to Duryodha,
who was sitting among his counselors. He said to them all,
"You mighty warriors, the old man has thrown away all that
we won with so much trouble. What now, O bulls of the
Bháratas?" Duryodha, Karna, and Shákuni were stung by his
words, for they were filled with pride and jealousy. They
talked together and made a new and wicked plan.

Then they went to the old king and spoke smooth and artful
words: "O slayer of your foes, the angry sons of Pandu are
even now planning to destroy us. They are whipping their
horses in order to return quickly to their city and to assemble
their armies. Even now Arjuna is driving his chariot, lifting
his mighty bow, and casting angry glances about him; Bhima
is whirling his heavy mace, and the twins have their swords in
their hands and their shields on their arms. How can they
forgive the injuries that we have done them? Who is there
among them that can forget the insults that Dráupadi suffered?

"Let us gamble again and let this be the stake: those who
lose must be exiled to the forest for twelve years and must
then spend a thirteenth year in some inhabited place, but unknown to anyone. If they are discovered during that year, they
must go into exile for another twelve years. The Pándavas
will surely lose, just as they lost before. We shall have their

kingdom and all their wealth during the thirteen years of their exile, and we can ally ourselves with all the kings of the earth and assemble a vast, invincible host. Then we can defeat them if they ever return and bring them under our sway. Therefore bring the sons of Pandu hither once more to cast the dice!"

"It shall be as you say," Kuru said. "Let the Pándavas return even if they have gone a great way. Let them come once more and cast the dice!"

Bhishma and Drona, Vídura and Gandhari all entreated the king, "Do not let the play begin again! Let there be peace!" But Kuru listened to his sons; he paid no attention to the wise advice of his friends and his wife, but summoned the sons of Pandu to return.

The royal messenger overtook Yudhistra when he was close to his own city of Indra Prastha and said, "Hear the words of your uncle, O King! The assembly is ready, O son of Pandu! O Yudhistra, come back and cast the dice!"

"Good and evil come at the will of the Creator, whether I play or not," said Yudhistra. "This is a challenge and, besides, the command of the old king. I cannot refuse, even though I know that it will injure me." Therefore he turned his chariot and retraced his steps, along with his brothers and Dráupadi. Although they knew full well the deceitful ways of Shákuni, the mighty warriors entered the assembly hall and sat down to gamble amid their sorrowing friends.

Shákuni said, "The old king has given you back your wealth, O son of Pandu. That is well, but there is still a stake of great value to be won. It is this: those who are defeated at dice must dress in deerskins, enter the forest and live there for twelve years. The thirteenth year they must spend in some inhabited place, unknown to anyone. If they are recognized, they must spend another twelve years' exile in the woods. But if these conditions be fulfilled, they shall regain their kingdom after the thirteen years are past. Either you five sons of Pandu, with Dráupadi your wife, will suffer this, or we shall. Therefore play with us, Yudhistra, and cast the dice."

At these words, all that were in the assembly raised their voices in distress, and one cried, "Alas! Fie upon the friends of Duryodha! Why do they not warn him of his danger?"

Yudhistra knew well what would come to pass, but he answered Shákuni, "O monarch, how can a king like me, who must always be mindful of the honor of his caste, refuse a challenge to a game? Therefore I will play with you."

He cast the dice and then Shákuni picked them up, cast them and said, "Lo, I have won!"

Then the vanquished sons of Kunti prepared for their exile into the forest, one after another casting off his royal robes and dressing himself in deerskins. When Dushasa saw them thus, he danced around them shamelessly, and Duryodha, too, could not hide his joy and imitated the lion-like step of Bhima as he left the assembly hall.

The proud and mighty Bhima beheld this insult but controlled his rage and said, "O fool, I shall remind you of this when I kill you and all your brothers! Arjuna will slay Karna and Sadeva will slay Shákuni, that cheater with the dice. Hear these proud words, for the gods will make them good when we fight with the sons of Kuru!"

"In the fourteenth year from this day, O Bhima," Arjuna said, "if Duryodha does not return our kingdom to us, I shall slay in battle this Karna and all those other kings who foolishly fight against me. May the Himalayas be removed from where they stand, may the maker of the day lose his heat and the moon his coolness, if this vow of mine be not fulfilled!"

Sadeva said, raising his strong arms, "O Shákuni, you disgrace of the line of Gandhara! Those dice of yours are sharp-pointed arrows which will turn against you and pierce you in the day of battle. I shall surely kill you if you remain in the fight."

The handsome Nákula spoke, "I shall send to the abode of Yama all those who, because they wished to please Duryodha, spoke harsh and insulting words to the princess of Panchala at the gambling match."

Then those tigers among men, when they had pledged themselves thus, went to King Kuru, and Yudhistra said, "I bid farewell to my old grandsire Bhishma, to Drona and Vídura, to Kuru and his sons and to his courtiers. I shall see you all again when I return."

Those who were present were so overcome with shame that they could not say a word to Yudhistra, but in their hearts they prayed for his welfare.

Only Vídura spoke to him, saying, "O child, one who is vanquished by sinful means need never be downcast by his defeat. Go hence with our leave and with our blessing! You love each other and delight in one another's presence; your enemies cannot separate you. Who is there that will not envy you? It will be good for you to be away from the world for a time; for after this experience no enemy in the world will be able to stand against you. Learn from the moon the power of giving joy; learn from the water the power of nourishing all things; learn patience from the earth, power from the sun, and strength from the winds! I shall see you return in safety and crowned with victory."

"So be it!" Yudhistra said, and bowing low to Vídura, Bhishma, and Drona, he went away with his brothers, to prepare for their exile.

When Dráupadi was ready to go, she took leave of the noble Kunti and the other ladies of the household, embracing each one of them, and a wail of sorrow arose from the inner apartments.

Kunti said to her in a voice broken by grief, "O child, go safely, blessed by my prayers! I need not teach you your duties to your husbands; they are fortunate that they have not been scorched by your anger. In the woods, watch over my son Sadeva, who is the dearest of all my children—dearer than life itself. See that his heart does not sink under this misfortune." Sorrowfully she followed Dráupadi and came upon her sons, shorn of their robes and ornaments, clad in deerskins and hanging their heads in shame.

She wept, lamenting their misfortune, and said farewell to them, while they comforted her as best they could. Then Vídura came and led her slowly to his house, for she no longer wished to live in Kuru's palace.

And the Pándavas, with Dráupadi, set out on foot for the woods, their hearts plunged in grief, their children, with Subadra and their servants, following them in their chariots. The sorrowing citizens followed them past the gates, blessing them as they went.

When the Pándavas had departed, King Kuru sent for Vídura, for he thought of the dangers that threatened his sons and was anxious and had no peace. He asked his brother fearfully, "O wise one, how did Yudhistra go away? In what manner did Bhima and Arjuna depart, and the twin sons of Madri? What did their priest do, and the noble Dráupadi? Tell me, O Vídura, all that they did."

"Yudhistra, the son of Kunti," answered Vídura, "went away, covering his face with his cloak; Bhima went, looking at his mighty arms; Arjuna followed his brothers, scattering grains of sand; Sadeva smeared his face; and Nákula, the handsomest of men, stained himself with dust. The large-eyed Dráupadi covered her face with her disheveled hair and followed in the wake of the king, weeping bitterly. And their priest, O King, walked along the road before them, with kusha grass in his hand, chanting the awful hymns of death."

"Tell me, O Vídura," said the king, "why did the sons of Pandu leave Hástina in these different ways?"

Vídura replied, "King Yudhistra is always kind to your children, even when he has been so deeply wronged by them, O lord of earth. He is filled with anger, but he will not show his face because he thinks, 'I must not scorch the people by looking at them with angry eyes.' Bhima looked at his mighty arms because he was thinking, 'There is none equal to me in strength; I will vanquish all our enemies with these arms.' Arjuna followed the footsteps of his brothers, thinking that he would scatter arrows upon his enemies as easily as he was then scattering the sand. Sadeva smeared his face because he did not wish anyone to recognize him in this day of trouble, and Nákula stained himself with dust, thinking, 'I must not steal the hearts of the ladies that look at me.' Dráupadi, disheveled and weeping, thought, 'The wives of those who have brought me to such sorrow shall fourteen years from now be weeping and disheveled, as I am now, for those whom they have lost.'

"Their learned priest, O King, held the sacred grass in his hand and sang the hymns of death because he thought, 'When the Kúravas are slain in battle, their priests and teachers will be singing these hymns, as I am doing now.' The citizens cried out in their grief, 'Alas! Alas! Our masters are leaving us. Shame upon the Kúravas for acting like foolish children, banishing the sons of Pandu out of greed! Now we shall have no masters, for how can we love the wicked sons of Kuru?'

"As the Pándavas left the city, lightning appeared in the cloudless sky, the earth began to tremble, meteors fell to the left of the city, and birds shrieked from the temples of the gods and from the tops of the sacred trees. These evil omens were seen and heard, O King; they are a warning of the doom that will follow the wicked acts of your sons."

In the Forest — 1

The Kámyaka Forest

Thus the sons of Kunti, defeated at dice, with anger in their hearts, set out from the city called after the elephant, with Dráupadi and her five sons and Subadra with her son Abimanyu. When they had passed beyond the gates they mounted their chariots, while their servants, carrying their bows and quivers and their other splendid weapons, and the maidservants, carrying Dráupadi's robes and jewels, rode in carts behind them. Many Brahmans walked beside them, and the citizens of the town followed them for a long way, wailing aloud in their sorrow.

At sunset they reached the banks of the Ganges, where a mighty banyan tree stood. They purified themselves in the sacred water and spent the night there taking nothing but water for their food. In the twilight hour, that is both beautiful and terrible, the Brahmans lit their holy fires and chanted the

Vedas, comforting Yudhistra and calming the anger in his brothers' hearts.

The next day they set out for the forest of Kámyaka, which lies to the west, on the banks of a broad river. Several of their friends and kinsmen overtook them after they entered the forest: Krishna, who had been away at war when the gambling match took place, Dráupadi's brother, Jumna, and other kings and Kshatrias who had heard of their exile with sorrow and anger.

"Alas," said Krishna, "if I had been at Hástina, O best of kings, this evil would not have befallen you, for I should have forbidden the game, either by persuasion or by force. The earth shall drink the blood of Duryodha and Karna, of Dushasa and Shákuni, for the wicked deserve to be slain."

And Jumna, comforting Dráupadi, said to her, "O sister, I will slay Drona, and our brother Shikándin will slay the grand-sire, Bhishma. We cannot be conquered even by the gods when we have Krishna's help; what can the sons of Kuru do to us?"

They talked together for a long time, and when the visitors were taking their leave, Yudhistra said, "O Krishna, take back with you the delicate Subadra, your sister, and Abimanyu, Arjuna's son. Train him in the science of arms, in the study of the Vedas and the duties of the Kshatria caste. And you, O Jumna, take these five sons of Dráupadi and care for them as if they were your own. They need not share the hardships and the dangers of our exile." The two heroic princes gladly did what Yudhistra asked; they mounted their shining chariots, taking Subadra and the children and their nurses with them, and drove back to their own cities. The other kings and warriors reverently saluted the Pándavas and returned to their realms.

Then the sons of Pandu and Dráupadi went deeper into the

The Pándavas and Dráupadi bathe in the forest.

forest to find a pleasant place where they could spend the twelve years of their exile. It was late summer, and they looked with delight at the tall trees covered with flowers or fruits, hummed over by swarms of black bees, while on the topmost branches birds poured forth their songs. As they drew near to the river's bank, they came upon a hermitage where men of pure soul, clad in the bark of trees, were living. The king, his brothers, and their followers stepped from their chariots and entered the hermitage with joined palms, and the holy men and forest dwellers came toward them, eager to behold that king who was devoted to truth. Yudhistra sat down in their midst at the foot of a mighty tree covered with flowers and creepers, as his father Pandu had done before him. Bhima and Arjuna, the twins and Dráupadi, tired by the journey, sat down around him and made that tree, bent down with its weight of creepers, look like a mountain with five great elephants resting on its side. There in that holy hermitage the Pándavas made their home.

They picked the forest fruits for their food, and the five brothers, each going in a different direction, went out every day with their bows in their hands to shoot the deer. They first gave a portion of the food to the Brahmans and the holy men and ate the rest themselves; the faultless Dráupadi fed her husbands and the Brahmans as if she were their mother, taking her own food last of all. No one who lived with Yudhistra was thin or ill or had anything to fear.

One evening the sons of Kunti and their beloved wife were seated under that mighty tree, talking sadly together. The beautiful Dráupadi, dear to her lords and devoted unto them, said to Yudhistra, "When I behold this bed of grass and remember what you had before, I grieve for you, O King, for you do not deserve any sorrow. What peace can my heart know when I behold you here? Alas, these brothers of yours were once dressed in rich apparel and fed with foods of the sweetest savor. I grieve for them, too, because now they live in the woods on what the woods may yield.

"Why does your anger not blaze up, O King, when you behold Bhima living in sorrow in the woods, though he deserves every happiness? Why does your anger not blaze up at the sight of Arjuna in exile, who alone in his chariot has vanquished gods and men and serpents? How can you forgive our enemies when you behold Nákula in exile, so fair and young and strong, the foremost of all swordsmen? Why does your anger not blaze up at the sight of the brave and handsome Sadeva living here in the woods, when he does not deserve any sorrow? And how can you forgive our enemies when you see me here in exile, the daughter of Panchala's king, the daughter-in-law of Pandu and the devoted wife of heroes? Every Kshatria should know what anger is, but you can have no anger if your heart is unmoved by the sight of your brothers and me in such distress.

"Forgiveness is not always to be admired, O son of Kunti. He who always forgives is looked down upon by his servants, by strangers, and by his enemies; mean-minded men cheat him, and no one respects him. Forgiveness and force should both be used, each at the right time. The wise say that you should forgive a man who has done you a service, even if he wrongs you deeply; that you should forgive those who do wrong because they are foolish or because they know no better, for it is not easy to be wise; and that a first offense should always be forgiven. But force should be used against sinners at all times except these. O King, the wicked and greedy sons of Kuru have injured us again and again and should not be forgiven. You should use force against them.

"O Yudhistra, there was a learned Brahman at my father's court. Sometimes, when I was a girl, I went out of the inner apartments and sat on my father's lap and listened to the wise words of that Brahman. He taught me these things."

"Anger is the slayer of men, O beautiful one," Yudhistra said. "He who controls his anger conquers the world. There is no sin that an angry man may not commit, no word that an angry man may not utter. In anger a man may slay one who should not be slain and may reward one who deserves death. How, then, can we let ourselves be angry?

"There would be no peace at all in the world if there were not some men who are as forgiving as the earth. If everyone returned evil for evil, if everyone who was punished wanted to punish in return, there would be nothing but sin in the world, and all creatures would perish. Creatures are born because there is peace, O lovely one; they enjoy life and happiness because there are men who are as forgiving as the earth. Therefore, we should forgive every injury. Forgiveness is goodness; forgiveness is truth; forgiveness is sacrifice and holiness; forgiveness is the power of the strong; forgiveness is peace of mind; by forgiveness the universe is held together. Whoever knows this can forgive anything. The forgiving man is always victorious, for the world belongs to him. Therefore, do not give way to anger, Dráupadi."

"I cannot see that victory or happiness are won by virtue or by forgiveness," answered Dráupadi. "Everyone knows that you are virtuous, and yet this unbearable misfortune has befallen you. I do believe that you would give up Bhima and Arjuna, these twin sons of Madri, and myself, before you would give up virtue; yet virtue does not protect you. Therefore surely you should act, O King, to remove this evil that has come upon us."

Then Bhima, breathing hard with anger, spoke to Yudhistra, "O King, what do we gain by living here like holy men, unable to pursue any of the three aims of life—duty, pleasure, and profit? Why must we endure this banishment, just for the sake of keeping a promise? Only cowards would do it and that is what people believe us to be. This grieves me more than death in battle. We cannot live as Brahmans do, because we are forbidden to do so. A Kshatria must win his wealth by strength and energy. Awake, O King, and understand the duties of the caste into which you were born! Kill your enemies and destroy the power of Kuru's sons! No man can bear the touch of Arjuna's arrows winged with vulture's feathers. No warrior or horse or elephant can stand the stroke of my mace in battle. Why, then, should we not wrest our rightful kingdom from our enemies, with the help of Krishna, of Dráupadi's father and brothers, and our many friends?"

Yudhistra, after a few moments, patiently answered his brother, "I cannot blame you, O Bhima, for piercing me with your sharp words. This misfortune has befallen you all because of my folly. You know well, however, that when Shákuni challenged me to play the second time, in the presence of all the court, he told me the stake that we were playing for, and I replied, 'So be it!' I made that agreement in the presence of those good men, so how could I dare to break it, even for the sake of a kingdom? Wait, O Bhima, for the return of better days, as the sower waits for the harvest!"

"If we wait for thirteen years, O King," said Bhima, "we shall only be so much nearer death. Life is uncertain, and we should try to regain our kingdom before we die. During the last year of our exile we must live, unknown to anyone, in some inhabited place. O son of Kunti, everyone in the world has known us ever since we were boys. How can we live without being recognized? And if our enemies, through their spies, discover us, we must live in exile for another twelve years. Anger is hard to control. I burn with it day and night and cannot sleep. Arjuna also burns with grief, although he lives here like a lion in his den because he wants to please you. The twins do not speak, but all of us long for battle. Why, then, O tiger among men, will you not act and slay your enemies? There is no higher duty for a Kshatria than a righteous battle."

Yudhistra sighed deeply and thought to himself, "I hear a great deal about the duties of kings and Kshatrias, but I know the path of virtue and I must follow it." Then he said to Bhima, "Courage is not enough, O slayer of foes, to give you what you desire. There must be well-laid plans. Our enemies are skilled in fighting and always ready for battle. Many kings whom we have injured will fight on their side. Bhishma and Drona love us as much as they do our cousins, but because of the favor and the wealth that they enjoy at Kuru's court, they must fight for his sons. They cannot be vanquished even by the gods; and there is also that mighty warrior, Karna, fierce and angry, master of all weapons. How can we slay Duryodha and his brothers, when they are protected by these tigers among men? I cannot sleep at night when I think of Karna's lightness of hand, for I think that no one can surpass him in wielding the bow."

At these words, Bhima was silent and sat there, thinking. While they were talking together, the holy sage Vyasa appeared among them and they rose to worship him. He said to Yudhistra, "I know what is in your heart, O sinless one, and I can free you of the fear of Bhishma and of Drona and of Karna, the Suta's son." He took the king's hand and led him apart and said to him, "The time will come, O best of kings, when Arjuna will slay all your foes in battle, but he will need even better weapons than those he now has. He must go to Shiva and to Indra, his father, and learn from them the use of heavenly weapons. He is pure and brave enough to behold them and to win their favor, and when he receives those divine weapons no one on earth will be able to stand against him." Then Vyasa bade him farewell and vanished as he had come.

Yudhistra called Arjuna to him; he took both his hands and looked lovingly at him, saying, "The whole science of arms, O Arjuna, is known to Bhishma, Drona, and Karna. The earth, with all its towns and villages, its seas and woods and mountains, is now under the sway of Duryodha. You are the only one who can win it back for us, if he will not return our kingdom to us when the thirteen years are over. You are our one hope. Let me tell you what Vyasa said to me: 'Arjuna must go to Shiva and to Indra and learn from them the use of all their weapons. When he receives them, no one in the world can stand against him.' O slayer of foes, devote yourself fiercely to discipline, so that you may win the favor of these mighty gods. Take your bow and sword, put on your mail, and go northward this very day and do not give way to anyone until you find them."

Arjuna's Sojourn in Heaven

The strong-armed Arjuna obeyed the command of his elder brother. That very day he took up his bow and his quivers and put on his mail and his finger guards made of lizard skin; he said farewell to his brothers and to Dráupadi and set out on his journey. He strode through the forests and over the mountains without rest, and all the creatures fled out of the path that he took. He walked day and night without wearying and crossed the Himalayas, passing many fearful and dangerous cliffs and rocks and rushing streams, until he reached the mountain of Indra.

As he climbed its slope, a voice said to him, "Stop!" He looked round him and saw a holy man, ablaze with spiritual light, sitting under a tree. The holy one said to him, "Why do you come here armed and dressed in mail? There is no need of weapons here, for there are no quarrels on this hill. Besides, you could not have come this far if you were not pure in heart and free of anger; therefore, O child, throw away that great bow of yours and choose whatever region of bliss you wish to dwell in."

"I cannot dwell yet in any region of bliss," replied Arjuna, "for I have left my brothers behind me in the forest, and I have enemies whom I must kill."

The holy one smiled and said to him, "O slayer of foes, I bless you! I am Indra; ask of me whatever boon you desire."

The heroic Arjuna bent his head and joined his hands, saying to that god of a thousand eyes, "O exalted one, this is the boon that I ask: let me learn from you the use of all your weapons!"

The god replied with gentle words, "O child, I will give you all the heavenly weapons when you are able to behold Shiva, the lord of all creatures, who carries the trident and has a third eye in his brow. Open the eyes of your soul, O Arjuna, and strive to behold the highest of the gods, for when you have seen him, all your desires shall be granted."

Arjuna stayed on in that delightful place, by the banks of a clear stream where swans and cranes abounded. He gave himself with fierce energy to mastering his mind and body so that the eyes of his soul might be opened. He sat on a black deerskin and ate the withered leaves that fell upon the ground. During the first month he ate these, with some fruits, every third night; the second month he ate every sixth night and the third month he ate once in a fortnight. When the fourth month came he lived on air alone, and trained himself to stand on tiptoe with his arms upraised for days at a time. The light of his soul began to shine through his thin body.

The great sages who live in heaven beheld his fierce discipline and went together to Shiva and told him what Arjuna was doing, but Shiva, smiling, said, "Do not grieve because of Arjuna! I know what is in his heart, and this very day I shall give him his desire." And the sages, glad at heart, returned to their dwellings.

Then Shiva, the cleanser of all sins, the wielder of the great bow, took the form of a hunter of tall and stalwart body, with a fine bow and quiver, and came down upon the mountain where Arjuna sat. His wife, Uma, came with him in the guise of a huntress, with a crowd of merry spirits. The mountainside suddenly blazed with beauty, because the god of gods came there; the birds stopped singing and even the brooks and springs were silent, awed by his presence.

At this moment Arjuna saw a mighty boar that rushed upon him as if to kill him. He sprang up, seized and strung his bow in an instant, breaking the silence with the thunderous twang of its string. He aimed at the boar, but Shiva cried, "Stop! This boar is my prey, for I aimed at it first." Arjuna paid no heed to his words, but let fly his arrow; Shiva shot at the same moment, and both arrows struck the heart of the boar, which fell dead before them.

Then Arjuna turned and saw the hunter, splendid as a golden tree, and asked him, "Who are you that wander in this lonely wood? Why did you shoot the boar that was my prey? You have not obeyed the rules of the chase, and therefore I must challenge you to fight me."

Shiva answered, smiling, "I aimed first at the boar and my arrow killed him. You were at fault and therefore shall not escape me. Now shoot your sharpest arrows, and we shall see who is the better bowman."

This answer angered Arjuna, and he accepted the hunter's challenge, pouring out a shower of arrows that blazed like the rays of the sun. But Shiva, the creator of the worlds, the bearer of the trident, stood unwounded, like a mountain under a shower of stones, and Arjuna wondered, thinking to himself, "Well done! Well done! This mountaineer bears all my deadly shafts without wavering. Is he Shiva himself, or some other god or demon?" He shot all his arrows and then lifted his great bow and struck the hunter with the end of it, but Shiva snatched the bow out of his hands. Arjuna drew his sword and with the whole might of his arm struck at the hunter's head; but that best of swords broke in a hundred pieces the moment it struck. Then the son of Pandu, his mouth smoking with anger, fell upon the invincible god with his clenched fists, striking him blows like thunderbolts, which the hunter returned. At last Arjuna closed with him, pressing him against his breast; and then the god, putting forth his might, crushed Arjuna's breath out of his body and ended the fight. Bruised and breathless, the son of Kunti fell down on the earth as if he were dead, and Shiva stood above him, laughing.

The god saw how thin Arjuna's body was because of his fasting and wondered at his strength. Looking down at him, he spoke in a voice deep as thunder, "O son of Kunti, I am pleased with this deed of yours. There is no Kshatria equal to you in courage and in patience. O sinless one, behold me now in my true form and ask of me any boon that you desire."

Then he took his own form, that shamed the sun with its glory. In this divine form the god had many faces and many eyes and looked everywhere; he was clothed in divine garments with wondrous jewels and garlands and perfumes, and he held, upraised in many hands, his shining weapons. He shone with the radiance of a thousand suns, and Arjuna could not bear to look at him for more than a moment. He bowed his head to the ground and worshipped Shiva, saying, "O god of gods, O cause of all causes, O pure one, giver of boons, forgive this rash deed of mine, this fight that I waged with you, not knowing you. I came to this mountain only to behold you, for I seek your protection. Therefore forgive me!"

Shiva, appearing again as a hunter, took his hands and raised him from the ground. "I have forgiven you," he said. "Now ask of me the boon that you desire."

"O lord of all created things," answered Arjuna, "I ask of you that fierce celestial weapon that you wield, the weapon that hurls forth thousands of darts and arrows like poisonous snakes, that weapon with which you will destroy the world when time ends. If I may use it, I can vanquish Karna, Bhishma, and Drona in the terrible conflict which must take place between us. My great desire is to be victorious in that fight."

"I will give you that weapon," Shiva replied, "for you are worthy to keep it, to hurl it and to withdraw it. But, O son of Kunti, beware of using it! If it were cast at a foe of little strength, it might destroy this universe. You may use it only when all your other weapons have failed."

Arjuna bathed and purified himself in the stream; then he stood before Shiva with rapt attention while the god taught him the use of that mighty weapon and the mysteries of casting and withdrawing it. Then, with joined palms and bowed head, he thanked the god, who forthwith left the blessed mountain and disappeared before the eyes of the son of Pandu, as the sun sets from the sight of the world. After that the divine weapon belonged to Arjuna as it did to Shiva; it could not be seen by men, but gods and demons saw it at his side.

Arjuna spent that night and the next day on the mountain-side, rejoicing that he had obtained that wonderful weapon and had beheld the god of gods. In the evening a pure, refreshing breeze began to blow, new and fragrant flowers blossomed around him on all sides, and he heard the chanting of hymns to Indra. The lord of heaven with his queen, seated on the back of a celestial elephant, alighted on a mountain peak like a second sun and spoke to him saying, "O child, prepare now to enter heaven. I shall send my chariot to take you to that blessed region where I will give you my divine weapons and teach you how to use them."

After Indra had returned to heaven, Arjuna purified himself by a bath in the river, worshiping the gods with libations of water. He wondered what sort of chariot Indra would send for him, and even as he wondered, the chariot appeared, dividing the clouds and filling the sky with blazing light and with the thunder of its wheels. It was drawn by ten golden horses as swift as the wind and driven by a charioteer adorned with gold who, stepping down from it, bowed before Kunti's son and invited him to mount it.

Arjuna first bade farewell to the mountain, with its caves, its valleys and its snowy peaks, saying, "O king of mountains, you who give shelter to holy and heaven-seeking sages! I have lived on your heights as happily as a child sleeps on his father's lap; I have eaten your savory fruits and drunk the sweet water that flows from your body. Every day I have spent here has been a happy one. Now I must leave you and I bid you farewell."

Then he mounted the chariot gladly, and it soared upward

through the sky, drawn by those steeds that had the speed of thought. When they had gone so far that they could no longer see the earth, they entered the region of the gods, where the sun and the moon do not shine, for it has its own brilliant light. He saw the stars, which look as small as lamps from the earth, ablaze with splendor and beauty, and on the stars he saw royal sages, heroes who had died in battle, and saints by hundreds and hundreds. He wondered much at the sight and asked the charioteer who these might be.

"These, O son of Kunti," the charioteer replied, "are men who have deserved to live in these blessed regions because of their virtue."

Thousands of other chariots moved through the heavens, and the Gandharvas and the Apsaras, who dance and make music for the gods, came out to greet them.

They drew near Indra's city, at whose gate the four-tusked celestial elephant stood, and Arjuna beheld gardens and sacred trees that seemed to welcome him among them, while all around he heard the sounds of drums and conchs. There was no heat or cold, no poverty or sorrow or weariness in that celestial city. No one could behold it who had not purified himself with hard discipline; no one could come near it who did not know the Vedas and had not performed sacrifices and made gifts. As he drove through it, gods and sages and Gandharvas greeted him courteously, blessing him as he saluted them. Then at last he arrived at the hall of Indra, which the sage Vyasa had described to him and his brothers, and he alighted there.

The lord of heaven, his father Indra, was seated under a white canopy held up by a golden staff; he was surrounded by bards and singers and Brahmans chanting the Vedic hymns. Arjuna drew near and saluted him, bending his head to the ground, and Indra raised his son, took his hand and seated him at his side upon the throne, caressing him and looking at him with delight.

Arjuna lived then in his father's palace, learning all the while how to use the divine weapons and how to bring them back to his hand after they had done his will. Indra gave him his own favorite missiles—the thunderbolt and the lightning which come forth when the heavy clouds appear and the peacocks dance; he gave him also other weapons belonging to Agni and to Vayu, the Wind-God, to the demons and the storm gods, for all were in Indra's keeping. Arjuna became the friend of the chief of the Gandharvas, who taught him the singing, music, and dancing that those heavenly minstrels practice. So the son of Pandu lived for full five years in heaven, surrounded by every joy and comfort; but his mind was never at peace, for he always remembered his brothers and Dráupadi and the unfair game of dice, and he thought with rage of Dushasa and Shákuni and Karna.

Arjuna's Return

After the five years had passed, Indra said to him, "O son, the time has come for you to return to earth; your brothers are sorrowing for you. You can now overpower every foe; neither Bhishma nor Drona, Karna nor Shákuni, nor any other Kshatria will ever be able to defeat you." He set on Arjuna's head a golden diadem, girded him with a coat of mail that no shaft could pierce, and gave him rare unearthly garments and jewels and a mighty conch to blow in battle. Arjuna bowed down to Indra and walked round him thrice; then he mounted the blazing chariot of the god, which sped like a meteor through the skies. The charioteer guided the golden horses to a peak of the Gandamádana Mountains, where Arjuna alighted.

After the high-souled Arjuna left them, his brothers and Dráupadi were filled with sorrow; they were like pearls loosed from their string or like birds whose wings were clipped. They often spoke of him and remembered how he could use his bow with his right or left hand equally well; they recalled his amazing deeds in battle, his sweet speech and forgiving temper, his high honor, and his mercy to a fallen foe.

One day, while they were talking thus, a holy hermit came before them. When he was seated and refreshed, Yudhistra said to him sadly, "O holy one, I have been robbed of my wealth and my kingdom by cunning gamblers who exiled me to this great forest with my brothers and my wife, who is dearer to me than my own life. I cannot sleep at night when I think of our misfortunes. Even when I have regained my kingdom, I may be challenged again to gamble and I may again lose all, for I am not skilled in play, and I cannot stoop to deceit. And now besides, I have lost the company of the large-hearted Arjuna, that wielder of the bow on whom our lives depend. When will he return to us, having mastered the heavenly weapons? Alas, I am the most unhappy man!"

"Be comforted, O King, and do not yield to grief," the hermit said. "I have heard from certain holy pilgrims that Arjuna is living on a peak of the Himalayas, engaged in fierce discipline of mind and body. He lives on air and speaks to no man; surely he will soon fulfill all his desires. You need not fear to be challenged again to a gambling match, for I know the whole science of numbers and will gladly teach it to you." And he taught the science of numbers to the high-souled son of Pandu, who learned it from him eagerly.

Many holy men and hermits lived within the Kámyaka forest, and many others came there from various parts of the country, or passed through it when they went on pilgrimages. One day one of the great sages, who shone with spiritual light, came to the forest, and the Pándavas received him reverently. They sat round him as the gods sit round Indra, and Yudhistra asked him whence he had come.

"A short time ago," he said, "I went to the palace of Indra, where I saw your heroic brother, who wields the bow with either hand, sitting on the very throne of Indra. Listen carefully, O King, for he sent this message to you: 'Tell my brother Yudhistra to devote himself to virtue and to discipline, for they will bring him victory. Counsel him to make pilgrimages to the sacred bathing places, with his brothers and Dráupadi, that their souls may be cleansed of any evil. And tell him that in five years' time I will come to that king of mountains, the Sveta Peak in the Gandamádana Mountains, where I will meet him.' He also asked me to go with you to show you the way to distant and difficult places, and to protect you from the mighty demons whom you may encounter there. I have twice made the pilgrimage, O son of Kunti, and I will gladly make it the third time in your company."

"My heart is so full of joy, O sinless one," Yudhistra answered, "that I can hardly find words to answer you. Who could be more fortunate than I, to have Arjuna for my brother and you for my guide? Let us start our pilgrimage on the first favorable day."

On the day following the next full moon those heroes, with Dráupadi, set out in their chariots, with the high-souled sage and the Brahmans who had lived with them in the forest, followed by their cooks and other servants in fifteen carts. They first turned their faces towards the east till they came to the sea where the river Ganges flows into it. There the Pándavas bathed in the holy waters; then they turned southward along the seashore and visited the sacred bathing places, one after another, plunging into the waters that cleansed their hearts of sin. They purified themselves also by fasting and by long days of thought and meditation. They passed through various countries and visited the shrines of all the gods, worshiping each one with offerings of flowers and water. After they had bathed in the waters of the Godávari and Nerbada rivers, the Indus, the Jumna, and the Sarasvati, they turned northward again; for four years had passed and the time for Arjuna's return drew near.

They reached the foothills of the Himalayas and were delighted to find there a kingdom abounding in horses and elephants, where huntsmen and horsemen dwelt. The king received them gladly at the borders of his land, and they lived in comfort with him until the sun rode high in the heavens and they were ready for their journey into the mountains.

Then Yudhistra said to Bhima, "Dráupadi always looks to you for protection, even when Arjuna is with us. Therefore, stay with her here and keep Sadeva also with you, while Nákula and I, carrying only our bows and swords, go forward on foot with the holy one."

"O tiger among men," Bhima replied, "this blessed princess has suffered much hardship and sorrow, but she will gladly go further if she hopes to meet Arjuna. You, who miss him so much, will be still sadder if Sadeva and I are not with you, and we cannot let you go alone through those steep and dangerous mountains. Let the Brahmans stay with our chariots and servants, but let us all go together to meet Arjuna. Do not be anxious; I will carry the daughter of Panchala if her strength fails her."

Dráupadi smiled and said, "Do not fear. I shall be able to go with you." And Yudhistra consented to their going.

So they left their chariots and servants with the king of that country and set out on foot for the mountains; the brothers kept their bows strung at full stretch, their quivers full of arrows within easy reach, and their lizard-skin gloves on their hands. As they walked along the mountain paths, their hearts were filled with delight, for the slopes were covered with blossoming trees that looked like garlands hung upon the mountain, and the birds, mad with joy, filled the air with their songs. Herds of elephants moved like clouds among the trees, and deer lifted their heads, holding the grass in their mouths, to watch the wayfarers. They walked beside lakes covered with lotuses, whose buds were like joined hands greeting them. The air was filled with the sweet hum of bees covered with yellow pollen and drowsy with the heady honey of the lotus. Peacocks danced and spread their splendid tails high in the branches, where they looked like crowns upon the trees. The Pándavas and Dráupadi, wide-eyed with wonder, went deeper into the forest.

When they reached the Gandamádana Mountains, the way became steep and rocky; they passed through mighty forests filled with tigers, boars, and monkeys. One day a violent storm arose that raised clouds of dust and dry leaves; trees fell and crashed round them, and they could neither see nor hear one another. They took shelter in a cave, and Dráupadi, who was not used to walking and was worn out by the storm, sank down on the ground, faint and trembling. They all turned to her; Yudhistra took her on his lap, comforting her, while the twins lifted her rosy-soled feet and rubbed them gently with their strong hands, scarred by the bowstring, until she regained her senses.

Then Bhima said, "Do not despair, O King of kings. I will carry her now over all the mountains that lie before us."

So saying, he lifted her in his mighty arms and they went quickly on, for the storm was over. Before many days had passed, they saw on the side of a great mountain a pleasant hermitage, well swept, fragrant with flowers, and echoing with the chanting of the Vedas. Many sages lived there, dressed in black deerskins, feeding on fruits and roots and wild honey, and these holy ones received the travelers joyfully, offering them fresh water, flowers, and fruit. So they rested there for seven days before going on their way.

When they were rested, they took the mountain path again, ever traveling toward the north. They climbed the steep and fearful rocks with ease, passing deep caves and towering cliffs, and neither the Pándavas nor their guide, the holy sage, ever grew tired. Suddenly, one day, they beheld the peak they sought and they stood still in awe at the sight: for the great mountain, dazzling in its brightness, with clouds stretching out from its sides, seemed to be dancing with outstretched wings. Its forests were more beautiful than any they had seen: its rocks gleamed with brilliant jewels, and streams, like strings of pearls, rushed down its sides.

High on its slopes, they came upon a solitary hermit, sitting like a skeleton bound together with naked muscles, for he had worn away his flesh with discipline. They stopped to greet him, and he said to Yudhistra, "Do not go beyond this place, O best of the Bháratas. The summits of these mountains are the playground of the gods and no mortal may set his foot upon them. Even here you may hear the drums and conchs of the Apsaras and the Gandharvas and the sweet notes of their songs. O child, stay here until you meet with Arjuna; live on the fruits and honey of this mountain and do not venture farther."

They spent a month in that high hermitage, beholding many marvels, performing the daily sacrifices, reciting the Vedas, and watching the rising and the setting of the sun. All the time they thought and talked about Arjuna, and every day seemed to them like a year, for they had known no joy since their high-souled brother left them in the Kámyaka forest.

One day the sky suddenly lightened, and looking up, they beheld the chariot of Indra, like a smokeless fire or a blazing meteor, drawn by horses bright and swift as lightning. Quicker than thought it alighted on the mountain, and Arjuna, radiant with beauty, decked with fresh garlands and bright jewels, leaped to the ground. He bowed down first to the sage, then to Yudhistra and Bhima, touching their feet, while the twins bowed down to him and touched his feet. Then he greeted his beloved wife and presented to her the rare, unearthly garments and the jewels that Indra had given him. They were exceedingly happy together as Arjuna sat in the midst of his brothers, his wife, and the holy one, and told them all that had happened to him in the five years that he had been away.

"Thus I have learned the use of the weapons of Indra and Shiva and all the other gods," he said at last. "Indra himself set upon my head this diadem, gave me this mighty roaring shell and this celestial mail."

When he had told them all these wonderful things and they had sat together far into the starlit night, Arjuna of the spotless deeds lay down and slept sweetly beside the twin sons of Madri.

In the Forest — 2

Krishna's Visit

When Arjuna, that prince among heroes, had returned from the abode of Indra, the Pándavas stayed in the forests of that beautiful mountain, caring nothing for wealth or fame. Now that they were together, their lives passed so happily that they spent four years there as if a single night had gone by. These four years, with the six that had passed before Arjuna's return, made ten years that they had spent in exile.

One day Bhima, the fierce son of the Wind-God, with Arjuna and the heroic twins, seated himself before Yudhistra and said, "We have stayed here in exile, O King, only out of obedience to you and for the sake of your honor and good name. Otherwise we should have slain Duryodha and all his followers long ago. This is the eleventh year that we have ranged these woods, robbed of our kingdom. Our enemies no longer fear us; therefore we shall surely be able to live out the thirteenth year undiscovered. Then we shall have our revenge on that most hateful of men, Duryodha; then we shall slay him and regain our kingdom. Now, O just King, let us return to the world, for if we live much longer in this place that is so like heaven, we shall forget our sorrows, and your fame will vanish from the earth, as a fragrant flower withers."

Yudhistra listened to his brothers and did as they desired. They left that splendid peak and sought out the path by which they had come. As they started down, the holy sage bade them farewell, counseling them as a father does his sons, and then left them to return to his abode in heaven. Those heroes went down the steep and rocky road until they reached the foothills and came again to the kingdom of huntsmen and horsemen where they had left their chariots and their attendants. They were welcomed joyfully by the king and by their servants and remained for a while in that pleasant kingdom. Then they mounted their chariots and drove back to the Kámyaka forest, where they had dwelt before Arjuna left them, and they stayed there for the twelfth year of their exile, spending their days in hunting.

They passed the hot season in those cool woods, and then the rainy season came, which ends the heat and is delightful to all living things. Hundreds of black clouds, like domes built up into the sky, thundered and poured down rain day and night without ceasing; the sun disappeared and the stainless lightning took its place. The earth was washed with rain and overgrown with grass; the rivers overflowed, hissing like serpents. Boars and stags, birds and insects, excited frogs and snakes, all welcomed with joy that happy season of rain.

Then the autumn came, with throngs of geese and cranes; the river water turned clear and was covered with lilies and lotuses. The nights were free of dust, cool with clouds, and beautiful with myriads of stars, the planets, and the moon. The season was joyous and pleasant for the sons of Pandu, who roved by the rivers and in the woods, wielding their powerful bows.

During that autumn season, Krishna and his beloved wife came to see them. They alighted from their chariots and saluted the Pándavas and were joyfully welcomed. Krishna, when he saw at last his dear friend Arjuna after such a long absence, clasped him in his arms again and again, while his wife embraced the princess of Panchala. Then Krishna and the sons of Pandu talked together for a long time, while Dráupadi and her friend, seated at ease in the hermitage, laughed happily together and told each other all that had happened to both their families.

"O Dráupadi," said the wife of Krishna, "do not be anxious and do not grieve. Do not lie sleepless at night, for you will surely rule the earth again with your godlike husbands. Your brave sons are well and have become skillful in arms. They are living with us, and Subadra cares for them as if they were her own sons. She makes no difference between them and Abimanyu, but delights in them all, grieving in their griefs and rejoicing in their joys. They are beloved by everyone and take the greatest delight in the science of arms and in horsemanship.

"Tell me now, O daughter of Panchala, how is it that you rule the sons of Pandu, those heroes who are as strong and beautiful as gods? How is it that they are so obedient to you, so anxious to do your bidding and are never angry with you? Do you use spells or drugs to keep their love, or is it because you always look so young and beautiful? Tell me how I, too, may keep Krishna ever obedient to me."

"How can I answer such a question, noble lady?" Dráupadi replied. "Only a wicked woman uses spells or drugs to keep her husband's love. If a man knows that a wife uses such things, he fears her as he would a serpent hidden in his bedchamber. How can a man who is troubled with fear have peace, and how can one who has no peace be happy?

"Hear now, O beautiful one, how I behave toward the high-souled sons of Pandu, those heroes who can slay their foes with a glance. My heart desires no others, whether they be gods, men, or Gandharvas. I serve the sons of Kunti with deep devotion and humility. I never bathe or eat or sleep until they have bathed or eaten or slept, until, indeed, our servants have bathed and eaten and slept. I rise and greet each of my husbands when he comes in from the field, the forest, or the town, and offer him a seat and water to wash his feet. I keep the house and all within the house well ordered and clean and serve the food at the proper time. I never speak angrily or fretfully; I am never idle; I do not laugh without reason, and I never linger at the door of my dwelling.

"Formerly many Brahmans lived in Yudhistra's palace in Indra Prastha, and I honored those Brahmans every day with food, drink, and clothing taken from the storehouses. There were hundreds of maidservants, adorned with jewels and gold, skilled in singing and dancing. I knew the names and faces of all those girls, what they ate and what they wore and what they did. The son of Kunti had hundreds of serving-men who used to feed his guests every day with plates of gold in their hands; hundreds more who took care of the horses and elephants that followed in his train when he ruled the earth. But it was I, O lady, who knew their number, planned their work and listened to all complaints about them. Indeed, I knew everything that all the attendants of the palace did, down to the shepherds and the cowherds. I alone knew how much wealth my husbands possessed and how much of it was spent on the management and the protection of that great kingdom with its hundreds of thousands of citizens. While my husbands were busy with their duties, I took charge of their treasury, which was as deep and unbounded as the ocean. This burden, so heavy for anyone of idle mind, I bore day and night, sacrificing my ease and comfort. I awoke first and went last to bed, devotedly serving the sons of Kunti.

"This, O lovely one, has been the charm that has kept my husbands obedient to me; this is the art that I have always practiced in order to keep their love!"

Krishna's wife listened to these excellent words and touched the feet of Dráupadi, saying, "O princess, forgive me for my light words; I spoke in jest, as one friend to another."

"Adore your husband Krishna," said Dráupadi, smiling, "with love and friendship and sacrifice, so that he may think 'She loves me truly with all her heart.' Serve him; even when he commands a serving-woman to do something, rise up and do it yourself. And make yourself beautiful for him with fresh garlands and jewels, anointing yourself with fragrant perfumes."

The Sage's Stories

After these friends had left, there came to the hermitage a great saint who had lived for many thousands of years, yet his life was so holy that he looked like a young man of twenty-five years.

As he sat among them like a friend, Yudhistra said to him, "O deathless one, all of us who are assembled here long to hear your most excellent words. You have seen thousands of ages pass away and have seen with your own eyes the acts of creation. You have beheld God himself with the eyes of your soul when you opened your pure and lotus-like heart to him; therefore you are deathless. When the sun and the moon pass away and God sleeps, you will still be there to worship him. Tell us stories of bygone times and teach us how kings and saints and women should behave."

The saint stayed for many months in that hermitage, delighting the hearts of the sons of Pandu with stories of gods and heroes and sages. He comforted them for their misfortunes, telling them the story of Rama, the heroic king of Ayodhya, who was also banished to the forest for fourteen years and then returned victorious to his kingdom. He gave them wise counsel about the duties of kings and warriors and told them the following tale:

"There was once a king so wise and virtuous that Indra and Agni decided that they would go down to earth to test his goodness. So Agni took the form of a pigeon, and Indra pursued him in the form of a hawk, and that pigeon fell upon the lap of the king as he sat on his throne. 'Save me, O King,' it said to him. 'Do not yield me up to the talons of the hawk! The highest duty of a king is to protect his subjects. Therefore save my life!'

"Then the hawk, clinging to the royal throne, spoke to the king, 'It is not right, O King, for you to keep from me the food that God has given me. If I have no food I shall surely die and then my wife and children will perish. If you protect this pigeon you will destroy many lives. This is not virtue, O King!'

" 'Has any man ever heard birds speak as these do?' the king said, wondering. 'How can I act rightly, having heard them both? One who gives up a frightened creature that seeks his protection will never live in heaven. On the other hand, one who refuses food to the hungry is also doomed. O hawk, you shall have a bull cooked with rice, instead of this pigeon, and abundant food shall be carried to the place where you live!'

" 'I do not desire a bull, great King,' answered the hawk, 'or any other food except this pigeon whom God gave me today for my prey.'

" 'O ranger of the skies,' said the king, 'I will bestow upon you a rich province of my kingdom or any other thing that you desire, except this one pigeon that has come to me for protection. Tell me what you will take in exchange for him.'

"The hawk said, 'If you really care so much for this bird, O mighty ruler of men, cut off a piece of your own flesh and weigh it in a balance against this pigeon. If you will give me a piece of your flesh that equals the pigeon in weight, I shall be satisfied.'

" 'You have done me a favor,' answered the king.

"Then the good monarch cut off a piece of his own flesh and placed it on one of the scales of a balance, putting the pigeon on the other scale. The pigeon, however, outweighed the piece of flesh, so he cut off another piece and still another and another but the pigeon was always heavier. At last the king himself mounted the balance cheerfully, willing to sacrifice himself in order to save the frightened bird.

"When the hawk saw this, he cried, 'Stay, O noble King! I am Indra, the wielder of the thunderbolt, and the pigeon is Agni, the smoke-bannered God of Fire. We came to test you and we are satisfied. Behold, these gashes in your body, where you cut off your flesh, shall be made the color of gold and shall give out a sweet fragrance. Your glory shall be known to all the earth, O King, and you shall dwell in the blessed regions after your death.' Speaking thus, Indra and Agni ascended into heaven, and the king, after filling heaven and earth with his good deeds, went to the regions of the blessed."

He told them about the creation of this universe and of many things that had happened long ages ago to the earth on which they lived.

"O King, foremost of men, there was once a powerful saint named Manu, who practiced severe and rigid discipline for many thousands of years in a forest by the side of a river.

"One day a fish came to the bank of the river and said to him, 'Worshipful sir, I am a helpless little fish and I am very much afraid of the big fishes, because it is the custom for the large ones to prey upon the small. O holy one, I hope that you will find it worth your while to protect me. I will reward you for your kindness.'

"Manu was filled with pity on hearing these words; he took the little fish, whose body gleamed like a moonbeam, and put it in a water jug. He tended it carefully, as if it were a child, and it soon grew so big that there was no room for it in the jug. So he took it out and put it in a pool and the fish lived there for a year, until it became so large that it could no longer play about in the pool.

"It saw Manu one day and said to him, 'O holy and adorable father, pray take me to the Ganges, that favorite wife of the Ocean, so that I may live there.' And Manu took it and put it into the river with his own hands and there it grew still more, until even the Ganges could not contain it.

"Then it said to Manu, 'Master, I can no longer move about in this river because of my great size. I beg you to take me quickly to the sea!'

"So Manu took it out of the river, and in spite of its great size he carried it to the sea and threw it in. Then the fish turned to him with a smile and said, 'Listen carefully to me, O sinless one. The time for the cleansing of the world is at hand. A fearful flood will overwhelm the earth and all creatures moving and unmoving will be destroyed. You must build a strong and massive boat and fasten to it a long rope that cannot break. When the water begins to rise you must get into it and take with you all the seeds that grow upon the earth and keep them carefully. Then wait for me, for without my help you cannot escape death. I shall appear to you with horns on my head and so you shall recognize me.'

"And Manu said, 'I believe all that you say, O mighty one, and I shall obey you.'

"Then Manu built the boat and gathered all the seeds that grew on the earth. The waters began to rise and he entered the boat and set sail upon the surging sea. He thought of the fish, and immediately it appeared to him, like a rock in the midst of the ocean. He saw that it had horns upon its head, so he tied the rope into a noose and threw it round the head of the fish, which towed the boat with great strength through the roaring, tossing sea. Nothing but water could be seen, and the boat reeled like a drunken man while the fish, for many days, towed it powerfully and patiently toward the highest peak of the Himalayas. There the fish told Manu to tie his boat to that peak—which is still called the Harbor—and Manu obeyed.

"Then it said to him, 'I am the Creator of all things; there is none greater than I. I have taken this form to save you from the flood. Now you must create again all beings—gods, men, and demons—and plant again all the seeds that you have brought with you. You can do this because of your spiritual power and because you have my blessing.' So saying, the fish vanished; and there, upon that mountain peak, Manu began to create all things in their proper order.

"This is the Legend of the Fish, and he who meditates upon it may be cleansed of all his sin."

The Legend of the Fish

So with many tales and much wise talk the Pándavas spent their last year in the forest.

The Riddles of the Crane

One day, toward the end of that year, a deer wandered into the clearing where the hermitage stood, and while it was butting its head about there, it chanced to catch in its antlers two sticks with which a Brahman made his fire by rubbing them together until a spark appeared. Thereupon the deer bounded swiftly away, carrying the sticks with it. Now the Brahman offered his daily sacrifice to Agni, God of Fire, with those two sticks, so he ran to the Pándavas and told them what had happened, begging them to follow the deer and to bring back his fire sticks, so that his sacrifice might not be hindered. They took up their bows and started out at once, and seeing the deer at no great distance, they shot barbed arrows and javelins at it but could not pierce it. They pursued it into the deep woods and at last lost sight of it. Tired and disappointed, hungry and thirsty, they sat down in the cool shade of a banyan tree, wondering why such mighty warriors and bowmen as they were should have failed to track down and to kill this one deer.

Yudhistra said to Nákula, "O son of Madri, climb this tree and see whether there is any water near us, for all your brothers are tired and suffer from thirst."

Nákula speedily climbed the tree and said, "I see trees that grow on watery ground and I hear the cries of cranes; therefore water must be near."

"Fetch water in our quivers, O kind one," said Yudhistra.

Nákula ran off and soon came to a crystal lake where many cranes were standing. He stooped to drink when a voice said to him, "O child, do not be rash! This lake is mine. Answer my questions first and then drink and take all the water that you desire." But Nákula was very thirsty; he paid no heed to these words and drank the cool water. No sooner had he drunk it than he fell down dead.

When Nákula did not return, Yudhistra sent Sadeva to find him and to bring the water, and Sadeva came to the lake and found his twin brother lying dead on the ground. He was torn with grief at the sight, but also very thirsty; so he stooped to drink, and as he did so he heard the same voice saying, "O son of Madri, do not be rash! This lake is mine. First answer my questions and then drink and take all the water you want." But Sadeva, too, paid no attention to the voice; he drank the water and fell dead beside his brother.

Then Yudhistra sent Arjuna to find his younger brothers, and Arjuna, with his bow in one hand and his naked sword in the other, came to the lake and found his brothers lying dead on the ground. Filled with grief and rage he raised his bow, looking round the wood for an enemy, but he saw no one. He thought, "Surely I shall have to fight, and I must first quench my thirst." And bending down to drink, he heard the same words that had been spoken to his brothers.

He leapt to his feet and cried, "Who is it that forbids me to drink? Come out of hiding! When you are pierced with my arrows you will no longer speak so insolently." And he shot his invincible shafts in all directions, even into the sky.

The voice said quietly, "Why take so much trouble, O son of Kunti? Answer my questions and then drink; for if you drink first, you shall surely die." But Arjuna was angry and did not answer; he drank and fell down dead.

Then the mighty Bhima came and suffered the same fate, falling beside his brothers.

Yudhistra waited for them a long time, his heart deeply

troubled. He rose up and entered the forest, listening for some human sound, but he heard only the hum of the black bees and the songs of warblers. He went on until he came to that beautiful lake, overgrown with lilies and lotuses, where he found his brothers, as glorious as gods, lying dead, with their bows and arrows strewn on the ground. He was overwhelmed with grief, and wept and lamented for them, wondering greatly who could have killed them.

"Alas," he said, "why do these unvanquished ones lie here upon the earth, their bodies unwounded? There are no marks of weapons here; no footprints on the ground. Some powerful being must have killed them, for each of them was like a mighty cataract. Who could have overthrown these four great mountains, who but Yama, the God of the Dead, who in due time takes to himself all creatures?"

He stepped down to the water in order to purify himself from the sight of death, and as he did so he heard a voice saying, "I am a crane that lives on tiny fish. It was I who sent your brothers to Yama's realm, because they drank of this water after I forbade them to do so. O prince, if you do not answer my questions before you drink, you will be the fifth to die. This lake is mine. Do not be rash, O son of Kunti!"

"I do not desire what belongs to you, O worshipful one," Yudhistra said. "You have done an exceedingly wonderful deed, for you have slain those whom neither gods nor demons could face in battle. I do not know who you are or what your purpose is, but I am filled with wonder and also with fear. I shall answer your questions as best I can; therefore ask what you will!"

The crane then said, "What does not close its eyes when it sleeps? What does not move after it is born? What has no heart? What grows as it moves?"

"A fish does not close its eyes when it sleeps," answered Yudhistra. "An egg does not move after it is born. A stone has no heart. A river grows as it moves."

The crane asked, "What always travels alone? What is reborn after its birth? What god is the guest of man? What is swifter than the wind?"

Yudhistra answered, "The sun always travels alone. The moon is reborn after its birth. Agni, God of Fire, is the guest of man. Thought is swifter than the wind."

The crane asked, "What, O King, is true knowledge? What is ignorance? What is mercy and what is the highest duty?"

"True knowledge is to know God," Yudhistra replied. "Ignorance is not to know one's duty. Mercy is to wish happiness to everyone. The highest duty is not to hurt any living creature."

"You have, O king of men," said the crane, "truly answered all of my questions. Therefore I shall give life to one of your brothers, whichever one you choose."

"Give life to this one who is tall as a tree, broad-chested and long of arm, O mighty one," Yudhistra answered after he had thought for a moment. "Give Nákula his life!"

"How can you forsake Bhima, who is as strong as a thousand elephants, and wish Nákula to live?" rejoined the crane. "How can you pass by Arjuna, on whom all the sons of Pandu depend, and wish Nákula to live? Bhima and Arjuna are so very dear to you; why, then, do you want a half brother to regain his life?"

"He who sacrifices virtue sacrifices himself also," Yudhistra said. "He who cherishes it is cherished by it in return. Therefore I always cherish virtue and never sacrifice it, lest we ourselves be sacrificed. My father had two wives, Kunti and Madri. There is no difference between them in my eyes and no difference between my brothers. But Kunti has a living son in me, and now there is no one to make offerings to Madri's spirit. Therefore give life to Nákula, her son."

"Since you know the true meaning of knowledge, duty, and mercy, O bull of the Bháratas, both in word and deed," said the crane, "I will let all your brothers live!" At these words the four brothers rose up, refreshed, their thirst and hunger gone, and they all embraced each other with great joy.

Then Yudhistra said, "O you who stand on one leg in the lake, what god are you, for surely you are no bird, O unconquerable one! Are you the lord of the gods, the wielder of the thunderbolt? Each of my brothers can slay ten thousand warriors and I know no god or man or demon who can slay so many. They are refreshed as if they had just wakened from sweet sleep. Are you a friend of ours? Are you, perchance, my father, Dharma?"

The crane vanished and in its place the mighty Dharma, the God of Justice, appeared before them, saying, "O child, I am your father, the lord of justice. I came here to test you, and I am well pleased with you. Now ask what you will of me, O foremost of kings, for I will grant whatever you desire. Those who honor me never come to harm."

"A deer carried away a Brahman's fire sticks," Yudhistra answered. "Let us find them, O exalted one, so that the Brahman's adoration of Agni may not be interrupted. This is the first boon that I ask, since for that reason we came to these woods."

"It was I, O son of Kunti," the lord of justice said, "who took the form of a deer and carried away the fire sticks, so that I might test you. Behold them here! Now ask another boon!"

"We have spent twelve years in the forest," said his noble son, "and the thirteenth year has now come. Let no one discover us during that year! That is my second boon."

The worshipful one replied, "I grant this second boon: you will spend this thirteenth year secretly and unknown, in the kingdom of Virata, the ruler of the Matsyas. Ask a third boon, O King!"

"It is enough that I have beheld you with my eyes, O god of gods," said Yudhistra, worshiping him. "May I conquer greed and folly and anger, and may my mind be ever devoted to truth and kindness!"

"Those desires are fulfilled by your own nature, O sinless one," answered the god. "May happiness and victory be yours!"

With these words he vanished from their sight. The Pándavas lay down and slept sweetly; when they awoke they returned to the hermitage and gave the Brahman his fire sticks.

They Plan the Thirteenth Year

Shortly after that day Yudhistra called his younger brothers and Dráupadi together and said to them, "Twelve years of our exile have now passed, and the thirteenth year, hardest of all to endure, has come. We must choose some pleasant region where we may live in secrecy, free of fear. The aged Virata, king of the Matsyas, is powerful, good, and generous. Let us spend this year in his city, serving him even as the adorable God of Justice has told us to. Tell me now, O sons of the Bháratas, how each of you can serve the king and how you will present yourselves to him."

"O god among men," Arjuna asked, "what service will you take in Virata's kingdom? It is hard for a king to bear trouble as an ordinary person does. How will you live unrecognized?"

"I shall present myself as a Brahman, skilled in dice and fond of gambling," Yudhistra replied. "I shall entertain that high-souled king and his friends in his court, moving ivory men on boards of gold and silver, or throwing jeweled dice. I shall call myself by another name, and if the monarch asks me who I am, I shall say that I was formerly the intimate friend of King Yudhistra. What service will you undertake, O Bhima?"

"I shall present myself to the king of the Matsyas as a cook," said Bhima. "I can cook skillfully, and I shall make him better curries than he has ever tasted before and carry mighty loads of wood for his fires. The king will be so pleased with me that he will give me charge of all his kitchens. I shall also break powerful elephants and bulls, and if any wrestlers come to the court I shall fight them and so entertain the king. If he asks me who I am, I shall say that I was formerly the cook and wrestler of the good King Yudhistra."

"What will Arjuna do," asked Yudhistra, "he who lived for five years in the shining halls of heaven, learning the use of all the heavenly weapons; he who is among warriors what the Himalayas are among mountains, what the ocean is among waters, and what the tiger is among the beasts?"

"O lord of earth," answered Arjuna, "it is hard to hide the scars of the bowstrings on my arms. Therefore I shall cover my arms with bangles, put brilliant rings in my ears, braid my hair, and call myself a eunuch who can teach singing and dancing to the ladies of Virata's palace. In the inner apartments I will entertain the ladies by telling them stories, and if anyone asks me whence I come, I will say that I taught music and dancing in Yudhistra's palace. Thus, O King, as fire is hidden in ashes, I will pass the year unrecognized in Virata's kingdom."

"O Nákula," Yudhistra said, "you are tender and graceful and worthy of every luxury. Tell me what you will do in the kingdom of the Matsyas."

"I shall become the keeper of King Virata's horses," answered Nákula. "Horses are very dear to me, as they are to you, O King of the Bháratas. I am skillful in training and tending them, as you know; even wild colts and mares become gentle under my hands and let me break them for riding and for drawing chariots. If anyone asks about me, I shall say that formerly I was employed by King Yudhistra and took charge of his horses. The king will give me charge of all his stables, and I shall spend my time delightfully there, where no one will look for me or recognize me."

"And you, O Sadeva," asked Yudhistra. "How will you present yourself before the king and what will you do in order to live in secrecy?"

"I shall offer myself as a cowherd, O lord of earth," answered Sadeva, "and take charge of all the king's cattle. I often watched over your herds, for I have a special knowledge of cattle and can tame the unruly ones. I am skilled in milking and keeping count of cows and take delight in working with them. I shall say that I was once a cowherd in your kingdom."

"This beloved wife of ours," said Yudhistra, "dearer to us than our lives, has always been cherished by us and has never left our sides. Now she, too, must serve strangers and live unrecognized in Virata's city. What will she do, who is so delicate and young?"

"I shall offer myself to the queen as a serving-woman skilled in dressing hair," Dráupadi replied, "and say that I served Dráupadi in Yudhistra's household. I will please her and she will cherish me; therefore do not grieve, O King!"

After they had talked thus and made their plans, they sought the advice of their priest. They decided together that he should return to Panchala, taking the holy fire with him so that he could continue their daily sacrifices; the maidservants and the cooks were to go with him, too, while the empty chariots were to be taken to Krishna; and all the servants were to say, "We do not know where the Pándavas have gone. They left us in the Kámyaka forest." Then the priest blessed them and performed the ceremonies of departure, and they saluted him and the other Brahmans in the hermitage, taking their leave of all. They girded on their swords and their lizard-skin gloves and, carrying their other weapons, set out on foot for the kingdom of the Matsyas, Dráupadi walking before them.

They left the forest where they had lived so long and came into open country, where there were footpaths and villages and fields with growing grain. They passed Dráupadi's home, the land of the Panchalas, and entered the kingdom of Virata, calling themselves hunters.

When they came in sight of the city, Yudhistra said to Arjuna, "Where shall we leave our weapons, before we enter the city? If we carry them with us, the people will be alarmed and wonder who we are; besides, your great bow, Gandíva, is well known to all men and would betray us. Remember that if even one of us is discovered, we shall have to pass another twelve years in the forest."

"I see yonder a burial ground that has a mighty tree with many branches that are hard to climb," Arjuna said. "No one will see us if we leave our weapons there and no one will find them in that dreary place that must be full of snakes and wild beasts. Let us put them on that tree, O son of Kunti, before we go on to the city."

Arjuna loosened the string of the mighty Gandíva, whose twang was like thunder, and his brothers unstrung those bows with which they had gone into the four directions and conquered the earth; they ungirded their long and flashing swords and their precious quivers, full of arrows as sharp as death.

Nákula climbed the tree and tied the weapons fast on those branches that he thought could never break, where the rain could not reach them. Then they entered the great city where they must remain undiscovered for the last year of their exile.

In Virata's Kingdom

Kíchaka's Insolence

King Virata was seated on his throne when Yudhistra came before him, looking like the moon hid in clouds or like a fire covered with ashes. The king said to his counselors and Brahmans, "Find out who it is that has just entered my court. He looks like a king of kings, a lord of earth, for he shines like Indra himself."

As he was speaking, Yudhistra came to him and spoke to him, "O great monarch, I am a Brahman who has lost all his possessions and comes to you for support. I am skilled in casting dice and can entertain your friends by gaming with them."

"I will grant you any boon that you desire," Virata replied, "for you look as if you deserved a kingdom. You shall have plenty of food and drink and clothing; you shall be my friend and ride in my chariot and all my doors shall be open to you. You need have no fear as long as you live with me." So

157

Yudhistra began to live in Virata's palace, highly honored by all men.

In the same manner the other sons of Pandu presented themselves, one by one, to the king, who marveled at their strength and beauty and gave to each one the place that he desired, not suspecting who they were. Bhima was put in charge of all the kitchens, while Arjuna, wearing bracelets and large earrings, with his thick hair braided, was sent into the maidens' apartments, where he taught the king's daughter, her friends and waiting maids the melodies and dances that he had learned in the halls of Indra. Nákula took charge of the king's stables and chariots and herds of horses, while Sadeva was made chief cowherd and was responsible for thousands of kine and all their keepers. They were treated kindly by the king, and made themselves dear to all who were in the palace.

Dráupadi bound her soft, black, curling hair into a long braid, hiding it under the single robe that she wore. Then she wandered through the streets of the city, looking very sad. The queen chanced to look down from her terrace as Dráupadi passed by and called to her, saying, "O beautiful one, who are you and what are you seeking?"

"I am a royal hairdresser, seeking employment, O Queen," answered Dráupadi. "I know how to dress the hair, how to pound sweet herbs for perfume, and how to make beautiful garlands of jasmine and lotus and blue lilies. Yudhistra's queen, Dráupadi, called me the maker of garlands."

"I fear that the king will forsake me when he sees your beauty," the queen said, "for see, all my maids are looking at you! How could any man resist you?"

"O fair lady," Dráupadi replied, "no man may make love to me, for I have five young husbands who are Gandharvas. They protect me so well that any man who troubles me will meet his death that very day. Therefore let no man rashly make love to me!"

"If that is true," said the queen, "I will take you into my household, O delighter of hearts." So Dráupadi lived in the queen's palace and no one suspected who she really was.

Those lords of the earth, the Pándavas, true to their promise, spent their days with perfect self-control, although they often suffered because of the false positions in which they lived. Yudhistra was now very skillful at dice, and entertained the king and his sons and courtiers so well that they sat in the gaming hall like a row of birds bound on a string, playing according to his pleasure. Unknown to the king, he shared with his brothers the wealth that he won at gambling. Bhima, on his part, brought them the food and sweetmeats that were given to him in the kitchen, and Arjuna divided with his brothers the money that he got by selling the castoff garments that the ladies gave him. Sadeva brought milk, curds, and butter to the others, and Nákula shared the wealth that the king freely gave him because of his skill in managing the horses. And Dráupadi, though she herself was waiting on the queen, secretly looked after the welfare of the brothers. Thus, taking care of one another, they lived for ten months in the city of the Matsyas, as safely hidden as if they were once more in their mothers' wombs.

When the year was nearly spent, the mighty Kíchaka, the commander of the king's army, chanced to see Dráupadi, for he was the queen's brother and often came to her apartments. He beheld his sister's hairdresser treading the earth like a goddess, and was smitten by the arrows of the God of Love. He went to her as a jackal might approach a lioness, and spoke to her in a winning voice, "Who are you, O beautiful one? Never before in the world have I beheld beauty like yours. But alas, blessed lady, your loveliness is now unused, like a fragrant garland that lies unworn. I pray you, sweet damsel, to marry me and to live with every luxury and joy. I will forsake all my wives and make them your slaves and I, too, will be your slave, ever obedient to you."

"It would be unworthy of you to marry a lowborn servant," answered Dráupadi. "Besides, your behavior is unseemly, for I am the wife of others. You must not bend your heart to sin, or misfortune will overtake you."

But Kíchaka, maddened by his desire, said to her, "You are unwise to scorn me, O graceful one, and you will repent of it. I am the real lord of this kingdom, for all its people depend on me to protect them. I will make you the mistress of it, and you can enjoy all the power and wealth that you desire. How can you choose to remain a servant?"

Dráupadi answered him reproachfully, "O Kíchaka, do not throw away your life. I have five Gandharvas for my husbands who will slay you in their anger. You could not escape them even if you were able to enter the earth or to soar into the sky. Why then do you desire me, like a baby lying on its mother's lap, crying for the moon? Be warned and save your own life!"

Kíchaka went to the queen, lamenting because Dráupadi had refused him, and begged for his sister's help. That gentle lady was touched with pity and said to him, "I will send the damsel to you, pretending that I need some wine. Then you can see her alone and perhaps she will incline her heart to you."

She called Dráupadi and told her to go to Kíchaka's house to fetch some wine, but Dráupadi fell down before her, weeping, and said, "O Queen, do not send me to Kíchaka's palace. You yourself know how shameless he is. You have many maids, O gentle lady; I pray you to send one of them and not me, for I know that Kíchaka will insult me."

Dráupadi spurns Kíchaka.

"He will not harm you when you come from me," said the Queen. "Now take this golden bowl and fetch the wine."

Weeping and filled with dread, Dráupadi went toward Kíchaka's palace, praying to the gods and thinking to herself, "I have never cared for any man except my husbands. Let that truth protect me from any harm at Kíchaka's hands!"

When that wicked man saw her coming toward him like a frightened doe, he rose up joyfully to welcome her, but Dráupadi said, "The queen sent me to get some wine. Pray fill the bowl quickly, for she is thirsty."

"Others will take the wine, O lovely one," Kíchaka replied, and he caught hold of her arm. When she turned to run away, he seized her garment, and Dráupadi, trembling with anger and unable to bear anything more, threw him to the ground. Then she ran to the king's court, followed by Kíchaka who seized her long hair and struck her in the presence of the king. Both Bhima and Yudhistra were seated there, but Dráupadi, even in her distress, was careful not to betray them and appealed to the king, reproaching him for letting her be so insulted.

Yudhistra and Bhima found it hard to control their fury, and the sweat stood on their foreheads. Bhima's eyes began to smoke, his eyelashes stood on end, and he gnashed his teeth with rage. He was about to rise, looking at Kíchaka as an elephant looks at a tree that it is about to uproot, when Yudhistra said to him, "Are you looking for fuel for your fires, cook? If you want fagots, go out and fell some trees."

Then he said to his beloved wife, "Do not stay here, O maker of garlands! Go to the queen's apartments. Wives of heroes bear great suffering for their husbands' sakes. Your Gandharva husbands will take the life of him who has wronged you, in their own good time. Meanwhile you are interrupting the play in the king's court."

"My husbands are indeed very kind," Dráupadi replied. "Since the oldest of them has a weakness for gambling, they are not in a position to help me." With these words, her eyes red with anger, she ran to the queen's rooms.

That night she lay weeping on her bed and thought to herself, "No one but Bhima can help me now." She rose and went swiftly to his room in the kitchen, put her arms around him and waked him, crying, "Arise, arise, Bhima! How can you sleep while the wretched Kíchaka lives?"

Bhima sat up, surprised. "Why have you come here so suddenly?" he asked. "Tell me quickly what you want, for you know that I will always save you from any danger. Then return to your bed before anyone wakes and sees you." Dráupadi hid her face on Bhima's breast and wept.

"How can you ask me what I want," she said, "you who know all my sorrows? Who but Dráupadi could go on living after suffering such grief? I have to behold Yudhistra, who used to be followed by a thousand elephants adorned with golden garlands, earning his bread by casting dice! I have to behold you, O bull of the Bháratas, doing the ignoble work of a cook, and when the king makes you fight with lions and bears I must look on, nearly swooning with fear, while the ladies and maidservants look sideways at me and believe that I have a secret love for you. Alas, I must see Arjuna, the terror of his foes, teaching dancing to King Virata's daughter, living among women and despised of men. How can I bear to live when I behold Sadeva, Kunti's favorite child, tending the cattle and sleeping at night on calfskins; and Nákula, before whom hostile armies fled, training horses to display before the king? But now I have greater griefs than these.

"You know, O Bhima, what happiness was mine. Alas, the whole earth with its belt of seas obeyed me once, but I must now obey the queen and stand in fear of her. I can bear this because the time of our exile draws to its end. But now the wicked Kíchaka asks me every day to be his wife and strikes me in the presence of the king. O slayer of foes, this I cannot bear, and my heart is bursting like a fruit ripened in its season. O Bhima, slay this wretch who has insulted me, as you would dash an earthen pot against a stone! If tomorrow's sun sheds its rays upon him, I shall surely drink poison, for I will never yield to him."

Bhima embraced her, comforted her and wiped the tears from her face. "I will do as you say, O lovely one," he promised. "I will slay him and all his friends. Arrange a meeting with him tomorrow in the dance hall when the dancers have gone home for the night. But do it secretly, so that no one else may know." Then they took leave of one another and waited impatiently for the day.

In the morning Kíchaka went once again to Dráupadi and begged her to marry him. She pretended to yield to him and asked him to meet her that evening in the dance hall. The stupid Kíchaka went home in great delight; he adorned himself with garlands, jewels and fragrant perfume, and his beauty flared up as a lamp does just before it goes out. The day seemed endless to him. When the appointed hour finally came, he entered the dance hall and saw through the darkness a figure sitting in the corner. He went toward it as an insect approaches a flame and began to speak, when suddenly the figure arose, and the mighty Bhima, laughing, seized him by the hair.

Kíchaka freed his hair, and the two warriors grappled with each other in the darkness in that lonely place. They were locked in each other's arms and fought like two powerful bulls or like two elephants in spring. At last Kíchaka grew tired and began to tremble. Then Bhima threw him down, seized his throat and, placing his knee on Kíchaka's chest, strangled him as he would a beast. He called Dráupadi and showed her what he had done; then he returned to the kitchen.

Dráupadi, with the greatest delight, woke the keepers of the hall and said to them, "Come and see what has befallen that wicked man who desired other men's wives! There he lies, slain by my Gandharva husbands."

They looked at him in amazement and ran to tell his kinsmen, who came and stood surrounding his body and wailing for his death. As they were carrying him out to prepare his funeral, they saw Dráupadi, leaning against a pillar.

"There is the wicked woman who caused his death!" they cried. "Let us burn her with him!" And they seized her, bound her with cords and placed her upon the bier of Kíchaka, to be burned with him. Dráupadi, terrified, screamed for help and Bhima heard her. He left the palace by another gate, ran toward the place where the funeral pyre was being raised and leaped over the wall. Near it was a tree; he uprooted it, laid it on his shoulder and rushed like an angry lion upon the family of Kíchaka, as they bore his body to the pyre.

When they beheld him they cried, "Lo, the powerful Gandharva is attacking us! Set the woman free!" And they unbound Dráupadi and ran away toward the city, Bhima pursuing them. They went to the king and told him what had happened and added, "Send this woman away from your kingdom, O Virata, or it will be entirely destroyed."

So when Dráupadi returned to the city, the people hid their eyes from her and fled in all directions; and when she came before the queen, that lady said, "O beautiful one, the king is filled with fear at what the powerful Gandharvas have done. Therefore leave us now and go whither you please, and may good betide you!"

"Suffer me to stay here just thirteen days more," said Dráupadi, for she knew that in that time the last year of exile would be over. "Then my Gandharva husbands will carry me away. They will be so pleased if you do this, that they will grant many favors to King Virata."

The Kúravas Steal the Cattle

During the course of this thirteenth year, Duryodha sent his spies far and wide, through the villages and the towns and cities of every country to search for the Pándavas. When they had done this they returned to Hástina and said to their master, "O lord of men, we have searched through the solitary wilderness abounding with deer and overgrown with trees and creepers; we have searched the mountaintops and the plains, and many kingdoms, provinces, and cities, but we have found no trace of the sons of Pandu. It seems that they have perished without leaving a mark behind them. Yet we have discovered one thing that will gladden your heart. The commander of King Virata's armies, Kíchaka of wicked soul, now lies slain. He was killed by invisible Gandharvas during the hours of darkness, O King of unfading glory!"

Now the mighty king of the Trigartas, a friend and ally of Duryodha, was sitting beside him when he received this news. He spoke at once, "My kingdom has been invaded many a time by the armies of Virata, led by the king's general, Kíchaka, a crooked and wrathful man, yet famous the world over for his might. If Kíchaka is dead, I believe that Virata will lose his courage and his pride. Let us therefore invade his realm and carry off his cattle and his wealth, O tiger among kings! Then we may divide his kingdom among ourselves."

Karna agreed to this, saying, "Let us forget about the sons of Pandu, who are either dead or have disappeared for good. Let us go at once into the kingdom of Virata."

Duryodha also agreed; he turned to his brother Dushasa and said, "Consult with the elders and then array our forces without delay! Let the Trigartas march first toward the city of Virata and seize his immense herds of cattle. Then, when the king has gone out to fight them, let us secretly invade the kingdom from another quarter and drive off all the cattle that we desire."

Therefore the Trigartas, on the seventh day of the dark fortnight of the moon, marched off with their chariots and foot soldiers to the southeast to invade the kingdom of Virata. As soon as they began to drive off the cattle, one of the herdsmen ran to the city, entered the court where the king was surrounded by his courtiers and the sons of Pandu and bowed down before him, saying, "O foremost of kings, the Trigartas are seizing your cattle by hundreds and by thousands! O, rescue them quickly, or they will all be lost!"

The king immediately arrayed his army for battle with its chariots and elephants, cavalry and foot soldiers. He and his sons put on their shining armor, yoked their white horses, encased in mail, to their chariots, and raised their gold-decked banners of various shapes and designs.

Virata said, "I wish the dice-player and the cook, the keeper of the stables and the chief herdsman to fight with us. Give them chariots and armor, banners and weapons, for I believe truly that they are warriors."

The four sons of Pandu were delighted to put on coats of mail, to handle weapons again, and to mount chariots, and they were willing to put off their disguise, for the very end of the thirteenth year of their exile had come. The king never thought of Arjuna, who spent his days in the women's apartments, singing and dancing.

The army looked very splendid with its elephants, chariots, and horses, as it marched out of the city to the place where the cattle had been stolen. The leaders easily followed the footprints of the herds and caught up with the army of the Trigartas in the afternoon. Then Virata's army and the Trigartas fought fiercely for the possession of the cattle; they raised great shouts and the encounter between them was terrifying. Chariots clashed against chariots, foot soldiers fought against foot soldiers, horsemen against horsemen, and elephants against mighty elephants, with great fury, neither side overcoming the other. The battle raged so madly and such clouds of dust arose that the warriors could hardly tell friend from foe.

Then the king of the Trigartas and his brother rushed toward King Virata, with their maces in their hands. They killed his charioteer and his two horses, as well as the soldiers who protected him, and took him captive, carrying him off the field in a chariot. His troops began to flee in fear in all directions when they saw their king taken captive, but Yudhistra said to Bhima, "King Virata is a prisoner. Rescue him, O mighty-armed one! We have lived happily in his city; put forth your strength and let us pay our debt to him!"

Bhima turned his chariot and rushed furiously after the king of the Trigartas, the twins driving on each side of him to protect his wheels. They overthrew all the chariots that tried to stop them; elephants, horsemen, and fierce bowmen were put to flight by Bhima as he rushed on. When Virata's warriors saw the Pándavas charging ahead, they returned to the fight and fell upon the enemy, driving them back and sending hundreds of them to the realm of Yama, God of the Dead.

Bhima overtook the king's chariot, slew the horses, and threw the driver upon the ground. Then he leaped from his own chariot, seized the hair of the king of the Trigartas and dashed him senseless to the ground. The whole Trigarta army was panic stricken and fled in all directions; Virata was rescued, and all the cattle were gathered in and restored. Bhima lifted up the king of the Trigartas, brought him before Virata, and made him say, "I am your slave." But Virata freed the vanquished king who, hanging his head with shame, saluted his victorious enemy and returned to his own kingdom.

Then Virata turned to the sons of Pandu and said, "O smiters of foes, I owe to you my kingdom and my wealth. It belongs now as much to you as it does to me. I pray you to stay here with me for as long as you live; I will bestow upon you all that you can desire." He sent messengers to the city to proclaim the victory at sunrise the next morning, and then all those mighty warriors lay down and slept on the field of battle.

Arjuna Fights the Kúravas

Now while King Virata was leading his whole army against the Trigartas, Duryodha was invading the kingdom from another quarter, as he had planned to do. Bhishma, Drona and his son Ashvattáma, Karna and all the brothers of Duryodha were with him, at the head of a great army. He drove away the cowherds and seized six thousand of Virata's cattle.

The chief cowherd, terrified, mounted a chariot and drove swiftly to the city for help, but only the youngest of the king's sons was there, for all the other princes had gone forth with the army of the king. This prince was not old enough to go to war; his name was Uttar, and he boasted loudly in the presence of the cowherd, saying, "I would set out this very day in pursuit of the cattle if only I had a charioteer. If anyone can be found who is fit to drive my chariot I will fight against all the Kúravas and make them say, 'Is it Arjuna who is fighting against us?'"

Now all that was said in the court was repeated in the inner apartments of the women. There Arjuna heard it, and he sought out Dráupadi and said to her secretly, "O beautiful one, go quickly to Uttar and tell him that I was formerly the charioteer of Arjuna and that I will hold his horses' reins today." Dráupadi stepped out bashfully from among the women and gave this message to the prince, who sent at once for Arjuna, ordered him to put on a coat of mail and to mount his chariot. Arjuna's pupil, the king's daughter, and her waiting maids crowded around him, and he pretended not to know how to put on the armor and made them laugh by trying to step into it.

The little princess said, "Bring us some rich, bright-colored robes from the field of battle, so that we can make some dresses for our dolls." Arjuna promised, smiling, that he would; then he mounted the prince's chariot and drove him swiftly out of the city, along the very road that the Pándavas had taken when they first came into the kingdom.

Before they had gone very far, they saw in the distance the army of Duryodha which looked with all its banners like a vast forest, and sent great clouds of dust into the sky. At the sight of it, Uttar cried, "Stop, O charioteer! I dare not fight with the Kúravas. See, my hair is standing on end, and I am faint with fear! My father has left me alone, and I am only a boy and know very little about war. I cannot fight against these great warriors. Turn back!"

"You ordered me to take you to battle with the Kúravas,"

Arjuna answered, "therefore I shall surely take you there, where those countless flags are flying. If you return now, after all your boasting, everyone will laugh at you. As for me, I have been Arjuna's charioteer; I cannot return until the cattle have been regained."

"Let the cattle perish!" cried Uttar. "Let the Kúravas have all our wealth and our kingdom and the city become a desert! Let everyone laugh at me! I will not fight!"

As he spoke, he leaped from the chariot and began to run away, throwing aside his bow and arrows. Arjuna ran after him, laughing, caught him by the hair and pulled him back, while the prince, wailing, offered him gold and jewels if he would set him free.

"If you do not dare to fight the foe, O tiger among men," said Arjuna, "come and hold the horses' reins while I fight them and recover the cattle." And he lifted the fainting prince into the chariot and gave him the reins.

They were close to that burial ground and to the great tree where the Pándavas had hidden their weapons. Arjuna said to Uttar, "Climb that tree, O prince of the Matsyas, and bring me some weapons that you will find there. These bows of yours cannot bear the strength and the stretch of my arms." Uttar dismounted unwillingly from the chariot and climbed the tree, while Arjuna, holding the reins, directed him. He found the weapons and cut the wrappings and the ropes that bound them to the branches.

First he beheld Arjuna's bow, Gandíva, with four others, shining with splendor as the planets do when they rise. He held them in his hands and looked at them with awe. "To what famous warrior does this excellent bow belong that has a hundred golden bosses and such shining ends?" he asked. "Whose bow is this, with golden elephants gleaming on its back? Whose is this splendid one adorned with threescore golden insects, and whose is this with the three suns that blaze so brilliantly? Whose is this beautiful bow inlaid with gold and jewels?"

He unbound the arrows and asked with wonder, "What great warrior owns these thousand arrows with golden heads, encased in golden quivers? Whose are these thick, long shafts of iron, sharp-pointed, well-tempered, winged with vulture's feathers? Whose is this black quiver bearing five images of tigers and holding boar-eared arrows? Who owns these hundred arrows shaped with heads like a crescent moon, and whose are these gold-crested ones, winged with parrot feathers?"

Then he unbound the swords and held them in his two hands. "What king of men," he asked Arjuna, "wields this excellent and terrible sword that bears the image of a toad; and whose is this, its blade inlaid with gold, in a sheath of tiger-skin, all set with tinkling bells? Who owns this handsome scimitar with polished blade and golden hilt, sheathed in a cowskin scabbard? Whose is this long and beautiful sword, with the sky-blue blade, mounted in gold, well-tempered, sheathed in goatskin? Who owns this broad and heavy blade— just longer than the breadth of thirty fingers—polished by the clash of other weapons, in a sheath as bright as fire? Whose is this scimitar covered with golden bosses, the touch of whose blade is like that of a venomous snake? Answer me truly, for I am filled with wonder!"

Arjuna answered, "These are the bows, the arrows, and the swords of the heroic sons of Pandu—of Yudhistra, Bhima, Arjuna, and the twins. The largest of them all is that powerful bow of Arjuna's called Gandíva, equal to a thousand other bows, handsome and smooth, without a knot or stain."

"Indeed, these weapons are exceedingly beautiful," Uttar

said. "But where then are the high-souled sons of Pandu, who have not been heard of since they lost their kingdom at dice? And where is Dráupadi, that jewel among women, who followed her husbands into the forest?"

"I am Arjuna," answered his charioteer. "Your father's dice-player is Yudhistra, and his cook is Bhima; the groom of the horses is Nákula, and Sadeva keeps the cows. That waiting woman for whom Kíchaka was slain is no other than Dráupadi, the beloved wife of the Pándavas."

When he heard these words, Uttar climbed swiftly down from the tree, carrying the weapons with him. He saluted Arjuna, saying, "Welcome, O foremost of warriors in the world! What good fortune is mine today! Command me now, for all my fears have vanished. I am a skillful driver and will hold the reins of these four horses that are equal to those of Krishna himself. Which part of the enemy's army do you wish to attack?"

"I am pleased with you, O mighty warrior," answered Arjuna. "Have no fear, for I will rout your enemies in battle and recover all the cattle. Bind these quivers to the chariot and take for yourself a polished sword."

Then Arjuna took the bracelets from his arms, drew on a pair of gloves adorned with gold, and wound a cloth about his curling hair. He turned toward the east and concentrated his mind on those celestial weapons that the gods had given him, and all the weapons came to him and said, "We are your servants, O son of Indra." Arjuna bowed to them and took them in his hands, saying, "Stay with me now." He took down Uttar's banner and thought of his own heavenly one that bore the figure of the gigantic ape with the lion's tail. No sooner had he thought of it than it seized upon his flagstaff, and the ape glared fiercely out, seeking his enemies. Arjuna strung his bow, Gandíva, and twanged the string, and the sound of it was like the collision of two mountains. The trees trembled and the birds flew madly about in the sky.

"Stand firmly on the chariot," he said to Uttar. "Press your feet down hard and hold the reins tight, for I am going to blow my conch." He took up the thundering shell that Indra had given him and blew it so loudly that the sound seemed to split the mountains and to shake the meteors from the sky. The horses fell on their knees, and Uttar sat down on the floor of the chariot, clinging to its side. Arjuna took the reins and raised the horses; he embraced Uttar and comforted him and said, "Now drive these white steeds with their golden bridles at their best speed, for I wish to meet this crowd of Kuru lions."

When the Kúrava warriors heard the twang of Gandíva, the blare of the conch, and the thunder of the chariot wheels, their hearts sank. Drona said, "This mighty bowman who is approaching us can be no other than Arjuna. Array the troops in order of combat and guard the cattle well! Expect a terrible slaughter, for there is no one among us who can withstand him!"

Karna said, "How you always praise Arjuna! He is not equal to a sixteenth part of Duryodha or of me."

"If this is Arjuna," said Duryodha, "I shall indeed be happy, for then the Pándavas will have to wander in the woods for another twelve years. This was their pledge, and the thirteenth year of exile is not yet over."

"I have calculated the days and fortnights, the seasons and the years," said Bhishma. "The thirteenth year has run its course, and the sons of Pandu have fulfilled all that they pledged themselves to, for they are all high-souled and follow the path of virtue. That is Arjuna's banner with its roaring ape; that is the sound of his conch. See, two arrows have fallen at my feet and another passed my ear. The wise and beloved Arjuna has finished the term of exile, and now he salutes me and whispers in my ear. Let us endeavor to withstand him, as the shore withstands the surging sea!"

While Bhishma arrayed the army, Arjuna drove forward, announced himself by name and covered the troops with countless arrows, thick as locusts. The soldiers could not see the earth or the sky and were so bewildered that they could not even run away. Arjuna blew his conch and twanged his great bow; the ape, high on his flagstaff, roared frightfully, and King Virata's cattle, terrified, turned and ran bellowing toward the city, their tails in the air. The Kúrava warriors were furious when they saw their army bewildered and the cattle lost, and they rushed upon Arjuna in their chariots, with their banners flaunting above them.

Then that great warrior, burning with anger, began to destroy the host of chariots as a mighty fire destroys a forest. The son of Virata drove the four swift steeds with great skill, and Arjuna ranged the field in all directions, routing his foes as the wind ranges at will in the autumn, scattering the clouds and the heaps of fallen leaves. He seemed to be dancing on the field of battle. Those brave bulls among men, the Kúravas, wounded by that braver one, wavered and trembled, and many fell on the ground like uprooted trees. The heroic Karna, however, met Arjuna's arrows with countless shafts of his own, pierced the four horses and the flagstaff, and wounded Uttar. Then Arjuna, like a lion awakened from sleep, took the keen, crescent-headed arrows from his quiver, drew his bowstring to his ear and pierced every part of his enemy's body until Karna, wounded and bleeding, left the fight and was carried in his chariot to the rear.

At once Duryodha and Ashvattáma, Drona and Bhishma surrounded the son of Kunti and poured arrows upon him. He did not wish to kill them; therefore he took up a weapon that Indra had given him and sent forth a shower of its bright-winged shafts which stupefied the senses of those great warriors and made them stand motionless in their chariots as if they were asleep; their horses, too, stopped and drooped their heads.

When he saw his enemies powerless, their bows dropping from their hands, Arjuna remembered the little princess and said to Uttar, "O best of princes, go down among those warriors and bring me the white garment of Drona, the handsome yellow one that Bhishma wears, and the blue cloak of Duryodha." Uttar gave him the reins, leaped from the chariot and took the garments from the unconscious leaders; then he ran back and drove Arjuna from the field.

Duryodha soon recovered his senses and saw Arjuna at a distance, standing on his chariot, looking like the chief of the gods or like the sun coming out of clouds. "Why have you let him escape?" he cried to Bhishma. "Strike him down now before it is too late!"

"Where was all your might when he escaped?" asked Bhishma, smiling. "You were unconscious, and your bow and arrows dropped from your hand. Arjuna might have killed us all then, but he cannot do a dishonorable deed. We owe our lives to his honor; therefore turn back, O King, to your own city, and let Arjuna depart with the cattle." Duryodha sighed deeply and was silent; the other warriors also heard the words of Bhishma and left the field, returning slowly to Hástina.

Arjuna followed them for a while, saluting each one of them with a beautiful arrow; with one last shot he broke into pieces the jeweled crown that Duryodha wore. Then he filled the three worlds with the twang of his Gandíva and blew his great conch, and the sounds pierced the hearts of the departing host. When they had disappeared like clouds scattered by a gale, he said to Uttar, "Turn back the horses, for the cattle are recovered and the enemy routed. Now let us return to the city. You are the only one, my child, who knows that the sons of Pandu are living in your father's court. Do not tell anyone and do not praise me when we enter the city, but proclaim this victory as your own."

"I cannot call this deed my own," Uttar said, "for what you have done is far beyond my power to achieve; but I will not tell my father who you are until you tell me to do so." He sent the cowherds to the city to proclaim the victory, while he and Arjuna returned to the burial ground to replace in the branches of the tree the weapons of those mighty bowmen. The terrible ape on Arjuna's banner leaped like fire into the sky; they set Uttar's banner on the pole again, and Arjuna, binding his hair into a braid, drove Uttar into his father's city.

There the prince entered King Virata's court while Arjuna went to the inner apartments and gave the princess the robes that he had brought for her dolls. She and her companions were delighted with the bright, rich garments and clapped their hands for joy.

The Thirteen Years Are Over

King Virata, when he had vanquished the Trigartas in battle and had recovered all his cattle, returned to his city with a glad heart, and the four Pándavas rode beside him. His subjects came to pay honor to him as he sat on his throne, and then he looked for his youngest son, asking, "Where has Uttar gone?" His chief minister had heard the tale of Uttar's victory from the cowherds, and he told it all to the king, who was overjoyed at the news. "Make all the highways gay with flags," he cried, "and let us worship the gods with gifts of flowers! Let the bellman ride swiftly on an elephant and proclaim the victory at every crossroad, while princes and warriors, musicians, poets, and dancers welcome my victorious son!"

When Uttar entered the court and touched his father's feet, Virata raised him joyfully and said, "O joy of your father's heart, I have no other son who is your equal! How could you, my child, encounter Bhishma, who cannot be conquered by men or demons? How could you, who are so young, vanquish in battle Drona and his son Ashvattáma, and Duryodha, who can pierce a mountain with his arrows? How did you rout those mighty warriors and snatch my cattle from them, as one who takes a tiger's prey from between its claws?"

"It was not I who vanquished the foe," answered Uttar, "nor did I recover the cattle. It was all done by the son of a god who mounted my chariot and pierced the Kúrava host with his arrows, and when he had routed them he laughed at them and robbed them of their clothes. He alone defeated all the great warriors of the Kúravas, as a tiger scatters a herd of deer."

"Where is that mighty and godlike hero who has saved both you and my cattle?" asked the king.

"He disappeared as soon as the battle was finished," Uttar said, "but I believe that he will reveal himself to us tomorrow or the day after that."

On the third day after the victory, the sons of Pandu bathed, put on white garments and decked themselves with jewels; then, led by Yudhistra, they entered the council hall of King Virata and took their seats on thrones reserved for kings, where they shone radiant as fires on a sacrificial altar. When Virata entered and saw them sitting there, he was angry and said to

Yudhistra, "You are employed by me as a dice-player. Why are you sitting on a royal throne, dressed in royal robes?"

Arjuna smiled and answered for his brother, "This man, O King, deserves to sit on a royal throne in the very hall of Indra, for he is no other than that bull of the Bháratas, the just King Yudhistra."

Virata answered, "If this be indeed the just King Yudhistra, the son of Kunti, which among these is his brother Arjuna and which the mighty Bhima? Which is Nákula and which Sadeva, and where is the matchless Dráupadi?"

"Even this one who is your cook," Arjuna said, "who killed tigers and bears here in your palace and slew the wicked-souled Kíchaka, is the mighty-armed Bhima. The manager of your stables is that oppressor of foes named Nákula, and Sadeva is the keeper of your cattle. And the queen's hairdresser, with the slender waist and eyes like lotus petals, is the princess of Panchala, for whom Kíchaka was slain. I am Arjuna, who am younger than Bhima and older than the twins."

"That is he," cried Uttar, "that dark-skinned youth with shoulders broad as a lion's and a tread like a mighty elephant's, who vanquished the Kúravas in battle and recovered the cattle! That is Arjuna, the foremost of bowmen, who ranged through crowds of hostile chariots like a lion putting to flight a herd of kine! The deed was his, not mine."

When he heard his son's words, the king of the Matsyas said, "May you be blessed, O Yudhistra, with all your brothers! It was Bhima who rescued me from the king of the Trigartas and my cattle were recovered by Arjuna. By the might of your arms we have been victorious. O King, if we have ever, out of ignorance, done or said anything to offend you, I pray you to forgive us."

He embraced the five brothers again and again and never

tired of looking at them. He made an alliance with Yudhistra and offered him his army, his kingdom, his treasury, and himself. He also offered the hand of Uttara, his daughter, to Arjuna in marriage. But Arjuna said, "O best of kings, let the princess be my daughter-in-law, but not my wife. For a whole year I have lived in the inner apartments, teaching her singing and dancing, and she trusts me as she would a father. It is not fitting, after this, that I should marry her. But my son, the mighty Abimanyu, skillful in war, beautiful as a god, the favorite nephew of Krishna, is worthy to be your son-in-law and the husband of your daughter. I welcome her as my daughter and rejoice in this added alliance between us."

"It shall be as you say, O wise son of Kunti," answered Virata. "He who marries his daughter to the son of Arjuna is indeed fortunate."

Yudhistra gave his consent to the marriage and invited all his friends and kinsmen to come to the wedding, as Virata also did. Krishna came, bringing with him Abimanyu and his mother, Subadra; the mighty king of Panchala with his son Jumna came and brought the heroic sons of Dráupadi. Great was the rejoicing as sons met their parents, who saw their children well grown and beautiful as gods. Many other kings came from different parts of the country, followed by thousands of elephants and chariots, horsemen and foot soldiers; and Virata received them all with a glad heart and entertained the troops and the servants as well as their masters, for he was greatly pleased to marry his daughter to Abimanyu.

When the wedding festival began, conches and drums, cymbals and stringed instruments resounded in Virata's palace. Rich foods and excellent wines were brought to the king's palace; poets and actors and singers waited upon the kings and sang their praises. The Matsya ladies, dressed in bright

robes and adorned with many jewels, came to the palace where
the wedding was to be held, and among them all Dráupadi
was the first in beauty and splendor. They led forth the princess
Uttara, decked with shining jewels and looking like a daughter
of the gods, and Arjuna welcomed her on behalf of his son.
Yudhistra also greeted her and caused the wedding ceremonies
to be performed between her and Abimanyu. Virata gave him
as dowry a thousand horses as swift as the wind, two hundred
fine elephants, and much wealth besides; while Krishna gave
him chariots and horses, and to each one of the sons of Pandu
jewels and robes and menservants and maidservants.

As this marriage was celebrated, uniting the family of the
king of the Matsyas with that of the Pándavas, the city of
King Virata, crowded with happy people, was one great festival.

Duryodha Breaks His Pledge

The Council

At sunrise on the day after the wedding of Abimanyu and Uttara, the Pándavas and those kings and warriors who were their friends met in the audience hall of King Virata. The kings of Matsya and Panchala sat on high thrones inlaid with jewels, with Krishna and Yudhistra beside them; behind them sat the sons of those kings with Bhima, Arjuna, and the sons of Madri. Abimanyu and the five sons of Dráupadi, who rivalled their fathers in valor, strength, and grace, sat upon excellent seats inlaid with gold. Those mighty heroes adorned with shining ornaments and splendid robes talked together for a while, and then sat silent and thoughtful, looking at Krishna and waiting for him to speak to them about the Pándavas.

At last Krishna said, "All of you know that Yudhistra was unfairly defeated at dice by Shákuni, and that he was robbed of his kingdom and sent into exile in the forest. The sons of Pandu were true to their pledge, although they could have won back their kingdom by force. For thirteen years they have carried out the cruel task imposed upon them and have spent the last year, the most difficult of all, in menial service here. It is for you to consider now what will be for the good of both Yudhistra and Duryodha and what will meet with the approval of all good men. These brave sons of Pandu ask only for what belongs to them and what they won in battle with other kings. We do not know what Duryodha thinks or what he may do. Therefore, let us send a virtuous and honest ambassador to him and ask him to give back the kingdom of Yudhistra, according to the agreement made at the gambling match."

The brother of Krishna spoke, saying, "The son of Kuru should of course give back the kingdom of Yudhistra; he should rejoice and be exceedingly happy that the quarrel he created can be so easily settled. He has, however, taken possession of the kingdom with a strong hand and has ruled the whole realm of the Bháratas for thirteen years. Let the ambassador, therefore, say nothing to provoke him, but let him speak words full of humility and friendliness. Do not seek war with the Kurus."

Another warrior rose up angrily and gainsaid this speech. "Yudhistra has fulfilled to the utmost the terms of the stake that he lost at dice. Why should he humble himself? I should ask for the kingdom not with words, but with sharp arrows, and force the Kúravas to prostrate themselves at the feet of the noble son of Kunti. Either Yudhistra must regain his kingdom immediately, or all his enemies must be slain."

"O mighty one," said the king of Panchala, "you speak wisely. Duryodha will never give up the kingdom willingly, and his foolish father, who dotes upon him, will do as he desires. He should never be addressed with mild words, for then the fool will think that he has won. Let us make preparations for war and send word to all our friends to raise their armies. Then let us send my priest, a learned Brahman, to Duryodha and ask him to give back to the Pándavas the kingdom that is theirs, according to the pledge that was made between them."

"These words are worthy of the chief of the Panchalas," said Krishna. "This, surely, is our best course. It is fitting that you should send a messenger to the Kúravas, for you are the foremost of kings, both in age and learning, and the father-in-law of the Pándavas. If they will make peace on just terms, all will be well; but if the wicked Duryodha haughtily and foolishly refuses, he will pronounce his own doom."

Then Krishna and the assembled kings returned, each to his own kingdom, while Yudhistra and his friends began to prepare for war. Virata and his kinsmen sent word to all their friends, asking for their support, and the king of Panchala did likewise. It was the custom among Kshatrias to grant the request of the person who was first to ask, and therefore they made haste before the Kúravas could hear what they were doing. At the request of the Pándavas and the two kings of Matsya and Panchala, many lords of earth with mighty armies came together with cheerful hearts. When the sons of Kuru heard of this, they, too, assembled their friends and allies, until the whole land was thronged with the armies of those heroes who were marching to fight for the Pándavas or the Kúravas. From all sides the horsemen and the elephants, the chariots and the foot soldiers poured in until the earth with its mountains and its forests trembled beneath their tread.

After they had sent messengers to the kings of various countries, Arjuna himself set out for Dváraka, the city of Krishna.

Now Duroydha heard that Arjuna was on his way to Dváraka to seek Krishna's help; therefore he, too, set out for the same city, drawn by horses swift as the wind. Those two tigers among men arrived on the selfsame day and entered the palace together to seek Krishna. Duryodha was the first to enter the room, where he found Krishna sleeping. He sat down at the head of the bed and shortly afterwards Arjuna came in and stood at the foot of the bed with joined hands. When Krishna awoke, therefore, his eyes fell first upon Arjuna. He greeted both cousins and asked why they had come.

Duryodha said, "I have come to ask for your help in the war that is coming. Arjuna and I are both your friends and are both related to you, but I was the first to come to you. All virtuous men grant the request of him who comes first; therefore I ask you, who are the most virtuous of all, to follow this rule of conduct."

"I do not doubt," answered Krishna, "that you came first, O King, but the son of Kunti is the one whom I first saw. Therefore it seems to me that I must help you both. I have a large army of cowherds of mighty strength, all of whom are able to fight in battle. These soldiers shall be sent to one of you, and I alone will serve the other, but I shall not fight. O son of Kunti, you may have the first choice, for it is the custom for the younger of two people to choose first."

Arjuna chose Krishna, even though he would not fight, while Duryodha took the great army of cowherds and was exceedingly pleased, even though Krishna would not be on his side.

After he had departed, Krishna said to Arjuna, "Why did you choose me, when you knew that I shall not fight for you?"

"O best of men," answered Arjuna, "I alone am able to slay all the Kúravas. But you are a wise and honored person, and your wisdom and honor will be with me. Besides, I have always longed to have you drive my chariot; I beg of you to do this for me."

"I will be your charioteer," said Krishna. "Your wish is fulfilled." And the two friends went back to Yudhistra with glad hearts, and many of the finest warriors among the Yadus chose to go with them.

At this time Shalya, the king of Madra, with his sons and his army, was traveling from his kingdom to join the Pándavas. He was their uncle, for he was the brother of Madri, the mother of the twins. His encampment covered a square mile, so large was his army, and he traveled by slow marches, giving rest to his troops and his animals. Duryodha heard that he was on his way and had pavilions built at different places along his route, and filled them with food and drink, flowers and entertainment, and pools of fresh water, for he knew that Shalya cared much for the pleasures of life. The king went from one to another of these pavilions, waited upon like a god by the servants of Duryodha, until he thought himself equal to Indra himself. He was exceedingly well pleased and asked the servants, "Where are those men of Yudhistra's who have prepared these pleasant places of refreshment for me? Bring them to me, for I wish to reward them."

Now Duryodha had been following the king, unknown to him, and waiting for the right moment to ask a boon. When he saw that the king was so flattered that he wished to pay for his pleasure, he came forward and showed himself to Shalya, telling him that it was he and not Yudhistra, who had taken all this trouble to entertain him.

Shalya embraced him and said, "Ask of me any boon that you desire."

"Be the leader of my army, O uncle!" said Duryodha.

"So be it!" answered Shalya. "How can I do otherwise, since I have bound myself? Return now to your own city. I must visit that best of men, Yudhistra, but I shall speedily rejoin you." Those two kings embraced one another; then Duryodha returned joyfully to Hástina, and Shalya went on to tell the sons of Pandu what had befallen him.

When he arrived at their encampment, the Pándavas received him with the usual gifts of honor, and he embraced with great delight the sons of Kunti and the twin sons of his sister Madri. Then he told them of his meeting with Duryodha and of the boon that he had granted.

Yudhistra said, "O brave king, you were right to grant the boon that you promised to Duryodha when you were pleased with what he had done for you, but I ask you to do one thing for my sake. At some time during the battle there will be a single combat between Arjuna and Karna, and I am sure that you will be asked to drive Karna's chariot, for you are equal to Krishna in handling horses. When that happens, O my uncle, you must do all that you can to discourage Karna and to protect Arjuna, so that victory may be ours. This is not an honorable thing to do, since you have promised to fight for the Kúravas, but still you must do it, O best of men, for my sake and for the sake of the twins, who are the sons of your sister, Madri."

"I shall do just as you ask me to do, my son," answered Shalya. "I shall speak to that vile son of a Suta in such a way that he will be discouraged and dispirited and can be easily slain. And I shall do anything else for you that I am able to do." Then he bade farewell to the five brothers and went with his army to the camp of Duryodha.

Other kings came to fight with the Pándavas, and their great armies were absorbed into the host of Yudhistra as small rivers are embraced by the sea. Seven armies, from many lands and many directions, came together to fight against the Kúravas and gladdened the hearts of the high-souled sons of Pandu.

In the same way, many kings from many lands, bringing with them multitudes of troops, like clouds driven by the winds, came to Duryodha, eager to fight against the sons of Kunti. Eleven armies assembled under the banner of Kuru's son; there was not room enough in Hástina even for the leaders of his host; therefore the whole of his kingdom, abundant with food and wealth, was covered by the warriors of the Kúravas, until the creatures of the earth were frightened and the trees trembled as they passed.

The Pándavas Claim Their Kingdom

At this time Yudhistra summoned the priest of Panchala to carry his message to the court of King Kuru.

"O learned one," said Yudhistra to that Brahman, "go now to Hástina to the court of King Kuru and in the presence of all the Bháratas and their friends and kinsmen say these words: 'O King, we, the sons of Pandu, greet each one of you according to your ages. We salute the ladies of the household and embrace the sons and daughters that have been born to you in the years that we have been away. We greet the menservants and the maidservants and all those among them who are lame or blind, dwarfed or imbecile, and ask about the welfare of each one.'

"Salute the mighty Kuru in our name, touch his feet and say to him, 'O King, we wish to live united. Do not let yourself be vanquished by your enemies.' Then, O holy one, bend your head in our name and salute the grandsire of the Bháratas, saying, 'O Sire, let your grandsons all live in friendship together!' Speak to Vídura, that wise counselor of Kuru, saying, 'Counsel peace, O amiable one, for Yudhistra's sake!'

"Then speak to that unforbearing prince Duryodha and say, 'The insults you offered to the innocent and helpless Dráupadi, when she was dragged into the assembly, we will quietly bear, because we do not wish to see the Bháratas slain. The other injuries, before and after that, we will quietly bear, although we are able to avenge them. You had us exiled, clad in deerskins; that also will be forgiven, because we do not wish to see the Bháratas slain. We do not desire war, but, O consumer of foes, we must have our just share of the kingdom. Turn your covetous heart from what belongs to others! Give back what should be given, according to the agreement at the gambling match! Give back Indra Prastha, and let our quarrel end! O Duryodha, let the Kúravas and the Pándavas meet with laughter and cheerful hearts. Let us make peace!' "

Then Arjuna, after asking the permission of his eldest brother, rose and spoke to the priest. He was fearless and ready to fight, and his eyes were red with anger. "Then speak these words of mine to Kuru's son, in the presence of all the Bháratas and of that foul-mouthed Karna, who wants so much to fight with me, and in the hearing of those kings who have assembled to fight against us. See that my words are well heard by them all: 'If the sons of Kuru fight, they will surely die. My bow Gandíva yawns without being handled; my bowstring trembles without being touched; my arrows leap from their quiver, eager to fly; my sword slides out of its sheath by itself, as a snake quits its skin, and on the top of my flagstaff terrible voices cry, "When will your chariot be yoked, O Arjuna?" As a blazing fire consumes a forest, I will leave no remnant of those who come to the field of battle.'

"Tell them this, O holy one," he added gently, "but let it not be so! I pray that the counsel of Bhishma and Drona and the wise Vídura will be followed and that the Kúravas may live long and happily."

The priest of Panchala was honorably received at Kuru's court, where all the kings and chiefs had assembled, anxious to hear the message of the sons of Pandu. When the Brahman had spoken, Bhishma, the eldest of the Bháratas, replied to him, "I rejoice that the Pándavas are well and that they desire peace with their cousins. Truly they have suffered long and deserve to receive their kingdom."

Karna interrupted him angrily and insolently, saying, "O Brahman, everyone knows all that you have told us. What is the use of repeating things over and over? Yudhistra went into the woods according to an agreement that he made; now let him return and live safely and in comfort under Duryodha's rule. If, however, he wishes to turn aside from the path of virtue and go to war, let him remember the mighty host that will be arrayed against him!"

"How foolishly you talk, O Suta's son," answered Bhishma. "Do you not remember how Arjuna, singlehanded, over-powered us all in Virata's kingdom?"

King Kuru spoke gently to Bhishma and rebuked Karna; then he said, "What Bhishma has said is best for us and for the Pándavas also. O Duryodha, give up this hatred! Half the realm is quite enough for you and for all your friends and followers. Give back to the sons of Pandu their own share! I do not want war, nor does Drona, nor Vídura; indeed, these warriors assembled here do not desire war. My child, incline your heart to peace!"

"I shall challenge the Pándavas to battle," answered Dur-yodha, "without depending on you or Bhishma or Drona or any others who think as you do. O Sire, Karna and I alone are ready to celebrate the sacrifice of battle, with Yudhistra as the victim. Three of us, Karna and my brother Dushasa and I, will slay the Pándavas. Either I, after slaying them, shall rule the earth, or they, when they have slain me, will enjoy it. O King, I had rather lose my wealth, my kingdom, and my very life, than share them with the sons of Pandu."

Then Kuru said, "I now cast off Duryodha, this son of mine. And I grieve for you, O kings, if you follow this fool into the realm of death. Already I can see the host of the Bháratas laid low by the mace of Bhima or put to flight by the arrows of Arjuna, like deer before hunting tigers. When you see your chariots, horses, and elephants felled like trees torn up by the roots, you will remember what I have said."

At these words, his passionate son, blazing with anger, cried, "You think that the Pándavas cannot be vanquished because they have the gods for their allies. Do not fear! They and all their followers will die as they approach me, like rivers entering the ocean. My power, my intelligence, my knowledge, and my wealth are all greater than those of the Pándavas."

Karna encouraged Duryodha and cheered the hearts of the assembled kings: "I alone," he said, "will slay within the twinkling of an eye the Pándavas, the Panchalas, the Matsyas, and all their other allies, and I will bestow upon you all the lands won by my weapons. Bhishma and Drona and all these kings may stay here while I go forth alone and slay our enemies."

"Your mind is clouded, Karna, "said Bhishma scornfully. "You speak mad words. Every weapon of yours will be consumed to ashes by the god-given weapons of Arjuna. Besides, Krishna, who has slain stronger foes than you, is protecting him."

"I now lay down my arms," said Karna, "for I can bear no longer the grandsire's cruel words. When his voice is silenced I shall take them up again, and the rulers of the world shall see my prowess." And he left the assembly and went in anger to his own palace.

Bhishma laughed aloud and said, "Behold how the Suta's son keeps his promise! He boasted that he alone would slay his foes, and now he lays down his arms!"

Kuru pleaded again with his headstrong son, but Duryodha would not listen. He sat silent; then he rose and left the hall, and the other kings went with him, each to his own dwelling.

Then the old king sent for a man whom he trusted, Sánjaya, his friend and charioteer. "O Sánjaya," he said, "go speedily now in a chariot to the encampment of the son of Kunti. Speak to him lovingly and tell him that Kuru desires only peace. Thus the hearts of the Pándavas will be softened, for they are righteous and kind. I have examined their conduct, and I have never been able to find a fault for which they could be blamed. No one hates them except this vile, dull-witted son of mine and the mean and insolent Karna. It is childish of Duryodha to think that he can rob them of their kingdom or beat them in battle. Who can withstand these mighty warriors and their friends? My heart trembles with fear when I hear that Krishna and Arjuna will be seated in the same chariot. Yet I do not fear Krishna or Arjuna, Bhima or the twins, so much as I fear the just anger of Yudhistra. Say anything to him, O Sánjaya, that will avert war!"

Sánjaya drove swiftly to the capital city of Panchala, where he found the Pándavas and those kings who were their allies. In the presence of them all he made obeisance to Yudhistra and gave him King Kuru's message, pleading for peace, but saying nothing about the return of the kingdom.

"Why should you think that I desire war, O Sánjaya?" asked Kunti's eldest son. What man is so cursed by the gods that he could wish to fight when peace is possible? Return now, and in the presence of the Bháratas say these words to Kuru's son: 'O Duryodha, we desire only peace. Give us even one province of the kingdom; give to your five brothers five villages, and this shall end the quarrel!' "

Krishna Pleads for Peace

After Sánjaya had departed, Yudhistra was deeply troubled and pondered the message that he had brought. He summoned Krishna and said to him, "O friend, only you can save us now. You heard what Sánjaya said in the name of Kuru and his son: they seek to make peace with us, keeping our kingdom for themselves. We have truthfully kept our pledge, expecting them to keep theirs, but now the covetous king has broken his word, forsaking his honor as a Kshatria. We cannot give up what justly belongs to us, for a Kshatria's duty is to govern and to fight. We must have our kingdom to govern and protect; we must have our wealth, for duty as well as pleasure depends upon it. For us poverty is worse than death, for what can be more sorrowful than this, O Krishna, that I cannot support my mother and my brothers and my friends? And yet, what good can there be in battle? Even if we win, we shall kill those whom we love. O friend, how can we be both just and virtuous? Only you can counsel us, who are so dear to us and who know the way of truth."

"I will go myself to the Kúravas," answered Krishna, "for your sake and theirs, and do my best to make peace without giving up what rightly belongs to you. If I can do this, I shall have saved the whole earth from the meshes of death."

The king and his brothers rejoiced at his words, and each of them added a message to what Yudhistra already had said. Only Sadeva did not counsel peace.

"Speak, O slayer of foes, for war!" he said to Krishna. "Since Dráupadi was dragged into the assembly, my wrath has never ceased to burn within me, and it will never be quenched until Duryodha is slain. If all my brothers are inclined to peace, I alone will fight Duryodha to the death!"

Then Dráupadi, her eyes filled with tears, spoke to Krishna, taking in her hand her long black hair, bound into a soft, perfumed braid, "Remember, O Krishna, how this hair of mine was seized by Dushasa's rough hands. If Bhima and Arjuna have fallen so low as to desire peace, my aged father and his sons and Sadeva will avenge me, and my five sons will fight the Kúravas, with Abimanyu leading them. Thirteen long years have I spent in the hope of happier days, hiding my anger in my heart like a burning fire. And now my heart breaks when I hear this talk of peace."

She wept aloud, and Krishna comforted her, saying, "Dry your eyes, O Dráupadi. I swear to you that if they do not listen to my words, the sons of Kuru will become the food of jackals, and their wives will weep as you do now."

The next morning Krishna mounted his splendid chariot, and his swift horses devoured the sky and drank up the road as they bore him to Hástina. The sun shone clear, and fragrant breezes blew; flocks of cranes flew above his head, and the fields were rich with grain, for it was late autumn. He was received with honor at Kuru's court and lingered there, talking and laughing with his friends and kinsmen; then he went to the house of Vídura and talked with him far into the starlit night.

At sunrise the next morning a messenger summoned him

to the court where Kuru awaited him with all the assembled kings and elders. Krishna entered and took a seat of honor there; he was dressed in yellow robes and looked like some dark jewel set in gold. When the assembly was silent, he spoke to all who were there, repeating what had been said before, warning them of the terrible slaughter that would follow if they refused the just demands of Pandu's sons, and reminding them that Yudhistra had asked for only five villages out of the great domain that had once been his. All those who heard praised his speech in their hearts, but none dared speak aloud in the presence of Duryodha.

That prince turned to Krishna and said, "You have found fault harshly and unreasonably with me alone, O slayer of foes. Indeed, my father, Bhishma, Drona, and Vídura all blame me and never anyone else, while I cannot find the least fault in myself. Is it my fault that in the match at dice, which he willingly entered, Yudhistra was defeated and his kingdom won? Is it my fault that he was again defeated and went with his brothers into the forest? What have I done to them that they seek a quarrel with me? Listen, O Krishna! As long as I live, that share of the kingdom that my father gave to the Pándavas shall never again be theirs! As long as I live, the Pándavas shall not have as much of our land as can be covered by the sharp point of a needle!"

Krishna was silent for a moment, his eyes red with anger; then he said, "O dull of understanding, how can you say that you have not injured them? You will not give them what they justly ask of you, but they will take it when you lie dead on the field of battle. O fool, who will not listen to the wise advice of your friends, you speak wicked and shameful words and with them you doom yourself to death."

When he heard this, the proud Duryodha, breathing hard

like a great snake, rose angrily from his seat; he paid no attention to his father and all the elders, but left the court. His
brothers, his counselors, and all the kings rose up and followed
him.

When he saw them do so, Bhishma said, "I see, O Krishna,
that the fate of all these Kshatrias is decided, for they have
foolishly followed Duryodha."

And Krishna answered, "You have all witnessed what has
happened here. With your permission I shall now return to
Yudhistra."

Before he left, Krishna sought out Karna. He took that
fierce warrior up on his chariot and drove slowly out of the
city.

"O bull among men," said Krishna, "you are the son of
Kunti, born in her maidenhood and begotten by Surya himself.
You are therefore by law the eldest son of Pandu. Come with
me today and let the Pándavas know that you are Kunti's son,
born before Yudhistra. Your five brothers will embrace your
feet and will crown you lord of the whole earth in the presence
of all the kings assembled in their cause. Let Yudhistra be
your heir and ride on your chariot, bearing the white fan,
while the mighty Bhima lifts the canopy over your head and
Arjuna holds the reins. The twins and the sons of Dráupadi
with Abimanyu, all the allied kings and I myself will walk
behind you. Let there be brotherly union between you and the
Pándavas today, O son of Kunti, and you shall rule the kingdom, surrounded by them, as the moon is surrounded by the
stars."

"I know already all that you have told me, O slayer of foes,"
said Karna. "I am the son of Kunti and therefore by law the
eldest son of Pandu. But my mother abandoned me as soon as
I was born and has never cared for my welfare. A Suta took

me to his home and performed for me the rites of infancy; he
and his wife think of me as their son and my heart is bound
to them with all the ties of love and gratitude. I cannot break
those ties, O Krishna, even for the sake of the whole earth or
for mountains of gold. Besides, Duryodha gave me the kingdom of Anga, which I have enjoyed for many years. He is
depending on me to fight Arjuna in single combat, and I cannot be false to him. I know, O Krishna, that you have spoken
to me for my own good, and I believe that the Pándavas
would do all that you have promised. Keep this talk of ours a
secret from them, for they would not fight against me if they
knew me for Kunti's first-born son. O sinless one, if we come
out alive from this great battle, may we meet here again;
otherwise we shall surely meet in heaven."

Karna embraced Krishna, clasping him tightly to his breast,
then stepped down from the chariot and returned to the city;
while the horses of Krishna, fleet as hawks, carried him back
to the camp of the five brothers.

After Krishna had gone, Kunti also sought Karna. She went
to the bank of the Ganges, for she knew that he came there
each morning to worship the sun. She heard his voice chanting
the Vedic hymns and saw him facing the east with upraised
arms. She waited for him to finish his prayers, standing
patiently behind him; but soon she began to suffer from the
sun's heat and moved closer to him, until she stood in the
shade of his broad shoulders. When Karna had done with his
prayers, he turned and beheld her with great surprise.

Saluting her courteously with joined palms, he said, "I am
Karna, the Suta's son. Why have you come here, noble lady?
What can I do for you?"

"You are my son," she cried. "No Suta brought you forth. It
is wrong that you should serve the sons of Kuru and not know

your own brothers. Let the Kúravas behold today the union of Karna and Arjuna! If you two are united, what is there in the world that you cannot achieve? O Karna, do not call yourself the Suta's son, but the eldest son of Kunti! The highest of all duties is to please one's father and mother; therefore listen to me, my child!"

"Noble lady," answered Karna, "I cannot believe that it is my highest duty to please you. You cast me off when I was born and have never cared for me; but now, for your own sake, you seek to lay your commands upon me. I cannot do what you ask, for the time has come when all those whom Duryodha has protected must stand by him and fight for him, and I shall fight for him against your sons to the best of my power. But I must not be hard, and your coming here shall not be in vain. I promise you that I shall fight only with Arjuna and that no other son of yours shall be slain by me. The number of your children will always be five: if Arjuna is slain, I shall be the fifth; if I am slain, Arjuna still remains."

Kunti, trembling with grief, said, "Remember this your pledge! May you be blessed!" And they both departed, going their separate ways.

The Field of Kuru Kshetra

When Krishna returned and the sons of Pandu heard all that had happened in Hástina, they gave up all hope of peace. Therefore they arrayed their troops for battle, and Yudhistra named the commanders of the seven armies. As the supreme leader of the host they all chose Jumna, Dráupadi's brother, who had been born to slay Drona. A great shout of joy arose at this choice. The troops began to move about; the neighing of horses, the roars of elephants, the clatter of chariot wheels, and the sounds of drums and conchs made a tremendous din. The Pándavas and all the mighty kings and warriors who supported them put on their coats of mail, mounted their chariots, and set out with their unconquerable host for the plain of Kuru Kshetra.

In the front of that army marched Bhima, Nákula, Sadeva, Abimanyu, and the five sons of Dráupadi, with Jumna at their head. Behind them came the army of the Panchalas. In the center marched Yudhistra, with the wagons carrying the food and fodder, the tents, the money chests, the weapons and machines of war, the skilled mechanics, and the surgeons and physicians, furnished with every medicine and remedy they needed. In the rear marched the army of Virata and his sons and the remainder of the host, and with it rode Arjuna, driven by Krishna. The din made by that joyful, marching host was like the roar of the ocean when the tide is highest on the day of the new moon.

When they reached the field of Kuru Kshetra, the army encamped on a part of the field that was level and open, abounding with grass and fuel, facing the east, beside the holy river Hiranwati. Jumna measured the ground for the encampment, where handsome tents, by hundreds and thousands, rose for the kings and warriors. They looked like palaces and were filled with food and drink and fuel. To every tent Yudhistra sent bows and bowstrings, coats of mail and weapons, honey and butter and water, fodder for cattle, chaff and coals. Each division had its hundreds of elephants, cased in plates of steel, its thousands of horses and foot soldiers, all camped upon that field.

Duryodha heard that Yudhistra was encamped on Kuru Kshetra and ready for battle; therefore he arrayed his own troops and appointed leaders for the eleven armies. Then,

with all those leaders, he went to Bhishma and stood before
him with joined palms, saying, "When it has no commander,
even a mighty army can be scattered like a swarm of ants. O
wise grandsire, be our commander! March at our head as
Indra leads the gods, and we shall follow you as calves follow
a mighty bull!"

"So be it!" replied Bhishma. "You know that the sons of
Pandu are as dear to me as you are, but I will fight for you,
as I have promised to do. Yet listen to me, O son of Kuru, for
there are things that you must understand if I am to command
your host. First, know that I am not able to kill the sons of
Pandu. I shall, however, slay their warriors day by day and so,
unless I am slain myself, I shall destroy their host. There is
a second thing that you must understand, O lord of earth.
Either Karna must fight first, or I, for the Suta's son so
boastfully compares his might with mine that I will not fight
by his side."

"As long as the grandsire lives, O King," Karna said, "I shall
not enter the battle. When he is slain, then I will fight Arjuna.
So I vowed among the assembled kings and so I shall do."

Then Bhishma said, "Still another thing I must tell you, O
King. I shall fight with all the lords of earth that may oppose
me, but I shall never strike or slay Shikándin, the son of the
king of Panchala, even if he rushes upon me with upraised
weapon."

"Why will you not slay Shikándin, O grandsire?"

"Listen to this story, Duryodha," answered Bhishma. "When
I was young, I made a vow that I would never marry nor sit
on my father's throne, but spend my life in study and meditation. I gained such power of soul that the gods granted me
the boon that I should not die till I desired death. I crowned
my younger brother king and set my heart on finding him a

beautiful and sweet-natured wife. I heard that the three daughters of the king of Kashi, who were all as beautiful as Apsaras, were about to choose their husbands at a *swayámvara* to which all the kings of earth had been invited. I went there and saw the maidens, who were so lovely that I wanted them all for my brother. Therefore I took them by force upon my chariot, challenging all the other kings to rescue them, in accord with Kshatria usage. Alone in my chariot, I drove them all back and brought the three fair damsels to my brother.

"The eldest damsel, however, had set her heart upon another suitor and was secretly betrothed to him, for she meant to choose him at her *swayámvara*. Therefore she asked me to permit her to marry him, and I sent her with an escort to his court. But her betrothed no longer wanted her since she had been taken away by me, and the unhappy maiden left his city, weeping bitterly and cursing me for causing her misfortune. She went to the forest and devoted herself to fierce discipline of mind and body in order to obtain a boon from the gods. After twelve years of fasting, prayer, and effort, she obtained from Shiva the boon that she might be born a man, able to slay me in battle; then she built herself a funeral pyre and, setting it afire, laid herself thereon.

"It is she, O son of Kuru, who was reborn as Shikándin, and I have vowed that I will never strike a woman or one whom I know to have been a woman in a former birth, or even one who bears a woman's name. Therefore, even if Shikándin attack me, bow in hand, I shall not slay nor smite him."

Duryodha pondered these words a moment and thought them just and proper. "O mighty-armed one," he asked, "in how many days can you destroy this host of Pandu's son, which abounds in elephants, men, and horses, and is protected by many godlike warriors?"

Bhishma carries off the three princesses.

Bhishma answered, "When I am standing in battle, shooting my great weapons that slay hundreds and thousands at a time, O foremost of the Kurus, I can wipe out that host in a month's time."

Duryodha turned to Drona, "And you, master? How soon can you destroy that host?"

Drona smiled and said, "I am old, O son of Kuru, but I, too, with the fire of my weapons, can destroy the army of the Pándavas in a month's time."

Now the spies that Yudhistra had placed in the Kúrava host told him all that these leaders had said. The son of Kunti called his brothers together. "O Arjuna," he asked, "in how much time can you destroy our foes?"

Arjuna of the curling hair looked at Krishna and replied, "Do not be anxious, O King! I can sweep away all living creatures with that terrible and mighty weapon that the lord Shiva gave me when I fought with him; but it is not right to use it against men, and we shall fight fairly. With Krishna as my ally, I believe that in one day I can destroy our foes."

The next morning, under a cloudless sky, the army of the Kúravas, led by Bhishma, set out for Kuru Kshetra and encamped on the opposite side of the plain from that of the Pándavas. Duryodha made his camp look like another Hástina, graced with hundreds of tents filled with provisions and weapons. He sent to all those kings who came with him excellent supplies of food for their horses and elephants and foot soldiers; he provided also for the bards and singers, the vendors and the traders, the spies and the people who came to watch the battle. The rest of the earth seemed to be empty of men, of elephants and horses, for the warriors who assembled on that field came from the whole earth over which the sun sheds its rays.

Thus those two great hosts were arrayed against one another, like two stormy oceans, on the east and the west sides of the plain of Kuru Kshetra. And beholding one another, the tens of thousands of warriors, filled with joy and delighting in battle, beat their drums and blew their thundering conchs until the earth and the sky resounded.

The Great Battle — Bhishma

Before the Battle

When the night had passed, the leaders of both armies arose
and shouted, "Array yourselves for battle!" Then on all sides
were heard the beat of drums, the neighing of horses, the
squeals of angry elephants, the shouts of men, and the clapping
of armpits. As the sun rose, each of the splendid hosts could
see the other, with its foot soldiers, its horsemen, chariots, and
elephants drawn up in their right places and armed with flashing weapons. Every warrior had his standard, bright colored
and decked with gold and gems, and these thousands of banners, blown by the wind, looked like fair damsels dancing.

The Pándavas looked across the field and beheld ten armies
led by ten tigers among men, while the eleventh great army,
made up of the Kúravas and their troops, stood in advance of
all the others, with Bhishma at its head. He was mounted on
a chariot of silver yoked with white horses; he wore a white

helmet and white mail, and a banner bearing the device of a
gold palmyra and five stars waved above him. He looked like
the full moon in the midst of clouds. They saw Drona, their
teacher and the teacher of almost all the kings assembled there,
on a golden chariot yoked with red steeds, his banner bearing
the device of a golden sacrificial altar and a water pot. His
son, Ashvattáma, was stationed with Bhishma at the head of
the host and carried a banner with the device of a lion's tail.
The king of Sind, at the head of his own troops, had on his
flag the emblem of a shining silver boar decked with golden
garlands. Shalya, king of Madra, led his army, bearing a
standard with the device of a golden plowshare, and the king
of Magadha carried one which depicted a golden bull. And the
flag of Duryodha, on whom all the rest depended, was decked
with gold and with a hundred tinkling bells and bore the
device of an elephant adorned with jewels. The host of the
Kúravas was arrayed in the form of a mighty bird: the kings
in their chariots were its head, the elephants its body, and the
horsemen its wings.

Seeing that formation, the sons of Pandu arrayed their armies
in the form called the thunderbolt, narrow and deep, for they
had less men than their enemies. Bhima and Jumna and the
twins led that host, while King Virata, with his brothers and
his sons, protected them at the rear. Behind Virata rode
Shikándin, eager to slay Bhishma, and then came Arjuna in
his golden chariot that shone like the sun and rang with a
hundred bells; it was drawn by his own white steeds, driven
by Krishna. In the center of the host Yudhistra took his place,
surrounded by huge and furious elephants that looked like
moving hills, while the king of Panchala, Dráupadi's father,
with his army, stood behind him. Above the chariots of all the
kings their banners waved, as bright as the sun and the moon.

Yudhistra's bore the device of a golden moon surrounded by the planets; on Bhima's banner shone the figure of a gigantic silver lion; on the tall, fierce standard of Nákula a deer with a golden back was portrayed; and Sadeva's bore the figure of a silver swan and was hung with bells. The five sons of Dráupadi had placed upon their flags the images of those gods who begot their fathers: Dharma and Vayu, Indra and the twin Ashvins. On the chariot of the young Abimanyu waved a standard with the device of a peacock, bright as heated gold. There were many others, adorned with gold and bells, that belonged to other warriors, and above them all rose the mighty ape with the lion's tail on the flagstaff of Arjuna.

As both armies stood at the dawn of day, waiting for battle, a wind began to blow and a gust of rain fell; although there were no clouds, the roll of thunder was heard, and the earth trembled. The banners shook in the wind, and their bells rang.

Arjuna said to Krishna, "O sinless one, place my chariot between the two hosts so that I may see those with whom I have to fight, who are here to do the will of the evil-minded son of Kuru."

Krishna drove the chariot out between the two armies, in view of Bhishma and Drona and all the kings of earth, saying, "Behold the Kúravas here assembled, O son of Kunti!"

And Arjuna, standing there, saw fathers and grandfathers, teachers and uncles, brothers and sons, comrades and dear friends in both the hosts. As he saw them thus opposed to each other, his heart was filled with pity, and he said, "When I see these kinsmen, O Krishna, ready to fight each other, my limbs become weak, my body trembles, I burn with fever and my bow, Gandíva, slips from my hand. I do not want victory, O best of men, or the kingdom with its pleasures. What joy would the kingdom give us, since those very men with whom we

wish to share its pleasures and its wealth are drawn up against
us here in battle? I do not wish to kill them, even though they
kill me, not even if the three worlds were offered to me, still
less for a kingdom of this earth. Alas, we are about to commit
a great sin! It would be better for me to lay down my arms and
to let myself be slain by the keen weapons of Kuru's sons."
With these words he cast aside his bow and arrows and sank
down upon the bench of the chariot, his heart shaken with
sorrow.

Krishna said to him, "Why have you become so faint of
heart, O Arjuna? It is neither glorious nor manly; it is
unseemly for a Kshatria. Shake off this weakness and arise, O
slayer of foes!"

"How can I loose my arrows against Bhishma and Drona,
who are worthy of all honor?" answered Arjuna. "It would be
better to beg my bread than to kill these men of great soul,
who are my elders and my teachers. I cannot tell which is
worse, to conquer them or to be conquered by them; for if we
conquer, we shall slay those without whom we shall not wish
to live. My vision is darkened; I no longer know what is right.
Teach me, for I am your disciple."

"You grieve for those who need no grief," Krishna said.
"The wise grieve neither for the dead nor for the living. There
never was a time when you and I and all these princes were
not living, and we shall never cease to live. These bodies of ours
belong to the eternal lord of the body—the soul, which cannot
be destroyed, O son of Bhárata. It does not kill and it cannot
be killed; it was never born and it can never die. As a man
throws away his worn-out clothes and puts on new ones, so
the soul, casting aside its worn-out body, enters a new one.
Weapons do not pierce it, nor is it burned by fire; waters do
not wet it, nor do the dry winds parch. This lord of the body

dwells undying in each one of us, O son of Kunti. Knowing this, how can you grieve?

"Do not shrink from the duty of your caste, O conqueror of wealth! Nothing is better for a Kshatria than a righteous battle, and this one has come to you unsought, like an open door to heaven. If you do not fight it, you will have failed in duty and in honor; and for one who has stood high in honor, ill-fame is worse than death. The warriors in their chariots will think that you have left the fight from fear, and they will speak ill of you.

"Each man reaches perfection by doing his own duty; he worships God—from whom all beings come, by whom this universe was stretched forth—by doing his appointed work, with no desire for its reward. You must do the work for its own sake and not for anything that it may bring to you. When pleasure and pain, gain and loss, victory and defeat are the same to you, you may go into battle without sin. If you dedicate your deeds to God, with no desire for reward, sin will not touch you, as a lotus leaf is not wet by water. God dwells in the heart of every creature, O son of Kunti, moving them all by his divine power. Take refuge in him with your whole heart, and you will find peace.

"Have you listened with singleness of heart, O conqueror of wealth? Has your weakness, which came from ignorance, vanished?"

"My weakness is gone, O sinless one," answered Arjuna. "I have listened to all that you have told me; my doubts have vanished, and I will do your bidding."

He rose and took up his arrows and Gandíva, and when they saw this, all the warriors of the Pándava host set up a shout and blew their sea-born conchs.

Then King Yudhistra took off his coat of mail and laid his

weapons down; he alighted from his chariot and went on foot with joined hands to the place where Bhishma stood. When his brothers saw what he did, they alighted also and followed him, amazed and anxious, asking him where he was going and what he meant to do. Yudhistra answered not a word, but walked toward the hostile army, which bristled with spears and arrows, and went to Bhishma and bowed before him, holding the grandsire's feet in his two hands. Surrounded by his brothers, he said, "I salute you, O unconquerable one! We must fight against you. Give us your permission and your blessing."

"If you had not come to me before this battle, O lord of earth," said Bhishma, "I should have cursed you and you would have been defeated. Now I am pleased with you, my son. Fight and be victorious! Men are the slaves of wealth, and so I am bound to the Kúravas by the wealth that they have given me. I must fight for your enemies, but if you will grant me that, I will give you any other boon that you desire."

"I bow to you, O grandsire," said Yudhistra, "as I ask you this. How can we conquer you who are unconquerable? Tell us how you may be slain in battle."

Bhishma said, "I do not know anyone, O King, who can slay me in battle. The time of my death is not yet known; therefore come to me again."

Yudhistra accepted Bhishma's words and, once more bowing to him, went with his brothers to Drona's chariot, through the crowds of soldiers who were looking curiously at him. Saluting him, he asked the master, "Tell me, O unconquerable one, how I may fight without sin and how, with your permission, I may defeat my foes."

"I am pleased with you and honored by you, O sinless one," Drona replied. "Fight and win the victory! I am bound to the Kúravas by the wealth that they have given me; I shall fight for them, but I shall pray for you. You will without doubt defeat your enemies, for where righteousness is, there is victory. What do you desire of me?"

"I ask you, O mighty-armed one," answered Yudhistra, "how we may vanquish you who are invincible?"

"You cannot win, O King, while I am in the battle. Therefore try to kill me as soon as may be."

"Alas that I must ask this!" Yudhistra said. "Tell me, then, how you may be slain. O master, I salute you as I ask."

"While I am standing in battle," Drona said, "no one will be able to slay me. Only when I am ready for death, withdrawn in meditation, shall any man be able to slay me; and I shall not lay down my arms or prepare for death till I am overwhelmed by sorrow."

Then Yudhistra saluted him once more and went with his brothers to where their uncle Shalya, the king of Madra, stood in his chariot. Bowing to him, the son of Kunti asked his permission to fight and reminded him of his promise to discourage Karna when the great battle should come between him and Arjuna. And Shalya blessed him, saying, "Go and fight, my son. I shall look after your victory."

The five brothers, coming out of that vast army, walked back to their own side of the field. Yudhistra, his heart at peace, put on his shining coat of mail, and those bulls among men mounted their chariots and took their places in the battle array. They caused the great drums and cymbals to be sounded, the trumpets and milk-white conchs to be blown. Krishna and Arjuna, standing in their chariot, blew their conchs called Fivefold and God-given; Bhima blew the Reednote, and Yudhistra his conch called Eternal Victory; Nákula and Sadeva blew theirs called Sweet-sounding and Pearlflowered, and all the mighty warriors blew their conchs until the sound pierced the hearts of the sons of Kuru and made the heavens and the earth resound.

The First Seven Days

On the morning of that awful day, the battle began that caused the death of so many noble warriors. The Kúrava host, reckless of their very lives, rushed with upraised standards against the Pándavas, and the Pándava host, led by Bhima, met them with cheerful hearts. The mighty shouts, the twang of bowstrings, the clash of weapons, the uproar of conchs and trumpets made the hair stand on end and shook those vast armies as forests are shaken by the tempest. As the din arose, Bhima began to roar like a bull till his shouts were heard above all other noises and struck fear into the hearts of the Kúravas.

Duryodha and his brothers, shaking their splendid bows, surrounded Bhima, covering him with arrows like snakes that have just shed their skins. Then the five sons of Dráupadi, with the twins and Abimanyu, rushed against the Kúravas, tearing them with whetted arrows as bolts of thunder shatter mountains. In that first encounter no warrior on either side turned back, and no difference could be seen between the two hosts. On both sides it was easy to see which warriors had been taught by Drona, because of their lightness of hand and their sure aim. Bhima and Duryodha fought fiercely, but neither prevailed over the other, for both were mighty warriors. On that first day Uttar, King Virata's young son whose chariot Arjuna had driven, was struck down by the king of Madra.

Dushasa attacked Nákula, striking him with many arrows, but the son of Madri laughed at him and cut down with his shafts the standard and the bow of his enemy. Yudhistra fought against his uncle Shalya, while Jumna sought out Drona. The king of Panchala fought with the king of Sind, and the battle between them was fierce and terrible. Thousands of single combats took place between chariots and elephants, horsemen and foot soldiers, for both sides fought as if possessed by demons. Chariot crashed against chariot; huge elephants with canopied seats and standards on their backs fought furiously against one another, or wounded and panic-stricken, dashed through the army, crushing chariots and horses under their feet. Many a young, heroic warrior fell from his car and lay prostrate upon the ground; many a horseman was carried from the field hanging dead from his saddle and still holding his bow. A thick dust arose and the din was deafening. Over the field the palmyra banner of Bhishma constantly waved, and the grandsire himself, on his great chariot, shone like the moon above a mountain peak.

On the second day the battle raged again, neither side prevailing over the other. On the third day Bhishma arrayed his forces again in the shape of a great bird, and the army of the Pándavas was counterarrayed in the shape of a half-moon, with Bhima at the right horn, Yudhistra at the center, surrounded by many kings, and Arjuna at the left horn. All that morning the warriors fought, and none of them gave way.

In the afternoon, Bhishma, with his bow constantly drawn to a circle, using celestial weapons, shot continuous lines of arrows in all directions and seemed to be everywhere at once. The Pándava warriors could not see him for the showers of arrows sent forth from his bow; they fell before his shafts like insects falling into a blazing fire. Even as he had said, the vast army of the Pándavas began to tremble and give way, in spite of the efforts of its leaders.

Then Krishna spoke to Arjuna, saying, "The hour is come, O tiger among men, when you must make good your promise to rout the Kúrava army and fight with Bhishma himself. Behold, your army is being scattered by him alone." And, with Arjuna's consent, he urged the white steeds to the place where Bhishma's chariot stood.

When they beheld him advancing, the Pándava host rallied, while Bhishma, roaring like a lion, covered the onrushing chariot with his arrows. Arjuna stretched Gandíva and cut the grandsire's bow in two; Bhishma seized and strung another, but Arjuna cut that one, too. Bhishma praised his quickness, saying, "Well done, O mighty-armed one! I am pleased with you. Fight hard with me, my son!" And with a third bow he sent forth a shower of arrows. Krishna, with great skill, avoided many of these by driving in quick circles, but many struck their mark, and he and Arjuna looked like roaring bulls with the scratches of horns on their bodies.

Now Krishna saw that Bhishma's arrows were again driving back the Pándava army, while Arjuna was fighting only mildly, out of respect for the grandsire. This made him very angry, for he feared that Yudhistra's army might not survive another attack; therefore he dropped the reins, leaped from the chariot and ran toward Bhishma, whirling his discus. But Arjuna also leaped to the ground, ran after him and threw his arms around his friend, stopping him after he had run but ten steps. "Stop, O Krishna!" he cried. "Remember that you said you would not fight; do not let men say you are a liar. I swear to you, O slayer of foes, by my weapons, by the truth, by my own good deeds, that I will destroy our foes. The task is mine, not yours, and I will fulfill it." Krishna, still silent and angry, mounted the chariot and took up the reins again.

Arjuna summoned a celestial weapon, drew Gandíva with

power and filled every side of the field with sharp and blazing shafts, causing a river of blood to flow from the Kúrava host. Every other sound was silenced by the thundering twang of his bow; the Kúravas were struck with fear, while the Pándavas rallied to the attack. As the sun set the Kúravas withdrew, Bhishma and Drona retreating with them, and the Pándavas set up a triumphant shout. Then all the warriors, talking about this great feat of Arjuna's, entered their tents, lighted without by flaming torches and within by countless lamps.

Every day for eight days the armies were arrayed for battle in different formations, each trying to get the advantage over the other. Each day these mighty warriors, after their wounds had been tended by skillful surgeons, returned to the fight, killing their enemies' troops, slaying brothers and sons, kings and warriors. Each day one of them gained added glory by his prowess in battle. Now it was Bhima, careering over the field in his chariot with his lion banner flying, or seated on the neck of a mighty elephant, or on foot, whirling his great mace till he looked like a wheel of fire, felling elephants and cavalry and foot soldiers, like Death himself. Now it was Arjuna, in his chariot with the ape screaming above him on the banner, the reins held by Krishna, Gandíva flashing like lightning, its shafts drinking the blood of countless heroes. Now it was Nákula and Sadeva, fighting together against their uncle Shalya and driving him off the field or falling upon the Kúrava cavalry, slaying so many of them that the rest broke and fled before them, as a herd of deer flees before two tigers.

The sons of Dráupadi, her brothers, and Virata's sons were all mighty warriors; and Abimanyu, beautiful as a god, was the equal of Arjuna in lightness of hand, sureness of aim, knowledge of weapons, and bravery, for his father had taught him all he knew. He was always in the midst of the battle and could fight with five or ten warriors at once; he made the Kúravas tremble, for they thought that there were two Arjunas on the field.

Every day Bhima slew one or two of the sons of Kuru, for he had sworn after the gambling match that he would kill them all. Therefore his brothers and his nephews, though they often fought against their cousins and struck them from their chariots or drove them, wounded, from the field, never slew any of Kuru's sons, so that Bhima might be true to his promise. Several times he and Duryodha fought like two mad bulls, each longing to kill the other; they were equal in might and neither prevailed. But Duryodha, when he went each night to his tent, was overcome by grief and wept for his brothers.

When the sun set each day, the field was strewn with gold-backed bows and winged arrows, broken swords with ivory handles, and shields inlaid with gold, loosened from the hands of the slain. Many a chariot warrior lay on the ground as if asleep, his weapons beside him; horses and elephants lay there dead, their blood staining the earth. Wheelless chariots and torn banners, embroidered blankets and elephants' housings, chains and ornaments and helmets scattered about made the plain of Kuru Kshetra look like the earth in spring when it is strewn with flowers or like the night sky bright with stars.

Both armies stopped fighting when the darkness came. The warriors, after placing their sentries and caring for their troops, went into their tents, praising one another's deeds. They plucked the arrows from their bodies, bathed their wounds and treated them with healing herbs. Brahmans performed the evening worship, poets sang the heroes' praises, and they enjoyed themselves for a while, not speaking of the battle, but listening to music and poetry. Then they slept deeply, and the two armies, with their sleeping warriors, elephants and horses, were beautiful to behold.

On the eighth day the army of the Pándavas gained the advantage and drove back the Kúravas with great slaughter. At night, after their tired and defeated troops had gone to rest, Duryodha and Shákuni, Dushasa and Karna met together to consider how the sons of Pandu could be vanquished. Duryodha said, "Neither Drona nor Bhishma nor Shalya fights with all his power against the Pándavas; therefore my forces are being destroyed and my weapons will soon be exhausted. I am doubtful of victory."

"Do not grieve, O chief of the Kúravas," Karna replied. "Let Bhishma withdraw from the battle, and as soon as he lays down his arms, I shall slay all the Pándavas before his eyes. Truly, he favors them every day. Go without delay to his tent and ask him to give up his command; then set your heart at rest, for I alone will vanquish your enemies!"

"As soon as Bhishma has consented," Duryodha said, "I will come to you, O chastiser of foes, and you will lead us to victory."

Then Duryodha, clad in fresh and handsome robes, adorned with his royal crown and many jewels, mounted his horse and rode to Bhishma's tent, while all his brothers who were left alive and the leaders of his armies walked behind him, and servants lighted their way with golden lamps fed with fragrant oil. He alighted and saluted the grandsire and then sat down on a handsome seat covered with a rich carpet.

With his hands joined and his eyes filled with tears, he said, "O slayer of foes, you promised that you would destroy all the armies of the Pándavas and therefore we entered with confidence into this terrible conflict. Make your words true,

O sinless one! Or else, if you are sparing our enemies because you love them or because you hate me, withdraw from the battle and allow Karna to fight, for he can vanquish the Pándavas themselves and all their friends and kinsmen."

The high-souled Bhishma was filled with grief when he heard these cruel words; he sighed deeply and was silent for a while. Then raising his eyes which blazed with anger, he said, "Why do you pierce me with such sharp words? I try, with my utmost might, to bring about your victory and am prepared to lose my life in battle. Arjuna alone overcame every one of us in Virata's kingdom and shamed us by taking away our robes. That should prove to you that we cannot slay him and all his brothers. It is you who have provoked the Pándavas to battle; therefore fight them yourself, O King, and let us see you act like a man! As for me, I shall do as I promised: I shall slay their troops and their allies. Sleep happily, O son of Gandhari! Tomorrow I shall fight so fierce a battle that men will speak of it as long as the world lasts!"

The ninth day dawned, and Duryodha called all the royal warriors, saying, "Draw up your forces! Today Bhishma, filled with wrath, is going to slaughter our enemies. Our duty is to protect him, for even the lion can be slain by wolves if he is alone in the forest. If we protect him, our victory is certain."

Bhishma arrayed his troops in a hollow square, taking his position in the center of the front, while all the Kúrava warriors, in chariots or on elephants, were ranged on each side of him, facing the Pándavas, whose host was arrayed in that best of forms, the hawk. When the battle began, the grandsire smote the Pándava host with blazing arrows, and his shouts and the clapping of his palms struck terror to their hearts. He was like a fire in dry grass, blown by the wind. He struck off the heads of warriors as a man knocks ripe fruit off a tree with stones. He felled elephants and chariots or struck their riders from them, and many an empty chariot was dragged from the field by its runaway horses; many a noble warrior, advancing fearlessly against him, was sent to Yama's realm.

All day long the terrible battle went on, while Bhishma took the lives of warriors as the sun sucks up water in summer. He broke the ranks of the Pándavas just as they had been breaking those of the Kúravas, and the routed soldiers, hopeless and heartless, could not even look at him, for he was like the midday sun, blazing with his own splendor. Indeed, the sons of Pandu themselves looked at him with awe because of the superhuman deeds that he was achieving, and the troops, fleeing in fear, found no protectors, but looked like bulls running wild, no longer held by the yoke. They cried aloud as they threw away their armor and fled with disheveled hair.

While Bhishma was still destroying the Pándava host, the sun, the thousand-rayed maker of the day, reached the western hills; the troops, tired out, withdrew to rest, and the night came, which steals away the senses of all creatures. In the fierce hours of darkness the Pándavas and their allies sat in Yudhistra's tent to consider what they should do, for all of them were wounded by the shafts of Bhishma and all were thinking of his mighty deeds.

"Behold," said Yudhistra, "the high-souled Bhishma is crushing my troops as an elephant crushes a mass of reeds, as a fire rages in dry grass! When I spoke to him before the battle he said to me, 'The time of my death is not yet known; come to me again.' Therefore let us all go to him again and ask him how we may vanquish him. He will tell us, for he brought us up when we were children and fatherless. And now we seek to kill him! Shame upon the Kshatria usage, which forces us to slay the grandsire, our father's uncle!"

The others all agreed with his decision, and so Yudhistra, his four brothers, and Krishna put off their armor and went on foot to Bhishma's tent. He welcomed them lovingly and asked them what they desired of him.

"Even if it be very difficult," he said, "yet I will do it with all my heart."

"O grandsire," answered Yudhistra, "tell us how we may vanquish you in battle, how we may have the victory and how our army may escape further destruction. How can we beat you in battle? Tell us, O lord of earth, how we may bring about your death, for you can never be vanquished!"

"It is true, O son of Pandu," said Bhishma, "that even the gods cannot defeat me when I fight carefully in battle. But there are those with whom I will not fight, and through them I can be overcome. In your army is Shikándin, a prince of Panchala, who is brave and powerful. He was a woman once, later reborn to manhood, and I shall never fight with him. Let Arjuna keep Shikándin before him and then pierce me with his shafts and cast me down from my chariot. Then your victory will be certain, for you can overcome the rest when I am gone."

The Pándavas, after saluting the grandsire, went back to their tents. Arjuna, overwhelmed by grief and shame, said to Krishna, "How shall I fight the grandsire, the eldest of our family, whose lap I climbed upon when I was a child, all dusty from my play? How can I slay that wise and honored one?"

"You will never win the victory unless you slay him, O conqueror of wealth," answered Krishna, "and you have pledged yourself to victory. It has been said that even an aged person worthy of all honor must be slain if he comes against one as an enemy. It is the eternal duty of a Kshatria to fight, to govern, and to sacrifice, but without hatred."

Toward the hour of sunrise, with beat of drums and cymbals and the blare of conchs, the Pándavas formed their troops into a terrible array and marched out for battle, putting Shikándin in the very front rank. Bhima and Arjuna protected his wheels; behind him came the sons of Dráupadi and Abimanyu; behind them marched Jumna with the warriors of Panchala, and after him came Yudhistra with the twins and all the armies of their allies. They marched directly against Bhishma, scattering their arrows as they went.

Bhishma Falls

That mighty warrior, the high-souled Bhishma, said to Duryodha, "Listen to what I say, O King! Today I shall either be slain myself or I shall slay the Pándavas. If I fail to slay them, I shall free myself from the debt I owe you for the food and the wealth that you have given me, by casting my life away at the head of your army."

Then he attacked the Pándava host, pouring upon them showers of long shafts, calf-toothed or crescent-headed, all sped with power and wrath, each one like an angry and poisonous serpent. On that tenth day of battle he shone resplendent as a fire without smoke, and the Pándavas could not look at him, for he was like the sun at the summer solstice, scorching their troops with his arrows and taking the lives of thousands as the sun sucks moisture from the earth.

All the warriors of the Pándavas rushed against him while the Kúrava warriors surrounded him to protect him, and a terrible fight was waged around him, for in that game of battle Bhishma was the stake on whom the victory of each side depended. Shikándin attacked him joyfully, striking him with three shafts, but these arrows caused him little pain, and he received them laughingly; indeed, he received them as a person in the heat of summer receives a shower of rain.

Krishna, holding the reins of Arjuna's white steeds, said to him, "Now put forth all your strength and slay the grandsire! See, he is breaking our ranks! None but you can bear his arrows and none but you can slay him."

Then the ape-bannered Arjuna, keeping behind Shikándin, drew near to Bhishma, cut his standard down with one arrow, and broke his bow with another. The grandsire took up another bow, but Arjuna cut it into three pieces with two broadheaded shafts. All the bows that Bhishma took up, the son of Pandu cut down, and then he pierced Bhishma with ten arrows and then another ten.

And the grandsire, deeply wounded by the keen-pointed shafts, said to Dushasa, who fought beside him, "These arrows coming toward me in a line, whose touch is like the thunderbolt's—these are not Shikándin's. They cut me to the quick, piercing my coat of mail, and strike my vital organs. These are not Shikándin's. They come like angry, poisonous snakes, like messengers of death. They are Arjuna's. No one can cause me pain but the heroic wielder of Gandíva, the ape-bannered son of Pandu."

After that, he fought no longer; but although he was sorely wounded, he stood calmly in his chariot and did not leave the battle.

Then Arjuna, at the head of the Pándavas, broke the center of the Kúrava army, and the troops and many of the warriors fled from the field, abandoning Bhishma. And the Pándavas surrounded that mighty hero on all sides, driving off the Kúravas who protected him, and covered him with their arrows until there was not on his body a space of two fingers' breadth that was not pierced by them. He began to weaken like an aged lion surrounded by the hunters. A little before sunset, in the sight of both armies, he reeled and fell down from his chariot, like a falling banner. Yet his body did not touch the ground, for it was held up by the many arrows that pierced it. Even as he fell, he remembered that the sun was approaching the winter solstice, so he did not allow his life to depart, for it is not well to die at that season. He had been given the boon that he himself should choose the hour of his death; therefore he held his life within him until the sun should move into the north, and he lay, with his mind given to prayer, on his bed of arrows.

When Bhishma fell, the hearts of all the Kúravas fell with him, and cries of sorrow were heard; while the Pándavas, having won the victory, stood at the head of their ranks and blew their conchs and trumpets. Dushasa turned his chariot and drove quickly to Drona, who commanded an army in another part of the field, to tell him of Bhishma's fall. Drona fell fainting from his chariot when he heard the evil news, but he recovered quickly and ordered the Kúravas to stop fighting. When they understood this, the Pándavas, too, sent fleet messengers to all their troops, commanding them to stop and announcing Bhishma's fall.

The kings of both armies and hundreds of other warriors put off their armor and came to where the eldest of the Bháratas lay. They stood around him and saluted him and Bhishma spoke to them: "Welcome, you mighty warriors! Welcome, you blessed ones! I am well pleased with you, for truly you are the equals of the gods." Then he said, "My head is hanging down. Pray give me a pillow." The kings ran to their tents and fetched many beautiful pillows made of delicate, soft fabrics, but the grandsire did not want these, saying, with a laugh, "These are not fitting for a hero's bed." Then, seeing that mightiest of warriors, the ape-bannered son of Pandu, he spoke to him, "O Arjuna, my head hangs down. Give me such a pillow as you think fit, my son."

Arjuna, his eyes filled with tears, took up Gandíva and three straight shafts. Stretching the mighty bow, he drove the arrows deep into the earth, then lifted Bhishma's head and laid it upon them.

The grandsire was pleased that Arjuna had guessed his thought, and said, "Thus should a Kshatria sleep on the field of battle. I will lie on this bed until the sun turns to the north, and then I will yield my body as a friend bids farewell to a friend. Let it be burned with these arrows still piercing it."

The kings of both armies were filled with wonder. They had laid aside their armor and their weapons, and they met now as in the days of old and cheerfully talked together. Bhishma bore his pain bravely, but soon asked again for Arjuna, who came and stood before him with joined palms. "My body burns and my vital organs are in agony," he said. "Give me water, O Arjuna." Arjuna mounted on his chariot and again stretched Gandíva, twanging its string with a sound like thunder. Then he placed an arrow on the string, speaking an incantation, and pierced the earth a little to the south of where Bhishma lay; and lo, a jet of water rose, pure and cool and sweet, and he gave it to Bhishma to drink.

"Only you could do so wonderful a thing, O son of the Bháratas," the grandsire said. "With Krishna as your friend, you will achieve many mighty deeds that the gods themselves could not equal." He turned his eyes to Duryodha and said, "O King, forget your wrath! See how Arjuna has created this jet of cool, pure water! None but him, who knows the weapons of the gods, can do such deeds. Make peace with him, O King, and let this battle end with my death! Let this remnant of your

Arjuna gives water to Bhishma.

brothers and of these warriors live! Let peace come when I die!"

But Duryodha said nothing; he refused this counsel as a dying man refuses medicine, and the kings and warriors returned to their tents after saluting Bhishma and placing guards about him to protect him.

After they had gone, Karna came, and when he saw that mighty hero lying with closed eyes on his arrowy bed, he fell weeping at his feet and said, "O chief of the Bháratas, I am the Suta's son, whom you have always hated."

The aged leader, slowly raising his eyelids and telling the guards to stand aside, embraced Karna with one arm and said, with great love, as a father speaks to a son, "Come, come! You have been my adversary, one who always challenged me and compared himself with me. I tell you truly, my son, that I bear you no ill will. I spoke so harshly to you only to abate your pride. I know your courage and your might, your generosity and your fairness in battle. You are not a Suta's son, but the son of Kunti, and the Pándavas are your brothers. O slayer of foes, if you wish to please me, join them today and let all the kings of the earth be free from danger!"

"I know all that you tell me, O mighty one," answered Karna, "but I cannot change now. This war must take its course. I have always tried to injure the Pándavas, and I cannot overcome my hatred of them. Therefore I shall cheerfully fulfill the duties of my caste, and I shall fight against Arjuna. Grant me your permission, O exalted one, and forgive me for any harsh words that I have uttered against you and for any rash and thoughtless acts."

"If you cannot find it in your heart to change, O Karna," said Bhishma, "then I permit you to fight. Serve the king without anger or pride, with no desire for revenge, with all your power and courage. For a long time I have tried to make peace between you and your brothers, but I have failed. Do as you desire!"

And Karna rose, saluted Bhishma, and went to the tent of Duryodha.

The Great Battle — Drona

Abimanyu's Sacrifice

Karna returned to the spacious encampment of the Kúrava army and spoke cheering words to the warriors, and they, beholding him, were filled with hope and welcomed him with shouts, the twanging of bowstrings, and the clapping of armpits. He and Duryodha agreed that Drona should be made commander of the host in Bhishma's stead, and the ceremony was immediately held, with hymns and the songs of bards and cries of "Victory!" With Karna and Drona to lead them, the warriors felt sure of winning, even without Bhishma.

Afterwards, in the midst of all the host, Drona said to the king, "Since you have honored me with the command of your host, what can I do for you, O tiger among men? What boon do you desire?"

"This is the boon that I ask of you, O master," Duryodha replied. "Bring Yudhistra here to me, alive!"

"Why do you not desire his death, O King?" asked Drona.
"It would be truly wonderful if you vanquished him in battle
and then made peace and gave him back his kingdom."

"O master!" cried Duryodha, "the victory can never be
mine if Yudhistra is slain, for Arjuna would never rest till he
had slain us all. Nay, bring him here alive so that we may
gamble with him once again and send the Pándavas into the
forest for as long as they live! Thus we can win a lasting victory."

Drona thought for a while about this crooked plan and
then said, "Yudhistra can never be taken even by the gods, so
long as Arjuna protects him. But if by some means Arjuna can
be taken out of the fight, O King, I will bring his eldest
brother to you before the day is over."

The king of the Trigartas spoke: "We are always being
humbled by him who wields Gandíva. I shall challenge him
tomorrow and take him from the field; then we shall surround
him and slay him. I swear now before you all that we shall do
this." And he took a solemn vow with his brothers and the
leaders of his troops that all of them would die rather than
return from the battle without slaying him of the white steeds.

The next morning Arjuna said to Yudhistra, "These men
have sworn to conquer me or die and have challenged me to a
battle that I cannot refuse. Therefore let Sátyajit, Dráupadi's
brother, protect you in my place. As long as he lives, Drona
can never capture you; but, O lord of earth, if he is slain, do
not remain on the field, even if all our host surround you!"

Yudhistra gave him his promise, embracing him lovingly,
and Arjuna rode out against the Trigartas like a hungry lion
longing to feast upon a herd of deer, while the Kúrava army,
rejoicing in his absence, set their hearts on taking Yudhistra
captive.

The Trigartas took their stand on a level field and formed an array in the shape of a half-moon. They were filled with joy and raised a great shout as they saw their enemy, with his shining diadem, come toward them; but Arjuna said to Krishna with a smile, "These men who are about to die seem to be very joyful when they should be weeping." He took up his great conch, the God-given, and blew such a blast that the Trigarta host stood as if turned to stone, and their animals, with staring eyes, and necks and ears thrust out, trembled with fear. The warriors recovered quickly, placed their ranks in order, and shot their arrows all at once, which fell upon the son of Pandu as bees fly to a flowering tree in the forest. He pierced his foes in turn with many arrows, cut down their standards and killed their leaders.

While Arjuna was fighting against these warriors in the southern part of the field, Drona arrayed his forces in the form of a great bird whose beak was himself, while the head was made up of Duryodha, his brothers, and Karna, who for the first time unfurled his shining banner that bore the device of an elephant's tail. Warriors eager to seize Yudhistra darted out from the wings and the body of the bird like lightning flashing from the clouds in summer, and a sound arose in the Pándava army like the sound made by a herd of elephants when their leader is attacked. Sátyajit rushed at Drona and they fought like demons, for both were powerful. But Drona took a crescent-headed arrow and cut Sátyajit's head from his body, and the great warrior fell from his chariot like a falling star. Then Drona rushed eagerly at Yudhistra, but the son of Pandu remembered his promise to Arjuna and turned his chariot, leaving the field. Bitterly disappointed, Drona attacked the Pándavas and their allies and drove their troops back like frightened deer. The battle raged until sunset, when Arjuna returned, having driven the Trigartas from the field. As his blazing banner with the shrieking ape drew near, the Kúrava army broke and many were killed when darkness came and both armies, broken and wounded, returned to their tents.

Since Yudhistra had not been taken captive and the army had been routed by Arjuna, the Kúrava warriors were filled with sorrow and sat silent in their tents like men under a curse, while Drona was deeply ashamed because he had not kept his promise. In the morning he said to Duryodha, "I do my best to bring you victory, O lord of earth, but no one can defeat the army that is protected by the diadem-decked Arjuna. I promise you, however, that today I will form an array that cannot be broken and that I will slay one of the foremost heroes of the Pándavas. If it is possible, take Arjuna again out of the battle."

The Trigartas, therefore, still eager to slay Arjuna, challenged him again in the southern part of the field, while Drona drew up his host in the great circular array. In the center of the circle stood Duryodha, resplendent under his elephant banner, with Karna and Dushasa beside him. At the entrance of the circle Drona rode his chariot; beside him was his son, Ashvattáma, and the mighty king of Sind, the gambler Shákuni, Shalya, king of Madra, and the brothers of Duryodha, those few who remained alive.

The Pándava warriors, headed by Bhima, eager to fight and blazing with wrath, hurled themselves against that immovable array; but like a mighty wave rushing against a rock, they were flung back by Drona. The strength of his arms was amazing and none could stand before the power of his weapons. When Yudhistra saw that nothing prevailed against him, he called Abimanyu, Arjuna's son, who was not yet of age but who equaled his father in beauty, bravery, and knowledge.

"O child," said the king, "we cannot break that circular array. Only Arjuna and Krishna and you know how to pierce it. O Abimanyu, for our sakes and that of all our host, take up this heavy burden; lead us through it so that Arjuna may praise us when he returns from battle."

"I will soon break that fierce array," said Abimanyu, "for my father has taught me how to do it. But I do not know how to come out of it again if danger overtakes me."

"Only break that array!" cried Yudhistra. "Make a passage through it and the rest of us will follow and protect you."

"I will follow close after you," shouted Bhima, "with Jumna and the twins, once the array is broken."

Encouraged by these words, Arjuna's son ordered his charioteer to drive him swiftly toward Drona's army. "Are you sure that you can bear this heavy burden?" asked his charioteer. "You are not used to battle, and Drona is the master of all weapons."

Abimanyu laughed. "Who is this Drona, O charioteer, and who are all these warriors? If my uncle Krishna and my father, if Indra himself came against me in battle, I should not fear. Drive swiftly on!" And in his chariot with its gold-decked wheels, its peacock banner flying, he sped toward the opposing army like a young lion attacking a herd of elephants.

When they beheld him coming toward them with the Pándava host following, the Kúravas advanced joyfully against him, and a fearful battle raged round him, like the eddy made in the ocean where the river Ganges meets it. Abimanyu, with great lightness of hand and a knowledge of the vital parts of the body, slew many of the advancing warriors, and as he fought, he broke through the array and entered the inner circle, where he careered through the Kúrava army like a fire playing in the straw. His bow, always drawn to a circle, looked like the sun's disk, the twang of his bowstring and the clapping of his palms sounded like thunder.

Yudhistra, Bhima, and the twins, with all the warriors of their army, followed close behind him, pressing in along the path that he had opened. But the Kúrava warriors, turning from Abimanyu, fought against those mighty heroes with all their strength, led by the king of Sind, who carried the silver boar on his banner. The king, for a few moments, held back the Pándavas and the army that followed them, and in that time the path that Abimanyu had cut through the array was blocked, and the son of Arjuna was left alone within the circle.

Surrounded on all sides, Abimanyu looked like Yama himself destroying all creatures at the world's end. He showered arrows in all directions, strewed the earth with the bodies of his enemies and drove back mighty warriors.

Shákuni said to Duryodha, "Let us ask Drona how we may overcome him!"

Drona said to them, smiling, "Behold the lightness of hand and the swift motion of this son of Arjuna! Can you see the least weakness in him? I rejoice in him, even though his arrows wound me sorely. You cannot pierce his coat of mail, for I taught his father how to put on armor, and he has taught his son. Therefore you must cut off his bow, kill his horses and his charioteer, and so make him powerless."

Then Drona and Karna and Ashvattáma with three more great warriors surrounded the boy and mercilessly slew his steeds and his charioteer and cut his bow in pieces. Drona cut the hilt from his sword, and Karna destroyed his shield. Then Abimanyu picked up a chariot wheel, lifted it high in his hands and rushed at Drona, but the warriors who surrounded him broke the wheel with their powerful shafts. He picked up a mace and with it slew the horses and the charioteer of Ashvat-támá and then those of the son of Dushasa. The latter, taking up his mace, leaped from his chariot and the two cousins fought fiercely with their maces, each striking the other to the ground. The son of Dushasa rose first, and while Abimanyu was rising from the earth, struck him on the head with all his power. Arjuna's son fell dead, like a wild elephant slain by hunters, like a tempest spent after destroying mountains, like the setting sun. Thus one was slain by many.

The Pándavas were fighting fiercely at the place where the circle had closed behind Abimanyu, but they could not break that close array, which was defended by many Kúrava warriors, led by the mighty king of Sind. When Abimanyu fell, a great shout of joy came from within the circle, and both sides knew that the boy was dead. The Kúravas rejoiced but the Pándavas were filled with grief and said, "Alas, this child, fighting alone, was killed by six mighty chariot warriors led by Drona and Karna. This was not a righteous fight."

The Pándava troops fled away, and since the end of the day had come, the warriors retired to their tents. Taking off their armor and laying aside their weapons, they sat around Yudhistra, thinking of their great sorrow; and Yudhistra, with a heavy heart, wept for Abimanyu and thought to himself, "What can I say to Arjuna?"

Arjuna's Vow

In the hour of twilight Krishna and Arjuna turned their victorious chariot homeward, for they had again defeated the Trigartas. As they drew near the encampment, Arjuna said, "Why does my heart sink, O Krishna, and my speech falter? The fear of disaster seizes my mind and I cannot shake it off. I wonder whether any evil has befallen my brothers and our friends."

When they reached the camp, they found it silent and joyless, and Arjuna, with a heavy heart, spoke again: "No trumpet sounds the victory today. I hear no stringed instruments, no clapping of hands, no songs of praise; and those warriors whom we meet turn away from me, their heads hanging in grief. Alas, Subadra's son has not come out to meet me, smiling, as he always does. What evil thing has happened?" He entered Yudhistra's tent and found his brothers and their sons sitting sorrowfully there.

"How pale your faces are!" Arjuna said. "Where is Abimanyu? Why has he not come to meet me? I heard that Drona formed the circular array today; did you send the boy to pierce it? Has that mighty bowman, that slayer of enemies, fallen so soon in battle?" Their silence told him that it was true.

"Alas!" he said, "that dear son of Subadra, the favorite child of Dráupadi and Krishna, beloved of Kunti; if he is dead then I, too, will die. That son with softly curling hair and eyes like a deer's, sweet of speech and wise for all his youth, generous, obedient, and fearless; if he is dead, then I, too, will die. What joy can my heart know if I never again behold his face or hear his voice? What can I say to Dráupadi and Subadra? For while he fought, surrounded by his foes, he must have thought, 'My father will come and rescue me.' Surely my heart is as strong as the thunderbolt, since it does not break in pieces here and now."

As he sat there weeping for his son, none dared to speak to him save Krishna and Yudhistra, whom he loved and reverenced most. Yudhistra told him all that had happened: how Abimanyu had broken the array, how they followed close behind him but had been stopped by the king of Sind, and how at last Abimanyu had been surrounded and slain by six chariot warriors.

Then Arjuna, pressing his hands together with rage and sighing deeply, said, "You bulls among men, I swear here before you all that tomorrow I shall slay that king of Sind. Listen now to another oath of mine! If tomorrow's sun sets before I have slain that villain I myself shall mount the funeral pyre! You demons and gods and men, you wanderers of the night, you birds and snakes, do not protect my enemy, for if he goes under the earth or into the heavens, I shall with a hundred arrows, before another night has come, cut off the head of Abimanyu's foe!"

He rose and stretched Gandíva, plucking its string, and the sound of the mighty bow rose above his voice and reached the very heavens. Then shouts and the blare of conchs and trumpets arose in the Pándava camp, making the earth tremble.

The Kúravas heard these sounds, and the spies of Duryodha hurried to tell their master all that had happened, as he sat among the leaders of his host. The king of Sind was stunned with fear.

He arose and said, "If Arjuna means to kill me, allow me, O lords of earth, to go back home and live! These shouts from the Pándava camp fill me with fear; I feel like a man drowning in the ocean. Therefore give me leave, I pray you, to go where the wielder of Gandíva may not find me!"

But Duryodha, thinking always of his own victory, said to him, "Do not fear, O tiger among men! You are a mighty hero, and we shall surround you on all sides and protect you with our eleven armies. Arjuna shall not touch you!"

Thus comforted, the king of Sind went that night to Drona, who had been his teacher. He touched the master's feet and asked, "O illustrious one, tell me exactly what is the difference between Arjuna and myself—in aim, in lightness of hand, and in strength."

"Both of you had the same teaching," answered Drona, "but because of Arjuna's hard life and the discipline that he has undergone, he is better than you in every way. However, do not fear to fight tomorrow, for I will protect you and form an array that the Pándavas cannot pierce. Do your duty and follow the path of your ancestors!"

In the morning Drona formed an array that was hard to break. First he ordered one shaped like a cart, and behind that another in the form of a lotus, and inside that a dense array called the needle. At the eye of the needle stood Duryodha and Karna and behind them thousands of the finest warriors, while at the point of the needle the king of Sind took his stand. Drona stood at the head of the whole host, and Duryodha, beholding that mighty army teeming with chariots and men, horses and elephants, took heart and rejoiced.

On the other side, Arjuna, eager to achieve his vow, clad in mail and decked with his golden diadem, brandishing Gandíva, placed his chariot at the very head of his army and blew his conch, while the ape on his banner opened its mouth and yelled. He attacked his foes like a pouring cloud of arrows, seeming to dance upon his chariot, drawing his bow so swiftly that no one could find the slightest chance to strike him.

He drew near to Drona's chariot, joined his palms and said, "Wish me well, O Brahman, and bless me! I must enter this unbreakable array and kill the king of Sind. You are like a father to me, like the just king Yudhistra or Krishna, and I ask for your permission, as your son might ask it. Let me pass, O sinless one!"

The master, smiling, said to him, "O Arjuna, unless you vanquish me, you will not be able to kill the king of Sind. Remember your pledge to me and fight hard against me!" He covered the son of Pandu and his chariot with a shower of arrows, and Arjuna fought back, shooting his mightiest shafts, but so wonderful was Drona's skill that not one arrow touched him, although many of his troops were slain and wounded.

Krishna was anxious that Arjuna's vow should be kept and said to him, "We cannot lose time, for a more important task awaits us. We must avoid Drona and press on!"

"Do as you think best!" answered Arjuna, and Krishna, passing Drona on the left, drove onward, while Arjuna turned around and shot backward.

"Why do you drive on, O son of Pandu?" shouted the master. "Must not a warrior fight until he has defeated his foe? Are you leaving the battle?"

"You are my teacher and no foe of mine," answered Arjuna. "I am your pupil and therefore like your son. Besides, no one can defeat you in battle, and I have other foes to kill." He drove swiftly on, with two princes of Panchala guarding his wheels, and began to penetrate the Kúrava host, careering over the field like an elephant among reeds, strewing the earth with the bodies of men and animals. Meanwhile the Pándava army, in full force, attacked the outer array where Drona was.

Duryodha beheld the slaughter and confusion of his troops and drove to the side of Drona. "Behold, that tiger among men has passed through our host," he said. "What can we do to prevent him from killing the king of Sind? No one believed that he could pass you by; if you had not promised to check him, I should have permitted the king to return home, as he desired to do. I am a fool to trust you, for you have always favored the Pándavas, even though I support you. O sinless one, do not be angry with me; only protect the king of Sind!"

"Krishna is the best of charioteers and Arjuna's horses are

the fleetest," answered Drona. "I am too old to follow them so far and so fast. Besides, the whole army of the Pándavas is upon us and Yudhistra is unprotected and may therefore be captured. I shall stay and fight here and you must go and fight with Arjuna. You are a king and a hero, his equal in birth and education. Go, then, and fight with him yourself!"

"I, fight against Arjuna," cried Duryodha, "when he has passed you by and no one in the world can vanquish him?"

"I will enable you to stand against him and to stop him," Drona answered. He spoke certain incantations and put Duryodha's armor on him in such a way that no weapon could penetrate it; then he bade him have no fear, and the mighty-armed king, trusting the power of Drona and surrounded by the Trigartas and many other great chariot warriors, set out in pursuit of Arjuna.

The son of Kunti was already near the place where the ruler of Sind stood in his chariot; he made a path through the enemy with his arrows, and Krishna drove the white steeds along that path. As they passed through that part of the host led by Drona, they looked like the sun and the moon coming out of the darkness. When at last they came in sight of the king of Sind, they shouted with joy and rushed toward him like two hawks swooping down on their prey. Just then, however, Duryodha sped past them in his chariot, turned his horses sharply and stood between them and their foe. Both warriors were confident and blew their conchs, eager to slay one another.

Arjuna coolly and quickly shot fourteen arrows whetted on stone and winged with vulture's feathers, but these fell down from the armor of Duryodha without piercing it. Krishna was amazed at this, but Arjuna knew that Drona must have put the armor on, for he alone knew the whole science of armor and had taught it to Arjuna. Therefore the son of Kunti attacked

Duryodha's steeds, his driver, and his bow, even shooting the
gloves from his enemy's hands and piercing his palms. Thus he
made Duryodha helpless, and other warriors, coming to his
rescue, bore him off the field. But Karna and Ashvattáma and
other kings and warriors surrounded Arjuna, trying to protect
the king of Sind, hoping that the sun would set before he could
be slain, for they knew that Arjuna would keep his vow and
kill himself if he had not kept his word. But the ape-bannered
son of Pandu, like a blazing fire, fought his way through them
all and at last reached with his arrows the man who had slain
his son and pierced him with nine of them. The king, who bore
the silver boar on his banner, was filled with rage and rushed
against Arjuna, speeding from his bow many a polished shaft
while the fight became more fierce as the Kúrava warriors
crowded round him to protect him.

The fearful fight raged all afternoon and the sun was sinking
to the western hills. Krishna said, "You cannot kill the king, O
best of men, till you have slain these warriors. Therefore I shall
shroud the sun in a cloud of darkness so that they will believe
it has set and be less careful." Through his soul's power he
created darkness that only those warriors perceived and they,
thinking that the sun had set, were filled with gladness and
stood with their heads thrown back, looking at the sky.

"Now quickly drive them off, O mighty one!" cried Krishna.
"Strike off the head of the king of Sind and fulfill your vow!
Strike quickly, for the sun has touched the mountains!"

Arjuna sent forth a torrent of arrows, wounding every one of
the warriors and scattering their troops, and they were so
amazed that they fell back and many fled away, abandoning
the king. Then the son of Pandu took up an arrow that looked
like the thunderbolt of Indra, terrible and fiery, and fixed it
on his bow, and that shaft, sped from Gandíva, snatched off the

head of the king of Sind as a hawk snatches a smaller bird from a treetop.

Krishna removed the darkness that he had made, and the Kúrava warriors, seeing that they had been deceived, wept with sorrow and anger, while Krishna and Arjuna blew their conchs triumphantly. At that moment the thousand-rayed sun set behind the hills, and Arjuna returned to Yudhistra to tell him that the victory had been won.

Duryodha was filled with despair and breathed deep sighs, like a snake with broken fangs. He bitterly reproached Drona and then ordered the troops again to battle, even though night had come. In the terrible hours of darkness the fight went on, while the jackals howled round the field and owls perched hooting on the flagstaffs. A fearful din arose, for in the pitch dark no one knew which was friend and which was foe; shouts and the neighing of horses and the clash of weapons filled the air. Bhima and Arjuna attacked the army of Drona and drove it back until the Kúrava warriors, terrified of the darkness and overcome by weariness, broke their array and began to flee in all directions.

Then Duryodha stopped them and rallied them with cheering words, crying, "Lay aside your weapons and take blazing lamps into your hands!" The foot soldiers ran to the tents and brought each one a burning lamp; they arrayed themselves again and placed on each chariot five lamps, on every elephant three, and one on every horse. The army, thus made radiant with light, looked beautiful, like the summer sky flashing with lightning, like trees covered with fireflies at twilight. The flames were reflected from golden ornaments, from armor and from bows, and flashed back from maces and from swords. When they beheld the Kúrava host so radiant, the Pándavas also bestirred themselves and lighted lamps. On each elephant

The night battle

they placed seven, on each chariot ten, and two on every horse, while the foot soldiers held blazing torches.

Midnight came while they fought. Animals and men were worn out and their eyes closed in sleep, for the night seemed everlasting. Some, blind with weariness, laid down their weapons and slept, on the backs of elephants, in their chariots, or on the ground, and many were slain before they waked and many slew those of their own side, so dazed were they.

Arjuna saw this and shouted to his men, "All of you and your animals are worn out with fighting. Therefore rest here on the field of battle. When the moon rises, you may fight again!"

The Kúrava warriors heard him and cried, "O King Duryodha, O Karna, stop the fight! The Pándavas are no longer attacking us!" And both armies lay down on the field, each warrior with his animal. The elephants, heavy with sleep, looked like hills as they lay there cooling the earth with the breath blown through their snakelike trunks, and the horses stood still in their trappings, softly stamping the ground. Warriors lay against their elephants' necks or on their chariots, while many men, in their armor and with their weapons beside them, slept on the ground. All were motionless and silent, like a forest unstirred by the wind.

In the early morning the moon rose, that delighter of eyes, the lord of lilies. It came like a lion out of its eastern cave; slowly its rays drove off the darkness and filled the earth and sky with radiance. The two hosts were awakened; they rose up as the ocean rises when its tide is summoned by the moon, and tired as they were, they fought again. Soon the chariot of the sun, vanquishing the glory of the moon, reddened the east and blazed into the sky. All the warriors of both hosts alighted from their chariots or their beasts and stood with joined palms, facing the lord of day, and worshipped him, saying their morning prayers. Then filled with new strength and joy, they dashed into the battle.

The Death of Drona

The same soldiers who had fought against one another before sunrise now fought again after the sun had risen, although some of them, weakened by fatigue and hunger and thirst, fell fainting on the ground.

Bhima drove his chariot close to that of Arjuna and said, "Listen to these words of mine, O foremost of warriors! This is the day when we must put forth all our might and bring about the death of Drona."

They beheld the master at the head of the Kúrava host, handsome and blazing with energy in spite of his eighty years, and the Pándavas attacked him together, while Duryodha, Karna, and Shákuni surrounded him to protect him.

Dráupadi's father and Virata, those aged kings, supported by their armies, were the first to attack him. Drona, with three sharp shafts, slew three of the grandsons of the king of Panchala and then put to flight the army of the Matsyas. The two kings, mad with rage, covered him with their arrows and with iron darts, whereupon the master with two well-tempered, broad-headed arrows sent both those aged monarchs to the realm of Yama.

When he saw his father fall, the high-souled Jumna swore a great oath in the midst of all the leaders, saying, "May I lose the reward of all my deeds if Drona escapes me with his life today!"

The two armies rushed against each other like two stormy oceans meeting, and it seemed amazing that any man could come out alive. There were single combats between Duryodha and Nákula, between Dushasa and Sadeva, between Karna and Bhima, who had already, during the night, slain the rest of Duryodha's brothers. Finally Drona and Arjuna met, and so wonderful was that battle between master and pupil that the other warriors lowered their weapons to watch it, for these two were the leaders, the refuge and the saviors of their hosts. The motions of their chariots, their swiftness, their sure aim, were beautiful to behold. Whatever weapons, human or divine, Drona used, Arjuna destroyed, and Drona was pleased in his heart, for he was proud that the greatest bowman in the world had been his pupil. As the other warriors watched these two heroes, wheeling like two hawks in the sky over a single prey, they said to one another, "Never has there been the like of this battle; no one can find any difference between these mighty ones. If Shiva divided himself in two and fought against himself, that fight would equal this one."

Neither could prevail over the other, so the battle became general again, and Drona attacked the Pándava army, killing many and driving back the rest. The Pándavas despaired of victory and said to each other, "Drona will consume us all like raging fire in a heap of straw. None can ever defeat him in battle except Arjuna, and he, who alone can do it, will never slay the master."

Then Krishna said, "The gods themselves cannot vanquish this leader of leaders, this foremost of chariot warriors. He has told us that if he were overcome by sorrow, he would lay aside his weapons, and that then he might be slain. I believe he would do that if he knew that his son, Ashavattáma, was slain. Therefore, you sons of Pandu, lay virtue aside and let some man tell Drona that Ashvattáma is dead. Only thus can we win the victory."

Arjuna did not agree with this advice, but the others did, and at last Yudhistra unwillingly gave his consent. Bhima slew with his mace a huge elephant that was called Ashvattáma, which means the "horse-voiced"; then, with his brothers, he drove close to Drona and, after hesitating a moment, cried aloud, "Ashvattáma has been slain!"

When he heard these words, Drona's limbs seemed to melt like salt in water, but he remembered the might of his son and did not believe what Bhima said. He turned to Yudhistra and asked him if this were true, for he believed that the son of Dharma would never lie, even to gain the whole earth.

Krishna quickly said to Yudhistra, "If Drona fights for another day, I tell you truly that your army will be wiped out. Lying is no sin when it can save life."

And Yudhistra, who longed for victory, was persuaded by Krishna and said, "It is true; Ashvattáma is dead and lies on the bare ground like a young lion." After the word "Ashvattáma" he added under his breath, "the elephant." Before he said this, Yudhistra's chariot had always stood above the surface of the earth, but after he told that lie, chariot and horses stood upon the ground.

Then Drona, overcome by grief, laid down his weapons and cried aloud, "Ashvattáma! Ashvattáma!" He sat on the bench of his chariot, his head bent and his eyes closed, and devoted himself to meditation, his heart fixed on God. Jumna, the son of Panchala's king, frantic to avenge his father, leaped from his chariot with his sword in his hand and seized Drona's white hair. Shouts arose from all sides: "Forbear! Do not kill him!" Arjuna leaped from his chariot and ran toward Jumna with upraised arms, crying, "Do not slay the master! Bring him here alive!" But Jumna now had two reasons for revenge: his father's defeat by Drona, which he had been born to avenge, and now his father's death. He whirled his sword and cut off Drona's head, holding it high for all to see. Then he cast it on the ground before the Kúrava host, and all the warriors, as if they themselves were about to lose their lives, fled from the field, crying, "Alas! Alas!"

When Ashvattáma heard of his father's death, he was mad with grief and rage. He pressed his hands together and sighed deeply, like a snake that has been trodden upon. "I have heard how my sire was slain after he had laid aside his weapons," he said to Duryodha, "and I have heard how he was deceived by Dharma's son. I do not grieve because he died in battle, for he met a hero's death and has surely gone to those regions where dwell those who never turn their backs to a foe. I grieve because while I was alive his white locks were seized in the sight of the whole army. This tears the very core of my heart. Shame on my might! Shame on my skill in arms, since Drona, having me for a son, had his white locks seized by that impious wretch! O tiger among men, I swear by the truth and by my own deeds that I shall slay Jumna and wipe out all the Pándavas with the divine weapons my father gave me! Let them beware today!"

At his call the Kúrava army rallied, and the leaders blew their conchs and had the drums beaten. The uproar made the earth and sky echo, and the Pándavas, when they heard it, assembled to take counsel.

"When Drona was slain, O conqueror of wealth," said Yudhistra to Arjuna, "the Kúrava army fled. What mighty warrior is causing this terrible uproar and leading the enemy host back into battle?"

"He who rallies the Kúravas, he who walks like an angry elephant and has a face like a tiger's, he who now roars so loud, O King, is Ashvattáma!" answered Arjuna. "He will never forgive Jumna for seizing the master's hair; he will never rest until he has slain him or been slain himself, and all of us together will not be able to save Dráupadi's brother. You, O King, told your teacher a lie for the sake of a kingdom. Drona thought, 'The son of Pandu is virtuous and besides he is my pupil; he will never lie to me.' It is because he trusted you and believed you that he met his death. Alas, we have committed a cruel and a heavy sin! I have already, O lord of earth, sunk into hell, overcome with shame, since we caused the death of one who was a Brahman, who was old in years, who was our teacher, and who had laid aside his arms and was engaged in prayer."

After Arjuna had spoken, the rest sat silent for a moment, and then Bhima said angrily, "You are preaching like a Brahman or a holy man. We are Kshatrias, whose business is battle and whose purpose is victory, O son of Kunti. It is true that we have slain our teacher, but that teacher sat indifferent beside his son when Dráupadi was dragged into the assembly; that teacher caused the child, Subadra's son, to be slain by six mighty warriors; and that teacher put Duryodha's armor on in such a way that he could not be slain while fighting with you! We need not fear the son of Drona. It is no sin to slay one's enemy, and Drona was our enemy."

Then Jumna spoke: "O Arjuna, the duties of a Brahman are sacrifice, study, and the teaching of the Vedas. Which of these duties did Drona perform? He called himself a Brahman, but he lived as a Kshatria and did his best to slay us all in battle. Why, then, should we not slay him? Long ago he wronged my father, and I was born to avenge that wrong and my father's death. Why, then, do you not praise me, instead of blaming me? You slew the grandsire, and now you reproach me for slaying this enemy of mine. That is not a right thing to do; yet I forgive you for the sake of Dráupadi and her children. Let us fight now! Victory will be ours."

Then those warriors went out again to battle with the Kúrava host, led by Drona's son. Terrible was the fight between them, for the Pándavas felt new strength because of Drona's death, while Ashvattáma, mad with fury, encouraged the Kúravas and led them on. When the two armies met, like two oceans or two mountains crashing against each other, the son of Drona loosed his most powerful weapon: thousands of arrows with blazing mouths flew through the air, and also iron balls which sorely wounded the Pándava host.

Then Krishna shouted, "Lay down your arms and lie flat upon the earth, all you who hear my words! Only thus can this mighty weapon lose its power!"

All those who heard obeyed him, excepting Bhima, who lifted his mace and rushed toward Ashvattáma. Arjuna, followed by Krishna, leaped from his chariot, ran swiftly after his brother, seized him and dragged him down to the ground in spite of his roaring and struggling. When all were lying down on the field, the terrible weapons of Ashvattáma passed harmlessly above them. Then they rose joyfully, eager to fight once more.

"Hurl that weapon speedily again, O son of our master!" cried Duryodha. "Our enemies are arrayed for battle."

"Alas," said Ashvattáma sadly, "the weapon can be cast but once, and Krishna knew how to make it powerless."

"Then fight them with other weapons," said Duryodha, "and let these slayers of their teacher be slain by his son!"

Thus roused again to anger, Ashvattáma went forth and sought out Jumna, whom he struck between the eyebrows with an arrow. The prince of Panchala sank down on the floor of his chariot, holding the flagstaff for support, and his charioteer drove him from the field to tend his wound, while Bhima and Arjuna and many others covered his retreat. Ashvattáma also slew Bhima's charioteer, and the horses, feeling the reins loosened, galloped madly away, carrying Bhima with them. But Krishna and Arjuna led the Pándava host and drove the Kúravas back, until night came and both armies retired to rest.

This was the fifteenth day of battle, the fifth day of Drona's command of the Kúrava host.

The Battle Ends

Bhima Fulfills a Vow

At the end of that day when Drona had been killed and his son had failed to avenge him, the Kúrava chiefs met with cheerless hearts in Duryodha's tent. Drona's son proposed that Karna be made commander of the host; Duryodha agreed and installed Karna with the usual rites.

"I have told you already, O son of Gandhari," said Karna, who looked as resplendent as the sun, his father, "that I shall vanquish the Pándavas and all their sons and Krishna. Have no fear while I command your host!"

At dawn, to the sound of music, he arrayed the host in the hawk formation, placing himself at the tip of the beak; and Jumna made a counterarray in the shape of the half-moon. The two armies advanced as if in a dance, and warriors leaped forth from the tips of the moon and from the wings of the hawk, eager to slay each other. Yet on that sixteenth day of

247

battle neither side prevailed until the evening, when all the Pándavas turned upon Karna and drove him back. He, fearing another night battle, ordered his army to retire, and the Pándavas retired, too, jeering at their enemy with shouts and derisive sounds of their conchs and trumpets, hoping for victory the following day.

Early the next morning before dawn, Karna went to Duryodha and said, "Today I shall fight with Arjuna, and I shall slay him or be slain by him. Listen, O ruler of men! My knowledge of divine weapons is equal to that of Arjuna, and in all else I am far better than he. Therefore rejoice, for I shall gladden your heart by slaying him today, and the whole earth will be yours! There is only one way in which he is superior to me: he has Krishna for his charioteer. Now Shalya, king of Madra, is the only man who equals Krishna in the knowledge of horses and skill in driving; therefore, O best of the Kúravas, give me Shalya for my charioteer, and I will be in every way superior to the son of Pandu."

Duryodha heard these boastful words gladly. He went to the king of Madra and spoke to him humbly, saying, "O ruler of the Madras, O hero in battle, O slayer of foes, I come to you today with joined hands and bowed head to beg a favor of you. Today Karna wishes to contend in single combat with Arjuna, but there is no charioteer equal to Krishna—save yourself—to hold his reins. Therefore I beg of you, O foremost of warriors, to drive his chariot and to protect Karna, even as Krishna protects Arjuna. With you as his driver, the gods themselves could not defeat him, and we shall win the victory."

Shalya was filled with rage at these words. He frowned and rolled his eyes in anger as he answered, "You insult me, O son of Gandhari, by asking me to drive the chariot of Karna, who is not my equal in battle or in birth. Give me a harder task, O lord of earth! I will, if you wish, fight the enemy singlehanded. Behold these arms of mine, as strong as thunder! Behold this excellent bow, this mace entwined with hempen cords and decked with gold! I can split the very earth, dry up the oceans, scatter the mountains with my strength, but I cannot hold the reins of a Suta's son. Nor can I fight, since I have been so humiliated; therefore permit me to return home, O king of kings." And that tiger among men stood up, meaning to leave the encampment.

Duryodha, however, held him and spoke sweet and soothing words to the angry king, "Listen, O ruler of men! I do not think Karna better than you in any way; indeed, there is none like you in might of arms or in learning. You are greater than Krishna himself, and therefore I am asking you to do for Karna what Krishna does for Arjuna. This is no insult, O mighty hero."

Shalya was flattered by these words and said, "I am pleased with you, O son of Gandhari, since you say that I am greater than Krishna. I will hold the reins of Karna while he fights against Arjuna. But let it be understood that I shall say in his presence anything that I please." Duryodha and Karna both agreed to this, and Duryodha joyfully embraced Shalya.

Then the king of Madra mounted the splendid chariot of Karna and took up the reins; Karna also mounted it, stretching his mighty bow, and those two heroes looked like Surya and Agni seated on a cloud. The Kúravas, filled with delight, raised a great shout and beat their drums and cymbals.

"Urge on the steeds, O Shalya," Karna said, "so that I may slay Arjuna and Bhima, the twins and Yudhistra! If all the gods should protect the sons of Pandu, I shall still vanquish them."

Shalya laughed aloud, for he remembered his promise to

Yudhistra before the battle. "Forbear, forbear, O Karna," he said, "from such bragging! How can you, O lowest of men, compare yourself with Arjuna, who is the foremost? Who but he could have challenged Shiva himself to battle? Who but he could have defeated all the Kúravas when they tried to seize King Virata's cattle? Why did you not slay him then? Now you have another chance, but I tell you truly, if you do not flee from this battle, you yourself will be slain!"

"Why do you always praise Arjuna?" Karna asked. "If he wins this battle, then you may praise him, but not until then. Drive on!"

Shalya urged on the eager horses and drove him onto the field. As soon as Karna met the Pándava troops, he said to the soldiers, "Whoever will show me where the ape-bannered son of Pandu is, to him I will give a cartload of gems and jewels. I will give a hundred cows with brass milking vessels to him who will show me that hero who has Krishna for his driver. Indeed, he who will bring me to Arjuna shall have all the wealth that son of Pandu leaves behind him after I have slain him."

"O Suta's son," cried Shalya, "do not give away jewels and hundreds of cattle in order to encounter Arjuna; you will see him soon enough and repent of your folly. When you challenge Arjuna to battle, you are like a hare that challenges a mighty elephant, you are like a man who fights a furious black cobra with a piece of wood, or like a jackal yelling at a maned lion; you are like a frog croaking at a thundercloud, or a dog which from the safety of his master's house barks at the forest-ranging tiger."

Karna was stung to fury by these words and answered, "I see that you are an enemy with a friend's face; you seek to frighten me. I know my own might. I have here one shaft that lies alone in its quiver in sandalwood dust. It is terrible as a poisonous snake; it is steeped in oil and beautiful to behold; I have worshiped it for many years. I have saved this shaft for Arjuna, and with it I shall slay him."

"Behold, O Karna!" cried Shalya. "Yonder comes the son of Indra, slaughtering his foes along the way! Yonder flies his banner, while yours is trembling on its staff! Hark to Gandíva and behold your army fleeing before him!"

Karna replied with rage, "See now, he is beset on all sides by those Trigartas whom he has not yet slain! He will escape me. He is sure to perish, plunged into that ocean of warriors."

"Who would try to slay the god of waters with rain or quench the fire by throwing fuel upon it?" answered Shalya. "Rejoice that you cannot fight him now and turn to some other foe; there stand the other sons of Pandu, eager for battle!"

As they were talking thus, the two armies mingled fiercely, like the currents of the Jumna and the Ganges meeting. Karna dashed through the Pándava host and attacked Yudhistra, and a fierce fight took place, while the warriors on each side surrounded their leaders to protect them. That mighty bowman, Karna, wounded them all with his blood-drinking shafts and was himself wounded in the brow and chest by Yudhistra. Filled with rage, he cut Yudhistra's armor from his body and broke his bow, but he did not try to kill that king of men because he remembered his pledge to Kunti. Yudhistra, deeply wounded, retreated from the fight, while Bhima and the twins hurled themselves against Karna, shouting angry and taunting words. Bhima, eager to make an end of Karna, drew his bowstring to his ear and sped a fierce and mighty shaft against him. It pierced through Karna's armor and he fell senseless in his chariot, whereupon Shalya drove him swiftly from the field, and Bhima, triumphant, routed the Kúrava host.

Dushasa saw the army terrified and sorely smitten, and he advanced fearlessly against Bhima, shooting showers of arrows. Blazing with anger at the sight of him, Bhima shouted, "O wicked one! Today I shall drink your blood!" Dushasa hurled an iron dart at Bhima, who whirled his terrible mace and flung it at his foe. The mace shattered the dart in mid-air and then struck Dushasa on the head, felling him to the ground. Bhima beheld him lying there and remembered how Dráupadi's hair had been seized, how she had been shamefully dragged into the assembly and how her clothes had been torn from her, and his wrath blazed up. Leaping from his chariot, he drew his whetted sword; he put his foot on Dushasa's throat and cut open his breast; then he bent down and drank Dushasa's hot lifeblood as he had sworn to do.

"The taste of this blood," he said, "is sweeter than my mother's milk or good wine mixed with honey." Looking again at Dushasa's body, he laughed softly and said, "What more can I do to you? Death has rescued you from my hands."

Arjuna and Karna

Meanwhile Arjuna had slain the last of the warriors who had challenged him. Returning to battle, he met the son of Drona and slew his charioteer. Ashvattáma took up the reins himself, but Arjuna, smiling, cut the reins with his sharp arrows, and the horses ran wildly off the field, carrying their master with them. Then Arjuna, gladdening the eyes of his troops, came among them and looked about him to see Yudhistra's banner, with its golden moon and planets. He could not find it and drove close to Bhima, asking, "Where is the king?"

"He has left the battle, sorely wounded by Karna's arrows," answered Bhima, and Arjuna, alarmed, asked Krishna to turn the chariot around and drive the horses swiftly toward the camp.

They found the king in his tent, lying alone on his bed, the arrows plucked from his body and his wounds tended. They were filled with joy at finding him alive and touched his feet, and Yudhistra, thinking that Karna must be already slain, welcomed them, hailing their victory and praising them.

"I have not yet met the Suta's son," Arjuna told him, "for I wished to come here to see that all is well with you. Now bless me, O lion among kings, for today I shall slay Karna and all our foes!"

Now Yudhistra was shamed by his defeat at Karna's hands, and he suffered sorely from his wounds; therefore he became very angry and spoke harsh words to his brother, saying, "You have deserted Bhima and come here out of fear of Karna! Long ago you promised me that you would slay him; why, then, have you left the battle? For thirteen years we have relied on you, O conqueror of wealth; will you betray us now? If you will not meet the Suta's son in battle, then give Gandíva to someone else who can use it better!"

When he heard these bitter words, Arjuna's anger blazed. He drew his sword, ready to avenge the insult his brother had offered him, but Krishna stopped him, saying, "Who is there here whom you must threaten, O son of Kunti? You came to find out how the king fares. Behold, he is well; now let us go to battle!"

But Arjuna, breathing hard like an angry snake and fixing his eyes on his elder brother, said, "I would cut off the head of any man who said to me, 'Give Gandíva to someone else.' Those words have been spoken by the king and I dare not forgive them. For this reason I have drawn my sword, O Krishna."

"The king is tired," Krishna answered, "and suffers from pain and grief, for Karna drove him from the field and wounded him. Therefore he spoke harshly to you and also because he wished to provoke you to fight with Karna."

Arjuna thrust his sword into its sheath and, hanging his head in shame, took his brother's feet in his two hands and said, weeping, "Forgive me, O King! The task shall be delayed no longer. Karna seeks to fight with me today, and today I shall slay him. I live only for your good, O King; this is the truth!"

Yudhistra raised his brother and embraced him, saying, "I was put to shame this day in the sight of all my troops by Karna. Forgive my harsh words, O mighty-armed one! Go forth and slay the Suta's son, and my blessing go with you!"

The brothers wept together until their hearts were free of grief; then Krishna turned the white steeds and drove Arjuna out into the battle, where Karna's banner, with the elephant's rope, waved above his chariot.

When those two great bowmen met with shouts and the clapping of palms and the twang of bowstrings, the warriors on both sides cheered them with cries and the blare of conchs and trumpets. They were much alike, for both were born of gods and were godlike in strength and beauty. One had Krishna and the other Shalya for his driver; both had white horses and resplendent chariots; both had shining bows and arrows, swords and darts and lofty standards. The Kúrava warriors crowded around Karna, for he was now their stake in that game of battle, while the Pándavas stood by the high-souled Arjuna, who was their stake, and the soldiers were the spectators of that great game. Fiercely the two heroes challenged each other and blew their conchs. The mighty ape on Arjuna's banner leaped from his place and fell upon Karna's standard, tearing the elephant's rope with his teeth and nails,

The fight between Arjuna and Karna

while the rope, hard as iron and decked with little bells, wrapped itself angrily about the ape. The horses, too, neighed at each other and stamped, eager for battle, while Krishna and Shalya eyed each other with keen glances.

Then to the sound of conchs and drums, the two warriors fought like two full-grown Himalayan elephants fighting for a mate, like two stormclouds or two mountains meeting one another. Showers of arrows, crescent-headed and boar-toothed, fell upon both chariots like birds flying into a tree at night to roost. Both warriors possessed divine weapons. Arjuna sped the Fire-God's weapon; it flew blazing through the air, setting fire to the mantles of the warriors who drew back from its path, but Karna quenched it with the weapon of the God of Waters and also covered the sky with black clouds to blind his foe. These Arjuna drove away with the Wind-God's weapon and, taking up another whose use he had learned in heaven, he sent forth hundreds of arrows with golden wings, which sped beyond the chariot of Karna and slew the fighters of the Kúrava host who surrounded him.

Then Karna, filled with rage, took out that keen and snake-mouthed shaft that he had kept for so long within its quiver in sandalwood dust and loosed it at Arjuna. Krishna knew its power, and as he saw it blaze through the air, he pressed the chariot down with his feet until it sank a cubit's depth into the earth. The horses, white as moonbeams and decked with gold, bent their knees and lay down on the ground, and that terrible weapon passed over Arjuna's head, sweeping off the splendid diadem, set with many jewels and famous in the three worlds, that Indra had given him. The diadem broke into pieces, but Arjuna stood unmoved and bound his curling locks with a piece of cloth. Krishna dismounted and lifted the chariot out of the earth, and the white horses rose to their feet again.

Now Arjuna cut the bright and costly armor from Karna's body and pierced his vital parts with whetted shafts. Karna reeled, clutched his flagstaff and dropped his bow, but Arjuna, mindful of Kshatria honor, did not kill him then when he was helpless. Karna soon recovered and sped an iron shaft at his enemy's breast, and the son of Kunti trembled like a mountain in an earthquake and lowered Gandíva. At that moment, one of Karna's wheels sank into the earth; his chariot reeled and stuck fast. Seeing that Arjuna was hurt, he leaped from his car and tried in vain to pull the wheel out of the ground. Then he looked up and saw Arjuna drawing his bowstring to his ear.

With tears of rage in his eyes, Karna cried out, "O Arjuna, wait until I lift my wheel! You are both brave and virtuous and know the rules of battle: a warrior on his chariot may not fight with one who is on foot and in distress!"

Then Krishna answered him, saying, "It is well, O Suta's son, that you remember virtue now! When the son of Kunti was unfairly defeated at dice, where was your virtue? When you laughed to see Dráupadi dragged into the assembly, where was virtue then? When the sons of Pandu returned after the thirteenth year, did you wish to see their kingdom restored to them? When the boy Abimanyu was surrounded by six chariot warriors, where was your virtue? Since you thought nothing of it then, why waste your breath speaking of it now?"

Karna, furious and ashamed, took up his bow and fought from where he stood, while Arjuna, whose anger flamed as he listened to Krishna's words, took up a razor-headed arrow winged with gold and struck down Karna's standard bearing the elephant's rope and hung with bells. Then he took up another terrible shaft, drew his bowstring to his ear, and cut off Karna's head. Unwillingly that beautiful head left its body, as an owner unwillingly leaves a rich and comfortable house.

Beautiful even in death, Karna lay on the earth as the thousand-rayed sun falls at the close of day. Clad in bright garments and golden mail, he was like a mighty tree with flowering branches felled by woodsmen, like a heap of gold, like a fire quenched by Arjuna's arrows. Surya, the Sun-God, when he beheld his son, touched him with his rays and then sank into the western sea, as if to purify himself from the sight of death.

The Kúrava army fled away in fear like a herd of stampeding cattle, crying, "Alas, Karna! Alas, Karna!" As they fled, they looked back at the lofty standard of Arjuna, each man fearing that the son of Kunti was pursuing him.

Shalya, standing alone in the chariot of Karna, cried to Duryodha, "Turn back, O King! The foremost of your warriors has been slain. The sun is setting; let your troops retire! This is destiny, O lord of earth; remember the cause of it!"

Duryodha, nearly senseless with grief, wept for his friend, crying, "O Karna! O Karna!" His friends tried in vain to comfort him and returned to their tents with heavy hearts.

Meanwhile Krishna and Arjuna lifted their snow-white conchs and blew them together, piercing the hearts of their retreating foes and gladdening the ears of Yudhistra. Then they turned the chariot, and, looking like two rising suns, they entered their encampment surrounded by their friends, followed by the praises of bards and warriors, and went to Yudhistra's tent to tell him that the victory had been won.

Duryodha Enters the Lake

Next morning the Kúravas put aside their grief, and undaunted by defeat, they made Shalya the leader of their array. They hoped that Shalya might still defeat the Pándavas, even though Bhishma and Drona and Karna, those mighty warriors, had all failed and had all lost their lives; and Shalya himself accepted the leadership with confidence and promised Duryodha that he would be victorious that very day. It was the eighteenth day of battle; both armies had lost many thousands of their troops and most of their bravest leaders. The Kúrava army was still much larger than that of the Pándavas, but the Kúravas had lost more of their great chariot warriors than their enemies had.

When the two armies were arrayed and the awful battle began again, Shalya said to his driver, "Yonder is King Yudhistra, resplendent as the sun. Take me to him speedily and then watch my great prowess! The Pándavas cannot stand against me in battle."

He drove toward Yudhistra and both kings challenged each other angrily and blew their conchs. Terrible was the encounter between them, and both were wounded and bleeding from each other's blows. Then Yudhistra killed the horses of the king of Madra and cut down with one blazing arrow the standard with the golden plowshare. Ashvattáma drove quickly to Shalya and took him up on his own chariot, but as they fled away, Shalya heard Yudhistra's triumphant shout, and he found another chariot and returned, roaring with rage, to the fight.

In his turn he killed the steeds of Yudhistra, and then leaping from his car, he rushed on foot against the son of Kunti. Yudhistra took up a dart whose handle gleamed with gold and jewels, a dart that the sons of Pandu had worshiped with perfumes and garlands, for it had been forged with care by the workmen of the gods. He hurled it at the king of Madra, and those who watched it saw sparks of fire fly from it as it sped like a meteor through the air. Shalya tried to catch it, but it pierced his fair broad chest as if his body had been water

and entered the ground beyond him, carrying with it the
world-wide fame of Madra's king. He fell down with outstretched arms, facing his foe, and the earth seemed to rise a
little to receive him, as a wife rises to receive her lord, for the
mighty Shalya had long enjoyed the earth, as one enjoys a
dear wife, and seemed now to sleep on her breast, embracing
her with his arms.

Then the warriors of Madra fell upon Yudhistra, eager for
revenge, while Arjuna and Bhima, the twins and Dráupadi's
sons surrounded their king and fought against the Madras,
driving them back and slaying many of them.

Shákuni rallied them, shouting, "Stop, you sinful ones, and
fight again! What use is there in flight? Fight here with all
your strength, and I will attack the enemy from behind."

He rode swiftly to the rear with a strong force of horsemen
armed with lances and attacked the Pándava troops, slaying
many and breaking their ranks.

Yudhistra said to Sadeva, "See how the gambler is destroying our forces in the rear! Take Dráupadi's sons, with the
elephants and horses, and kill Shákuni, while your brothers
and I fight here against the chariots!"

Sadeva eagerly did as the king commanded him. His forces,
led by the sons of Dráupadi, fell upon Shákuni's cavalry and
routed them, driving them from the field like frightened deer.
Sadeva, angry to think that Shákuni was still alive, sought him
out and found him fleeing, protected by his horsemen. The
son of Madri pursued him on his chariot, striking him with
many whetted arrows winged with vulture's feathers, and calling out to him, "O fool, do you remember how you rejoiced
in the assembly when the game of dice was won? I told you
then that your dice were arrows that would turn against you
and pierce you. Reap now the harvest of your deeds, O dull of

understanding! Today I shall cut off your head as a man plucks fruit from a tree. Be a man and fight against me!"

These words filled Shákuni with rage; he turned and attacked Sadeva with his lance, but the son of Madri cut the lance in two with one broad-headed arrow and pierced also the strong arms of his enemy. Then, with an iron arrow winged with gold sped with care and power from his bow, he cut Shákuni's head from his body, the head that had hatched the evil plan of the gambling match and had sent the sons of Pandu to the forest. When they saw their leader lying headless on the ground, his troops fled, and the Pándavas blew their conchs, praising Sadeva and rejoicing that the wicked Shákuni was at last dead.

Meanwhile the other sons of Pandu had slain the last of the Kúrava host. Of all the thousands of famous warriors who had fought against them, not one remained alive save Duryodha, Ashvattáma, and two others. Arjuna, standing on his chariot and gazing over the field, which looked like a forest laid low by a tempest, said to Krishna, "Behold, O friend, the course of destiny! The army of Kuru's son, once as vast as the ocean, is now no larger than a pool caught in the hoofprint of a cow. If Duryodha had only made peace when Bhishma fell, all would now be well; but he foolishly would not cease fighting. Nor would he cease when Drona fell, or Karna, but still kept up the useless battle. Today, at last, our task will be ended and King Yudhistra will be free of all his foes, for today Duryodha will lose both his kingdom and his life."

On the other side of the field Duryodha, sorely wounded, his horses slain, looked around him on all sides and saw the earth empty of his host. He saw not a single warrior of his own, for Ashavattáma and his two companions were far off. He heard his enemies shouting aloud in triumph and saw himself alone without a single companion; so he left his steedless chariot and laid aside his armor; he took up his mace and fled on foot toward a lake to the east of the battlefield. That lord of eleven armies fled alone on foot toward the east.

On his way he met Sánjaya, the trusted messenger of King Kuru, and said to him, "O Sánjaya, none are left alive save we two. Tell the blind king, my father, that I have lost all my friends, my sons and my brothers; that I myself have escaped alive from the awful battle, though I am sorely wounded, and shall rest for a while within the waters of this lake." With these words, he cast a magic spell upon the waters, and entering the lake, he made a place for himself in its depths and lay there resting.

While Sánjaya stood there wondering, Ashvattáma and his two companions came to that place, their horses weary and they themselves exhausted and badly wounded. They came to Sánjaya and cried, "Well met, Sánjaya! Is our king, Duryodha, still alive?"

"He lives," answered the messenger of Kuru, "though his heart burns with grief and he is wounded. Behold, he is resting now within the waters of this lake."

"Alas, alas!" cried Ashvattáma, "the king did not know that we are still alive. With him to lead us, we can still fight and conquer."

They drove their chariots to the lake and spoke to that ruler of men who lay within its waters, saying, "Arise, O King, and fight with us against the Pándavas! Their forces also are weak, for many have been slain by us, and those that remain are sorely wounded. They cannot stand against you when we are fighting at your side."

Duryodha answered them from beneath the water, "I am glad to know that you are alive, you bulls among men. After we have rested for a while, we shall meet and conquer the enemy. Your hearts are noble and your devotion is beyond measure, but this is not the time for bravery. Let me rest for one night, and tomorrow I shall join you in the fight."

"I swear by all my good deeds," cried Ashvattáma, "by the gifts that I have made, by my silent meditations, that I will not put off my armor until I have slain the Pándavas! May all my sacrifices be vain if this night passes away before I have slain my foes! Believe me, O ruler of men!"

While they were talking together thus, some hunters came to the lake to quench their thirst and to rest, for they were tired of carrying the weight of the animals that they had killed. These men went into the woods every day to provide meat for Bhima. As they sat on the edge of the lake, they heard every word that was said by the three warriors and Duryodha, and they realized with wonder that the king lay hidden under the water.

One whispered to the other, "Let us tell the Pándavas that Duryodha is here, and they will reward us with great wealth. Let us quickly tell Bhima and he will pay us well. Why should we wear ourselves out with hunting every day?"

They took up their burdens joyfully and hastened to the Pándavas' camp. Those mighty warriors had looked everywhere for Duryodha and had sent their spies in every direction, but no trace could be found of him, and Yudhistra was troubled, for his victory was not complete if Duryodha still lived. Just then the hunters came to Bhima and told him all that they had seen and heard. Bhima rewarded them richly and hastened to Yudhistra to tell him the welcome news. Then the king and all his brothers were filled with joy; they mounted their chariots and drove swiftly to the lake where their enemy lay. A great noise arose in their camp as the news spread, shouts and the blare of conchs and the rattle of chariot wheels. The five brothers and their five sons, Jumna and Shikándin and all the warriors who remained alive mounted elephants or chariots and moved toward the lake, raising a cloud of dust and making the earth tremble.

Duryodha, lying in the depth of the water with his mace beside him, heard the noise, for indeed it sounded like thunder. The son of Drona and his two companions heard it, too, and said to the king, "Hark! The Pándava army is coming here; give us permission to leave." Duryodha answered, "Do as you desire!"

Sorrowfully the three warriors took their leave of him and drove far away into the forest, where they stopped under a banyan tree, for they were very tired. Sad at heart, anxious about the king, they loosed the horses from the yokes and lay down to rest.

The Duel with Maces

When the Pándavas arrived at the lake, Yudhistra dismounted from his chariot and stood on the bank, looking over the water. Then he spoke to the wicked king, saying, "Why, O Duryodha, have you caused and seen the slaughter of your sons and brothers, your kinsmen and friends, and then entered this lake today to save your own life? Arise, O King, and finish the battle! Where are your pride and honor? Men call you a hero, but they speak falsely, for heroes never flee at the sight of a foe. Surely you forget yourself! Arise, cast off your fears and fight! Either vanquish us and rule the wide earth or be slain by us and lie on the bare ground! Remember the duties of your caste, O mighty warrior!"

From the depths of the lake, Duryodha replied, "It was not

to save my life, it was not from fear, it was not from grief, O King, that I entered these waters. My horses were killed, my quivers were empty, I was alone without a single warrior to stand by me in the battle. I was very tired and came here to rest. Do you also rest awhile, O son of Kunti, with your followers; then I will rise from here and fight you all in battle."

But Yudhistra said, "We have no need of rest, although we were searching for you far and wide while you were lying here. Rise even now, O Duryodha, and give us battle!"

"All those for whose sake I desired the kingdom—my brothers and sons, my kinsmen and my friends—lie dead on the field," Duryodha said. "This earth is a widow, bereft of her wealth and her pride. Take it, O Yudhistra! Who could desire a kingdom without kinsmen and without friends? I shall go into the forest, dressed in deerskins, for I have no further desire for life. Go, O King, and rule this empty earth as you desire!"

"What foolish words are these?" answered Yudhistra angrily. "When you ruled the entire earth, you would not give me as much of it as could be covered with the sharp point of a needle, but now when you have lost it, you want to give me the whole of it. I do not wish to take the wide earth as a gift from you, but I shall enjoy it greatly when I wrest it from you in battle. Rise, rise, O slayer of the Bháratas, and fight!"

Duryodha could not bear these words, as a highbred horse cannot endure the whip. He breathed long and heavy sighs from within the water, like a snake within its hole, and answered, "You Pándavas, all of you have friends and chariots, horses and weapons. I am alone, without a chariot or a horse and with only one weapon. I cannot fight on foot against you all; therefore fight me one at a time! I do not fear any of you and shall meet you one after the other, as the year meets with all seasons; as the sun destroys the light of the stars at dawn, I shall destroy you all."

"Well said, O prince of the Bháratas!" cried Yudhistra. "At last you accept the duties of a Kshatria; at last you speak like a hero and challenge us all to battle. Fight any one of us and choose your weapon! The rest of us will watch the fight."

Churning the water, the king rose like a prince of elephants from the lake, breathing hard with anger and shouldering his mace. He stood there, dripping with water, frowning and biting his nether lip; then he said in a voice as deep as thunder, "This mace that I hold in my hand is the weapon that I choose. Let any one of you that thinks he is a match for me come forward on foot, armed with a mace! You must come one at a time, for it is not fitting that one should fight against many at the same time, especially when that one is tired and wounded, without armor, chariot, or horse."

"Why did you not think of that, O Duryodha, when six great warriors together slew the boy Abimanyu?" asked Yudhistra. "Take whatever armor you need and bind your hair! I shall give you yet another advantage over us: if you can slay any one of the five Pándavas, you shall be king. Otherwise, slain by him, you shall reap the reward of your deeds in the next world."

The Pándava warriors gave Duryodha golden armor and a diadem set with jewels. While he was arraying himself in these, Krishna spoke angrily to Yudhistra, "What rash words have you spoken, O King? Why did you say, 'If you slay any one of us, you shall be king?' Do you not know that for these thirteen years Duryodha has practiced with his mace on an iron image of Bhima so that he might slay him? Bhima is the only one of you who is a match for him with this weapon, and even he, though he has greater might and courage, is not so skillful as his cousin. In a contest between might and skill, the skillful always wins. What if he should challenge you or Arjuna or one of the twins? You have put us all in great danger, O best of kings!"

Meanwhile Duryodha had prepared himself, and he spoke to his cousins, saying, "Let any one of you five brothers take up a mace and fight with me now. Today we shall reach the end of this long battle, for I shall slay you one after the other. Within this very hour my words shall be proved true."

Then Bhima said to Yudhistra, "Permit me to accept this challenge, O King! Today I shall pluck out the thorn that has lodged so long in your heart; today I shall win back your crown of glory, for this day Duryodha shall yield up his life and his kingdom." With these words he stood up for battle, and his brothers, seeing him stand there like a mountain peak, were filled with joy. Duryodha also stood like a prince of elephants and felt no pain or fear.

Bhima said to him, "Remember now, O wicked one, all the wrongs you have done us! Remember what happened at Varanávata! Remember how Dráupadi was dragged into the assembly and how Yudhistra was unfairly defeated at dice! It is because of you that Bhishma, the grandsire of us all, lies now upon a bed of arrows. Drona has died, and Karna, and Shalya, and Shákuni, the root of all this evil. Your heroic brothers and your sons have all been slain. You alone, the destroyer of your line, remain alive, and you shall die today."

"What use has a Kshatria for words?" answered his foe. "Do you not see that I am waiting here to fight you? Up to this day I have never been vanquished in fair fight on the field of battle. If you defeat me unfairly, your name will be forever dishonored. Do not roar any longer like an autumn cloud that gives no rain, but put forth all your might and do battle with me!" All the warriors who stood there watching applauded these words with shouts and the clapping of hands, and Duryodha's heart was gladdened.

He rushed furiously against Bhima with a roar, and they met each other like two charging bulls, while the clash of their maces sounded like thunderbolts and sent out showers of sparks. Both were skillful in the use of the weapon and were beautiful to watch. They moved in circles; they advanced and retreated. They dealt blows and warded them off; they avoided blows, sometimes by crouching low and sometimes by leaping over the other's weapon. Now they ran to the right and now to the left, now straight at one another, and it seemed as if they were playing a game together. They rested a while and then returned to the fight.

Duryodha circled to the left, swung his mace and struck Bhima on the chest, stupefying him for a moment; then Bhima, filled with rage, struck his cousin on the side and made him fall to his knees. A great shout arose from the Pándavas, and when Duryodha heard it, he rose up, furious, and seemed to burn Bhima with his glance. Then he rushed at him and struck him on the head, but Bhima, though his blood flowed down, stood as firm as a mountain. Each struck the other down again, and Duryodha's last blow broke Bhima's coat of mail. When they saw this and saw Bhima rise, wiping the blood from his face and steadying himself with a great effort, fear entered the hearts of the Pándava warriors.

Arjuna asked Krishna, "Tell me truly, which of these two is the better, O you who know all things?"

"They received the same teaching," answered Krishna. "Bhima is stronger, but Duryodha has greater skill. Bhima will never win if he fights fairly; therefore he must be unfair. Even the gods have been known to deceive their enemies. At the time of the gambling match, O son of Pandu, Bhima vowed that he would break the thigh of Duryodha in the great battle. Let him keep that vow now, even though the blow be a foul one. Yudhistra has put you all in danger by saying that only one of you need be vanquished. Your foe is a great warrior and doubly dangerous because he is desperate. If Bhima does not slay him unfairly, he may yet keep the kingdom."

Arjuna heeded these words; he caught Bhima's eye and touched his own thigh, and Bhima understood him. Both the cousins were sorely bruised and bleeding from many wounds. They rested for a moment, and then Bhima rushed furiously against the king, eager to strike him down. Duryodha leaped into the air to avoid the blow, and as he leaped, Bhima swung his mace with all his power and broke the two thighs of the king, who fell to the earth like a great tree uprooted by a tempest.

Bhima stood above him, holding his mace on his shoulder, and said to him, "O wretch, you who laughed at Dráupadi in the assembly, bear now the fruit of that insult! We use no poison or fire, we do not cheat at dice, but by the might of our own arms we fight our foes." He touched with his left foot the head of Duryodha, then turned and faced Yudhistra, saluting him with joined palms. "The earth is yours today, O King," he said, "without brawls to disturb its peace, without a thorn! Rule over it with all its forests and mountains and seas, for now you have no living enemy."

When they beheld Duryodha struck down, like a wild elephant killed by a lion, the Pándava warriors rejoiced; some blew their conchs and beat their drums; they shouted and laughed aloud with joy. But others of righteous soul were not pleased when they saw Bhima touch the head of the fallen king with his foot, and one said angrily, "Shame on Bhima! O shame, that in a fair fight a foul blow was struck! No limb below the navel should be struck with a mace. This is the rule, and Bhima knows it well."

Krishna soothed the speaker, saying, "He and his brothers suffered many cruel wrongs from this king, and Bhima's heart was grieved because of them. Remember, too, the vow that he made; now he has paid his debt and kept that vow."

Duryodha was so angry when he heard these words that he tried to rise. Sitting up and leaning on his hands, he looked angrily at Krishna and said, "Have you no shame, O sinful one, that you justify this deed that you yourself advised? Do you think that I did not see the sign that Arjuna gave his brother at your behest? You, too, caused the death of Drona by persuading Yudhistra to tell a lie. When Karna's wheel was sunk in the mud, you caused him to be slain. If you had fought fairly with us, you would never have won the victory. Are you not ashamed of these unrighteous deeds?"

"O son of Gandhari," answered Krishna, "you have been slain with all your kindred and your friends because of the sinful path on which you trod. You met your death when, from greed, you refused to give the sons of Pandu their rightful share of the kingdom. Bear now the fruits of all your evil deeds."

Duryodha said, "I have performed sacrifices and made gifts and governed the wide earth with all its mountains and seas; enjoyments worthy of the very gods have been mine. Who is so fortunate as I? I have conquered hostile kingdoms and laid my commands on great kings; I have given wealth to my kinsmen and pleased my friends. Who is so fortunate as I? My life has passed in happiness, and death in battle—the death desired by all Kshatrias—is mine. Who, then, is more fortunate than I? I am going now to heaven with my brothers and my friends, while you, torn with grief, will live on in this unhappy world."

The Pándavas were grieved and wept as they listened to him, for they remembered those heroes who had been slain unrighteously, but Krishna said to them, "Those four great warriors, headed by Bhishma, could not have been slain by the gods themselves in fair fight. If I had not advised deceitful ways of battle, you would never have won the victory, your kingdom, or your wealth. Do not take it to heart that this last enemy has been slain unfairly; all that he has suffered he brought upon himself. We have won the victory and it is evening; let us return to our tents and rest, and let the troops and the elephants and horses also rest."

Those kings and warriors returned to their encampment, their hearts at rest, blowing their conchs as they went. They loosed their animals and rested for a while; then Krishna said, "Tonight, in order to purify ourselves, let us bathe in the sacred waters and sleep on the bare ground." Therefore, for that night, he and the five brothers slept on the bank of the Ganges.

The Aftermath

Ashvattáma's Revenge

A huntsman brought the news of Duryodha's fall to the son of Drona and his two companions as they rested under the tree. They mounted their chariots and drove swiftly back to the bank of the lake, where they found the king lying on the bare ground, covered with dust and blood and writhing in pain. Around him prowled fierce animals, which he kept at bay with his strong arms. The three warriors alighted and sat beside him and their anger blazed up as they saw him in such a plight.

Ashvattáma wrung his hands and said in a voice hoarse with grief, "My father was slain cruelly and unfairly by these wicked men, but even that does not grieve me so deeply as it does to see you here, O lord of earth. Listen to me! I swear by all my gifts and my good deeds, by truth itself, that I will send the Pándavas and all the Panchalas this very day to Yama's

271

realm. Give me leave to do this, my lord, and I will still bring you the victory!"

Now one of Ashvattáma's companions was a Brahman and was therefore able to perform the rites. "Bring a pot of water from the lake, O Brahman," said Duryodha, "and make the son of Drona the commander of my forces." The ceremonial water was brought, and Ashvattáma was solemnly installed as commander. He rose and raised a mighty shout that rang through the air in all directions; then he embraced the king and drove away with his companions, leaving Duryodha to face the fearful night alone.

Those heroes drove toward the south and secretly entered a forest close to the Pándava camp. Going deeper into the woods they came upon a gigantic banyan tree with thousands of branches and there they loosed their horses and said their evening prayers. Seated under the tree they talked sorrowfully of all that had happened, while around them the night-wandering animals began to howl and darkness fell. They were wounded and very tired, so they lay down on the ground, and Ashvattáma's two friends soon fell asleep; but he, burning with anger and the desire for revenge, could not close his eyes and lay wide awake, sighing deeply.

As he looked up into the tree, he saw hundreds of crows roosting among the branches, perched side by side and sleeping peacefully. Suddenly an owl appeared, with a huge tawny body, green eyes, and a long beak and claws. It flew swiftly, uttering little cries, and came secretly among the branches, where it slew several of the sleeping crows. It tore their wings, cut their heads off or broke their legs with its sharp beak, and soon the ground was covered with the feathers and the bodies of the dead birds. Then the owl was filled with delight.

"This owl has taught me a lesson," thought Ashvattáma. "I

Ashvattáma sees the owl kill the crows.

cannot slay the Pándavas in battle, and yet I have sworn, in the presence of the king, to slay them. If I were to fight openly with them I should lose my life at once, yet with guile I may still defeat them, as this owl has done to the crows. Tonight the Pándavas and the Panchalas will sleep deeply, happy in their victory and worn out with fighting. I shall attack their camp and kill them all while they are sunk in sleep."

He woke his companions and told them this wicked plan, but neither of them could answer him for shame. At last the Brahman said, "Do not do anything that you will repent of afterward, O son of Drona! It is a wicked thing to kill sleeping men, or those who have surrendered, or those who are disarmed. Our enemies will be sleeping trustfully, their armor laid aside, for they do not know that we are alive; anyone shameless enough to attack them would suffer for that deed in this world and the next. You have never done a dishonorable deed; rest tonight and sleep; tomorrow in broad daylight, go to their camp, proclaim yourself and slay them all in battle, with our help!"

"How can I sleep," answered Ashvattáma angrily, "when my heart is burning with rage and grief? I cannot sleep until I have slain Jumna, who killed my father when he was unarmed and seated in meditation. The Pándavas have broken every rule of battle and have torn down the barriers of virtue; why should not I do likewise? If I can slay them in their sleep, I do not care what happens to me, in this life or the next, and until I have done it, I cannot rest."

He yoked his steeds and mounted his chariot, and his two friends, seeing that they could not dissuade him, followed him to the Pándava camp. When they reached the gate, Ashvattáma whispered to the others, "Wait here and let no man escape, while I enter the camp and sweep through it like Death himself. It will not be hard to kill this remnant of the army while it is fast asleep."

He entered the camp softly and went at once to the tent of Jumna. All the Panchala warriors were tired out and slept side by side in perfect confidence. Ashvattáma entered the tent and saw his enemy lying on a perfumed bed strewn with flowers. He woke him with a kick and, when Jumna tried to rise, threw him down and seized him by the throat.

"Slay me with a weapon, O son of my teacher," Jumna gasped, "so that I may die a Kshatria's death!"

"O wretch," answered Ashvattáma, "those who slay their teachers have no right to a happy death." With this he strangled his enemy and, going out of the tent, set up a mighty shout. Then he sought out the other Panchala warriors.

These warriors and the guards, wakened suddenly, began to put on their armor, shouting, "Who is there?" "What is this noise?" "Is it a man or a demon who attacks us?" "Alas, the king is slain!" All were dazed and did not know what had happened or what they should do. Blinded by sleep and terrified by the sudden danger, they did not know who their enemy was and ran hither and thither, trying to find him. Elephants and horses broke their tethers and ran about, trampling upon men and raising dust that made the night more dark. Meanwhile Ashvattáma sought the tents of Jumna's brothers and slew them as if they had been animals in a sacrifice. He stormed along the different paths of the camp, carrying his splendid sword and his bright shield with a hundred moons upon it, and slew the unarmed, tired warriors who lay within their tents.

He came at last upon the sons of Dráupadi, who had heard the alarm and knew that Jumna was dead. They had risen and held their weapons and fought against him bravely, but

Ashvattáma, remembering his father's death, roared with rage and fought with the strength of a demon. One after another he cut down Dráupadi's sons and then went on to attack Shikándin, whom he cut in two with his sword. He careered through the camp like Death himself, slaying everyone he met with his mighty sword, covered with the blood of his enemies.

In the darkness and confusion, the Pándava and Panchala warriors, unable to recognize anyone, began to slay one another, while some, full of fear, threw away their weapons and ran out of the camp, but they were met at the gate by Ashvattáma's friends, who slew every man who tried to escape and let not one get by. Then those two set fire to the camp in three places, and the flames gave light to the son of Drona as he finished the slaughter, killing those who lay huddled on the ground and those who sought to flee. No one escaped except the charioteer of Jumna, who fled past the two at the gate and out into the night.

At last the shouts and shrieks and the clash of arms died down; the dawn came, and Ashvattáma, bathed in blood, with his hand stuck fast to the hilt of his sword as if they were one thing, looked about him and strode out of the camp. It had been silent when he entered it, for all within it had been asleep; it was silent again when he left it, for all were dead. Since he had kept his vow and done what no man had ever done before, he forgot his grief for his father's death and met his two companions joyfully, telling them all that had been done that night, while they told him how they had slain those who tried to escape.

The three warriors mounted their chariots and drove swiftly to the place where Duryodha lay. They saw that he was not yet dead, so they dismounted and sat beside him. "If there is any life still left to you, O King," said Drona's son, "listen to the good news that I bring you! Jumna and his sons and brothers, Dráupadi's five sons, the Panchalas and the Matsyas have all been slain this night! The Pándavas are now childless. On their side only six remain alive, the five brothers and Krishna; on our side, only we three. Behold the vengeance that has been taken for all that they have done!"

Duryodha rallied all his senses to reply to these welcome words. "O scorcher of foes, you have done what Bhishma and Karna and your father failed to do, since you have slain that low wretch who led the Pándava host and his brother Shikándin. Now I consider myself the victor. Good betide you! We shall all meet in heaven." With these words, casting off his grief for his slain brothers and kinsmen, the king of the Bháratas gave up his life.

His three friends took leave of one another and went their separate ways: the Brahman returned to Hástina; his companion went back to the land of the Yadus, whence he had come; and Ashvattáma mounted his chariot and drove into the forest, for he intended to take shelter in the hermitage of Vyasa, which was close to Kuru Kshetra.

The Last Debt Is Paid

At dawn, the charioteer of Jumna, who had escaped death within the camp, ran to Yudhistra to tell him the evil tidings. The king, hearing that all his sons had been slain, fell down upon the earth and wept grievously, as his brothers did also.

"Alas," he cried, "although we vanquished our foes, we ourselves have been vanquished in the end, and the vanquished are the victors. Those great warriors who stood against Bhishma and Drona and Karna have been slain through our carelessness!"

He sent Nákula to bring Dráupadi, who was living in her father's household, while he and his other brothers went to the camp. When they saw their sons, their friends, and their allies lying on the ground, their bodies mangled and bloody, the souls of the Pándavas were overwhelmed by sorrow.

Before the day was over, Nákula brought Dráupadi, who stood like a plantain tree shaken by the wind, her heart rent by the slaughter of her sons. Bhima took her in his arms. Weeping, she said to Yudhistra, "It is a happy thing, O King, to obtain the whole earth when all our sons are slain! O son of Kunti, grief burns me as if I were on fire. If Drona's son is not made to reap the fruit of this deed of his, if you do not take his life this very day—listen, you sons of Pandu—I shall sit here and fast until I die! I have heard that Ashvattáma was born with a jewel in his head; if that jewel is brought to me before the sun sets today, I can bear to live, but otherwise I die!" Then turning to Bhima, she said, "O Bhima, you are always our refuge! Slay now this evil man!" Then she sat down beside the bodies of her sons and concentrated her mind on her resolution.

Bhima mounted his chariot, taking Nákula as his charioteer, and his horses, fleet as the wind, carried him away from the camp, following the track of Ashvattáma's wheels.

When he had gone, Krishna said to Yudhistra, "O son of Pandu, of all your brothers Bhima is dearest to you, yet you let him go off alone to fight the son of Drona. When Drona gave to Arjuna that weapon that can destroy the world, his son, who was always jealous of Arjuna, begged to have it, too. His father gave it to him unwillingly, for he knew that Ashvattáma was headstrong and that he might not walk in the path of virtue. He commanded him never to use it against human beings even in the midst of battle, even when overtaken by the greatest danger. But he will use it now against Bhima, unless Arjuna protects his brother."

Krishna mounted his splendid chariot drawn by swift horses and carrying a banner with the device of a great bird; Arjuna and Yudhistra went with him and sat beside him. The horses carried them as fast and easily as a bird flies, and they soon caught up with Bhima, who did not stop but galloped on, following Ashvattáma's tracks. These led them to the bank of the Ganges, where they beheld the sage Vyasa sitting in the midst of a group of wise and holy men, among whom was Ashvattáma, his dust-stained body clad in a garment made of grass.

Bhima took up his bow, fixed an arrow on the string and walked toward Drona's son who, seeing that mighty bowman bearing down upon him and his two brothers standing in Krishna's chariot, thought that his last moment on earth had come. Then he remembered the heavenly weapon that his father had given him, telling him never to use it against a human foe. He picked a blade of grass and changed it, by speaking mighty spells, into that weapon. Burning with anger, he said, "Let this destroy the Pándavas!" and loosed the missile, which blazed with a blinding fire that seemed able to destroy the three worlds.

Arjuna leapt to the ground and summoned the same weapon; he blessed in his heart the son of Drona, his brothers, himself, and all the worlds, and loosed it, saying, "Let this stop Ashvattáma's weapon!" Then both those missiles blazed up with terrible flames into a huge sphere of fire; peals of thunder were heard, the earth trembled, and all living creatures fled into hiding.

When Vyasa beheld these celestial fires scorching the three worlds, he rose and stood between the two warriors. "What rash act is this, you heroes?" he cried. "Those famous warriors who fell in battle knew the use of this weapon and many others, but they never used them against their human foes. Why have you done it?"

Arjuna joined his hands humbly and said to him, "I used the weapon to stop Ashvattáma's, O holy one; if I withdraw it, he will consume us all."

The son of Drona said with a heavy heart, "I used it to protect my life from Bhima, O sinless one. Bhima slew Duryodha in a wicked way; I wished this weapon to destroy him and all his brothers."

"Arjuna also knew its use, my child," answered Vyasa, "yet he loosed it not from anger or from the desire to destroy you, but only to make yours powerless. Any place where this fearful power is let loose suffers a twelve-year drought. Therefore withdraw it and cast off your anger! Give the Pándavas the jewel that is in your head, and they, in turn, will give you your life."

"This jewel," said the master's son, "is worth more than all the wealth heaped up by both the Pándavas and the Kúravas. He who wears it need not fear any weapon or disease or hunger; neither gods nor demons can destroy him. Nevertheless, O exalted one, I must obey you. Here is the jewel; this blade of grass, turned into such awful power, I withdraw."

Both warriors withdrew their weapons. Ashvattáma gave Bhima the jewel from his head, then turned and went into the forest with despair in his heart. The Pándavas and Krishna, taking Vyasa with them, drove swiftly back to the camp and went to the place where Dráupadi sat. Bhima gave her the jewel, saying to her, "The slayer of your sons is vanquished, O beautiful one! We did not slay him, because he is a Brahman and our teacher's son. Rise now, cast off your sorrow and remember the duties of a Kshatria princess! Remember the bitter words you spoke when Krishna went on his mission of peace to Hástina and you desired war! The last debt that we owed our enemies is now paid."

"I only wished to pay the debt of injury that we have suffered," answered Dráupadi. "I respect the master's son as I did the master himself. Bind this jewel on your head, O son of Kunti!" The king took the jewel from her and bound it on his head, and Dráupadi, who was strong of soul, rose and once more took up her life.

Lament for the Dead

In Hástina, King Kuru had been told by his messenger and charioteer, Sánjaya, all that took place on the battlefield, day by day. When Duryodha was slain and the battle ended, Sánjaya came to the king and said, "The kings who came from many lands to fight for you, O ruler of men, have all gone to the realm of the dead, together with your sons. Duryodha, who refused all offers of peace, who wished to end his quarrel with the Pándavas by slaying them all, is himself dead and has made the earth empty of warriors. Now, O King, perform the funeral rites for your sons and your kinsmen."

When Kuru heard these terrible words, he fell down upon the ground like an uprooted tree and lamented for his sons, his kinsmen, and his friends.

"Cast off your grief, O King," Sánjaya said. "Your own mind, like a sharp-pointed sword, has wounded you. You always listened out of greed to evil counselors and refused to follow the advice of the wise and good. You always favored your eldest son, who was foolish, proud, and quarrelsome. His friends were men of wicked souls; none of them cared for virtue; battle was the one word on their lips. You were as an umpire between them and the Pándavas, but you did not give them one word of good advice; you held the scales unevenly between them, always tipped in Duryodha's favor. You must repent of that now. Therefore do not grieve for what has happened; the man who carries a lighted coal in the folds of his dress and then weeps when he is burned is called a fool. Grief of mind is cured by wisdom, as grief of the body is cured by medicine."

Vídura also, who had done all he could to prevent the calamity that had happened, came to the king and comforted him with wise words. At last Kuru rose from the ground and ordered his chariot to be yoked. He sent for Gandhari and Kunti and all his sons' wives, who were wailing loudly in their sorrow. Followed by those weeping women in their chariots, he set out from the city, while cries of woe arose from every house. Brahmans and men of the Vaisya and Shudra castes, who had taken no part in the battle, followed them and all went together to the field of Kuru Kshetra.

Yudhistra, with his brothers and Krishna and Vyasa, went to meet them as soon as they heard that Kuru had set out from the city; Dráupadi also, with the women of Panchala, all grieving for the loss of sons, husbands, and fathers, went with him. Near the banks of the Ganges they met. The women of Hástina surrounded Yudhistra with their arms raised aloft in sorrow and cried to him, "Where is the virtue of the king, since he has slain fathers and brothers, teachers and sons and friends? What good is the kingdom to you, O son of Kunti, when you have lost all your sons?"

Yudhistra did not answer them, but went to his uncle and touched his feet; his brothers followed him, each one speaking his own name as he did so. Kuru, his grief burning within him, unwillingly embraced Yudhistra and spoke words of comfort to him. Then he heard Bhima's voice, and his wrath blazed up as he thought of the death of Duryodha. Krishna understood what was in the old king's heart, and by his magic power he summoned the iron statue of Bhima on which Duryodha had practiced with his mace for thirteen years. He pulled Bhima aside and put the statue in his place. The king, strong as an elephant, seized the image in his two arms and broke it into pieces, but also bruised his own breast and fell bleeding to the ground. Sánjaya lifted him, and when Kuru came to his senses, his rage had passed and he wept, thinking that he had slain Bhima. When he found that hero alive before him, he embraced him, weeping, and welcomed Arjuna and the sons of Madri, blessing them.

Then the Pándavas and Krishna saluted the faultless Gand-hari, naming themselves to her, too, for her eyes were always covered. Gandhari sorrowed bitterly for all her sons and wished to curse Yudhistra, but Vyasa read her mind and said quickly, "Hold back the words that are on your lips, Gandhari! Forgive instead of cursing! Do you remember how your son Duryodha, before he went to battle, besought you, saying, 'O Mother, bless me now and pray for my victory!' and how you always said to him, 'He that is righteous will be the victor'? Remember your own words, O Queen, and withhold your anger!"

"I do not wish ill to the sons of Pandu, O holy one," said Gandhari, "for I know that they were not to blame for the death of all the Bháratas. But my heart is sore for the loss of my sons, and there is one deed of Bhima's, done in the presence of Krishna, that I cannot forget. He knew that Duryodha was more skillful than he with the mace, and therefore struck him a foul blow below the navel and killed him. Why should heroes do what is wrong to save their own lives?"

Bhima looked frightened as he answered the queen, "Right or wrong, O Lady, I acted out of fear, to defend my life. Your mighty son could not have been slain by anyone in fair battle. He caused Yudhistra to be beaten unfairly at dice and always acted treacherously toward us. He was the only warrior left fighting against us, and until he was dead we could not regain what was rightfully ours. Therefore I acted as I did. You never corrected his evil ways, and so you should not blame me but forgive me."

Gandhari was pleased that Bhima praised her son's might, but she still reproved him, saying, "You have slain every son of this old man. O why could you not have spared one son to this old couple, who have lost all they had; why could you not have left one child to guide these blind old people? Yet, even though you had slain them all, I should not grieve so if you had done it righteously." Her anger flared up anew and she asked, "Where is the king?"

Yudhistra came before her and stood with joined hands. "Here is the king," he said, "that cruel slayer of all your sons. Curse me, O faultless one, for I am the cause of all this slaughter. I have no further need of life or wealth or kingdom."

In her heart Gandhari knew the truth; therefore she said nothing to Yudhistra; but she sighed deeply and looked down, under the folds of cloth that covered her eyes, and saw the tip of his toe as he stood humbly before her, and her glance burned his toenail, which pained him ever after. Seeing this, Arjuna stepped behind Krishna, and the other sons of Pandu moved uneasily from one place to another. But Gandhari's anger passed, and she embraced the Pándavas and comforted them, for she had always thought of them as her own sons.

Last of all, the five brothers turned to their mother, Kunti, who had not seen them for all those thirteen years and had grieved so long for them. She covered her face and wept; then looking at them and seeing the scars of many wounds on their bodies, she embraced and caressed them and rejoiced that they still lived. She welcomed Dráupadi with love and wept with her for the loss of all her sons.

Then Kuru and his queen and his sons' wives went to that battlefield that was strewn with the bodies of men and animals. Gandhari, led by Krishna, went from one of her dead sons to the other and came at last upon the body of Duryodha. She threw herself upon it and wept bitterly, even though she knew that all this slaughter had come about because of his evil heart. She remembered all her sorrows and allowed anger to flood her heart again; she turned to Krishna and cast all the blame on him.

"The Pándavas and the Kúravas have both been destroyed, O Krishna," she cried. "Why did you not care? You could have prevented all this slaughter, for you had a vast army and many followers, and yet you did not stop it. Nay, more—all those unrighteous deeds, whereby the Pándavas slew Bhishma and Drona, Karna and Duryodha, were done at your behest, urged on by you. Therefore you shall reap the fruit of those acts. With the soul-power that I have gained by faithfully serving my husband, I curse you, O wielder of the discus and the mace! Since you did not care to stop the slaying of these cousins, you shall be the slayer of your own kinsmen. Thirty-six years hence, O Krishna, you shall cause the death of your sons and friends and kinsmen and perish yourself in a shameful way. The women of your realm shall weep as the women of the Bháratas are weeping now!"

Krishna answered her with a faint smile, "You have cursed well, O Queen! None but myself could ever slay the Yadus. It will be as you have said, even though you are blaming me for what is truly your own fault. Duryodha was wicked, jealous, and exceedingly proud, but you never restrained him. Now arise, Gandhari, and do not grieve, for one who grieves for what cannot be undone brings upon himself more grief. A Kshatria mother bears sons in order to have them killed, and all your sons have died bravely, facing the foe."

When the women had had their fill of lamentation and had seen all they desired to see of that dreadful field, King Yudhistra said, "Now let us perform the funeral rites of all the slain, so that no one may perish from lack of care." Then Vídura, Sánjaya and many others fetched sandal and aloe wood, oil and perfumes and costly robes. Great heaps of dry wood were raised and covered with the robes and the perfumes, and on these the bodies of the slain kings were laid in proper order according to their ages and their honor. Those among the dead who came from distant countries and were unknown and friendless were laid together on heaps of wood and burned with the proper rites. The funeral fires, smokeless and bright, burned far into the night, while the Brahmans chanted the hymns of death and women wept quietly for the slain.

The next morning Yudhistra, giving the place of honor to Kuru, followed by his brothers and the citizens and the women, went to the Ganges and in that holy river they performed the water rites for their sons and lords and sires.

There Kunti, overtaken by sorrow, said to her sons, "That great bowman who battled with you, that warrior who loved glory better than life, who shone like the sun himself as he commanded the host of Duryodha, that hero whom you took for a Suta's son and whom Arjuna slew, was your eldest brother, who was born of me by the sun-god, Surya. Therefore make offerings of water to Karna also, my sons!"

These words pierced the hearts of the sons of Kunti like

sharp arrows. "O Mother," cried Yudhistra, "was that great warrior whose might held us all in check, whom Arjuna alone could vanquish, truly our eldest brother? How could you hide him from us, like one who holds a burning fire in his hands? Alas, because you hid him we have been undone, for if we had known him, this battle would never have taken place. If he had been with us, if I had had both him and Arjuna to help me, I could have stormed heaven itself. Now I have caused my brother to be slain, and my heart burns with a greater grief than I have ever known."

His mother said, weeping, "Do not give way to grief, my son! I told Karna that he was your brother and Krishna did also. All that could be said to persuade him we both said to him, but he would not reveal himself to you or fight for you. He hated you and was bound to kill you all. Therefore I tried no longer to change his heart, and he made me promise not to tell you the truth."

But Yudhistra would not be comforted and said again, "Because you hid him from us, this great misfortune has overtaken us." And he added, "Henceforth let no woman be able to keep a secret!" Then he summoned Karna's wives and the other members of his family and performed with them the water rites in honor of his brother.

Yudhistra's Sorrow

The Pándavas and the old king and queen, Vídura and the ladies of the court stayed there by the sacred river for the full month of mourning, and many of the great sages and many noble Brahmans with their disciples came there to praise the king and to comfort him with wise words. But Yudhistra would not be turned from his grief and sat among them like a fire covered with smoke, unable to forget the deaths of sons and kinsmen, for all of which he blamed himself. "O scorcher of foes," he said to Arjuna, "if we had stayed in the forest, if we had been content to beg our food, we should not have the sorrow today of having slain our kinsmen. Fie upon power and strength and bravery, since they have brought us this misfortune! Blessed are forgiveness and self-control, humility and truthfulness, which forest dwellers practice! Those who have died should not have been slain even to gain the whole earth— no, not for the three worlds! I have committed great sins because I desired a kingdom; therefore give me leave to abandon it and to go to the woods, leaving all things both dear and hateful, harming no creature, casting off desire, fear, and anger, until I cast off life itself."

His brothers were deeply pained by these words of his, and each of them spoke to him, urging him to take up the duties of his caste and to rule wisely the earth that he had so righteously won.

"The highest duty," said Arjuna, "is that of the king, for he protects all the four castes and even the animals. Yet no man becomes a king without slaying others; indeed, I do not know of any creature in this world that lives without doing injury to others. Animals live upon each other: the mongoose eats the mouse; the cat eats the mongoose; the dog eats the cat, and the dog is eaten by the spotted leopard. Some creatures are so small that we cannot see them, yet we kill them when we wink our eyes. The wise man, therefore, does not lose heart because of death. Nothing can bring the slain to life again. Arise, O King, perform sacrifices, give alms and protect your people!"

Bhima was angry with his elder brother, yet tried to be patient with him. "How is it," he said, "that you who are the ruler of the earth, who know the right and the wrong paths

of this world, let your mind be so clouded? It is not the duty
of a king to go to the forest unless he is too old to rule or has
been defeated by his enemies; it is his duty to rule his kingdom
wisely. You have fought a great battle, O King, but there is
another that you must still fight, in which there is no need of
arrows nor of friends nor kinsmen, for you must fight it in
your own mind, alone. If you should die before you win the
victory, then in another life you will have to fight these very
foes again, but if you win it, you will have reached the goal
of life. Therefore fight that battle this very day and give your
whole mind to finding the path that you must follow, the
path that your ancestors have trodden. We are your servants
and await your decision."

Dráupadi added her pleas to theirs, and all of his brothers
spoke to him again, but Yudhistra still sat with bowed head,
plunged in grief.

Then Vyasa spoke to him, "O child, your brothers have
spoken the truth. You know the duties of a Kshatria, who
lives by warfare. A king who has righteously played his part
should not be overcome by grief. You were forced by the faults
of others to fight them, and you did it most unwillingly and
now grieve for it. It is not time for you to go to the woods;
it behooves you now to take up the duties of your caste and to
bear like an ox the burden of your ancestral kingdom."

"I do not doubt your words, O holy one," said Yudhistra,
"for all things are known to you. But my heart can find no
peace since, for the sake of that kingdom, I have caused so
many to be slain. This sin burns and consumes me."

"O Bhárata," answered Vyasa, "is God the doer, or is man?
Is all that happens the result of chance, or do we enjoy and
suffer the results of our own actions? The Kúravas sinned and
have been slain by you. When a tree is cut down, the axe is

not blamed, but he who wields it. You were the axe in the hands of Destiny, O King, and have no cause for grief. But if you cannot throw it off, then atone for what you believe that you have done. Rise, Yudhistra, and perform the great Horse Sacrifice, which cleanses the hearts of kings."

For the first time, the king was comforted and raised his head to answer Vyasa. "The idea of atonement fills me with joy," he said. "I will perform that sacrifice. But tell me first the duties of a king and those of all the four castes of men. It is hard to be a king and yet always to do what is right; my mind is not clear about this problem."

"If you wish to know the duties of a king," answered Vyasa, "go to Bhishma and ask the old grandsire of the Bháratas before he dies, for nothing is unknown to him. Behold now these brothers of yours and Dráupadi, who stand before you beseeching you as men beseech Indra for rain at the close of summer! The people of all castes in your kingdom await you, O delighter of the Bháratas. Do what they desire and what is best for the whole world!"

Then Yudhistra rose from his seat and cast off his grief. He set out for Hástina, surrounded by his brothers and by the sages, as the moon is surrounded by stars. He mounted a white chariot covered with deerskins, drawn by sixteen white bullocks. Bhima joyfully took up the reins and Arjuna held over his head a canopy bright as a sunlit cloud, while the twins fanned him with yak tails as white as moonbeams and flashing with jewels. Kuru and Gandhari were borne in litters at the head of the procession, Krishna rode in his own golden car, and the ladies followed in their chariots. Behind them came more chariots, elephants, and horsemen.

As they approached the city, the hum of innumerable voices were heard. The streets were decked with banners and flowers and thronged with citizens waiting to see the king. The palace was fragrant with powdered perfumes, flowers and sweet-smelling plants, and hung with wreaths and garlands. As the son of Pandu entered the city by its principal gate and passed through the streets and squares, the crowds swelled as the ocean does at the rise of the moon, and shouts of joy arose. On the terraces of the houses the ladies stood, praising the Pándavas with their soft voices. They also said, "Worthy of all praise are you, too, O blessed princess of Panchala! Your deeds and prayers have borne their fruit, O Dráupadi!"

Thus Yudhistra, graced with victory and the blessings of the people, entered the courtyard of the palace of the Bháratas and descended from his chariot.

The Horse Sacrifice

The Death of Bhishma

The royal son of Kunti, after the grief and fever of his heart had been healed, was seated on a golden throne and crowned with due ceremony king of the Bháratas. He made Bhima his heir and Vídura his chief minister. Sánjaya, the friend and charioteer of Kuru, was given charge of the treasury, and Nákula saw to all the needs of the army, the training, feeding and supplying of the troops, while Arjuna, as commander, protected the kingdom from all foes. The king kept Sadeva always at his side, for he could not do without the knowledge and advice of his youngest brother.

The beautiful palace of Duryodha, with the consent of Kuru, was given to Bhima, and the palace of Dushasa, abounding in wealth, to Arjuna, while Nákula and Sadeva were given two equally splendid mansions belonging to two of Kuru's sons. The king always treated Kuru and Gandhari with the same honor that they had had before and told his ministers to consult the old king in everything they did. He provided for all those women who had lost their husbands and sons in the battle; he gave rich gifts in the name of all the dead and gave food and shelter to the helpless and the blind.

As soon as this was done, he bethought himself of Bhishma, the grandsire of the Bháratas, who still lay upon his bed of arrows, waiting for the sun to turn to the north. One day Yudhistra called for his chariot and drove with his brothers and Krishna to the field of Kuru Kshetra. They dismounted on that field, where so many high-souled Kshatrias had cast away their lives, and went on foot to the spot where Bhishma lay. On the plain there was many a hill formed by the bodies and bones of elephants and horses, while human skulls lay scattered over it like conch shells. With the remains of countless funeral pyres and heaps of armor and weapons, the vast plain looked like the drinking garden of Death himself, as if he had been reveling there and had just departed.

Bhishma lay where he had fallen, stretched on his arrowy bed. He was surrounded by the holiest of the sages, Vyasa and many others, and at a distance stood the soldiers who guarded him night and day. The Pándavas approached the grandsire with joined palms, but none of them dared to speak to him; so Krishna spoke.

"O best of men," he said, "have you passed the night happily? Is your mind unclouded and your heart without pain?"

"All fatigue and pain have left me, O wielder of the discus," answered Bhishma. "I am strengthened by meditation and feel as if I were a young man again. My mind is unclouded. I see all that is past, present, and future as if it were a fruit placed in my hands."

"The son of Pandu has come to question you about the

duties of all men, especially those of a king," said Krishna, "but he is overcome by shame because he caused your death and does not dare to speak to you."

"A Kshatria," answered Bhishma, "should slay sires and grandsires, brothers, teachers, and kinsmen, if they fight against him in an unjust war. Let the son of Pandu, who is ever devoted to peace and truth, ask me whatever he desires."

Yudhistra came forward when he heard those words and took in his two hands the feet of Bhishma, who welcomed him lovingly and said, "Do not fear, my son, to question me."

Saluting him then with joined hands, Yudhistra asked, "Tell me, O grandsire, what are the duties of all castes of men and what way of life should be followed by each of them. What are the special duties of the king?"

"There are four castes, O King," said Bhishma, "the Shudra serves, the Vaisya lives by farming, herding, or trade, the Kshatria fights and governs, while the Brahman teaches and performs the sacrifices. As the footprints of the smaller animals are covered by that of the elephant, so the other three castes are sheltered and protected by the Kshatria, for the Kshatria supports the Shudra, the Vaisya, and the Brahman. The highest duty is that of the Kshatria, O King.

"There are four steps in life which are like a ladder or a flight of stairs leading to heaven.

"A man spends the first part of his life as a student; he lives with a teacher, whom he serves reverently while he studies the Vedas and the duties of his caste.

"When he has finished his studies and paid his teacher's fee, he returns home and becomes a householder. He marries and lights the sacred fire of his home and has sons and grandsons. He earns his living in honest ways; he never turns a guest from his door or refuses food to a Brahman.

"When the householder sees wrinkles on his face and white hair on his head, when he beholds his children's children, then he should go to the woods, carrying with him his sacrificial fire. The forest dweller eats only once a day; he sits and sleeps on the bare ground. He bears with patience heat and cold, rain and wind, and so burns his sins away as with fire and purifies his heart.

"In the fourth or last part of life, a man may leave the forest dweller's life for the last step—the way of freedom, the search for God. He casts away his sacred fire, for his sacrifice after that will be in his own heart, and his very self is the offering. He calls nothing his own; he eats what is barely necessary and roams over the earth, sleeping at the foot of trees. He fears no creature and no creature fears him; he beholds all things in himself and himself in all things. Cheerful, fearless, and silent, his mind fixed on God, he frees himself from death and rebirth and enters the regions of everlasting bliss. This last way of life is very hard to attain, O best of kings; few men are able to reach it. Indeed, the last two steps need not be taken by any but Brahmans, for the Kshatria often dies in battle before his hair is white, and the other castes finish their lives doing their appointed duties; but men and women of all the castes, if they feel able to do so, may take these last two steps and free their souls.

"Your duty now is to live the life of the householder, O Yudhistra. It is the best of all ways of life, for all the others—the student, the forest dweller, even the seeker for God—depend upon the householder. As the footprints of all the smaller animals are covered by that of the elephant, so the other ways of life are sheltered and protected by that of the householder."

Then he told Yudhistra the duties of a king, saying to him, "Kingly duties are the highest of all, for all the castes and all those who follow the different steps in life depend upon the power and protection of the king. The protection of his subjects is his first and highest duty; he must guard them from enemies both outside and inside his realm, and wield the rod of justice. You are very gentle, Yudhistra, and inclined to mercy; you must also be stern. People look for protection to one who is courageous, who can strike hard, who is both merciful and just.

"Take care of the weak and never make enemies of them, for it is said that no man can bear the eyes of the weak or the eyes of a snake or those of a saint, when they are angry. Do not take wealth from the poor. Tax your kingdom as the bees take honey from flowers, as a good cowherd takes milk from a cow, without hurting her udders and without starving her calf."

With these and many other wise words, Bhishma made clear to the king all his high duties, enlivening his talk with many tales of men and gods, of animals and birds. Day after day the Pándavas sat round him in the company of the holy sages, asking him ever more questions and listening with rapt attention to his answers, for they wished to store in their hearts the wisdom that would vanish from the world when Bhishma left it. At last the sun drew near the end of its southward course, and one day the grandsire said, "My mind, my eyes and ears are dulled today; the time is near when I shall cast off my body. I have answered all your questions, O king of men; now return to your city, and when the sun turns north, come here again."

When the day came for Bhishma's departure, Yudhistra took perfumes and garlands and silken cloths, sandal and aloe wood and jewels, and the Pándavas went again to Kuru Kshetra with Vídura, the old king and queen, Kunti and Dráupadi. They stood beside the old hero, who lay with closed eyes, like a fire about to go out. When he opened his eyes and beheld them all, he took the strong hand of Yudhistra and said in a voice as deep as thunder, "I wish to cast off my body now, O King. Pray give me leave." Then he embraced them all, and as they watched him, they saw his spirit come forth from his head and flash up into the sky like a meteor, disappearing at last from their sight. They built a funeral pyre of fragrant woods, and wrapping his body in silken cloths, they laid it on the pyre and burned it there, Kuru and Yudhistra standing at the feet.

An Heir Is Born

When the Pándavas returned to Hástina after the death of Bhishma, Vyasa said to the king, "It behooves you now to prepare for that greatest of sacrifices, the Horse Sacrifice, even as your ancestor, the exceedingly mighty King Bhárata, that lord of the earth, performed it. Only a monarch who has conquered the whole earth is worthy to carry out this king of rites. It will cleanse your heart of any grief or sin and because of it your kingdom will prosper and endure."

"I believe that this sacrifice purifies and blesses kings," answered Yudhistra, "but, alas, during this ceremony the wealth of the whole world must be given away, and since I have caused this great slaughter of my kindred, I cannot make even small gifts, for I have no wealth. Duryodha laid waste the earth for the sake of wealth, and now his treasury is empty. I cannot ask tribute from the young sons of the kings who were slain, for they are in distress and their sorrow is yet green; I cannot levy taxes when the world has been drained of its men and its treasure. What shall I do, O sinless one?"

"Your empty treasury shall be filled, O son of Kunti," answered the sage. "In the Himalaya Mountains there is a great heap of gold, left there long ago by the Brahmans after a famous sacrifice, because they could not carry it all away. A king in olden days, who was righteous and of great renown, celebrated a sacrifice on a golden hill on the northern side of the mountains. He caused his goldsmiths to make thousands of shining vessels and bowls and seats and ornaments, so many that not half of them could be taken from that place. You must collect all that was left and perform the sacrifice, worshiping the gods with due ceremony. I will show you where it lies."

Yudhistra was delighted to hear these words and summoned his brothers to go in quest of the treasure. They left the kingdom in Vídura's care and set out with joyful hearts, guided by the island-born sage and followed by a great train of men and animals, all in high spirits. They shook the earth with the clatter of their wheels, while the tread and the voices of men and animals seemed to fill the sky. Yudhistra rode in his chariot with the white canopy held over his head, and he heard the shouts and blessings of the people as he went on his way. He and his company crossed many rivers, forests, and mountains and reached at last the northern side of the Himalayas. Vyasa led them to the place where the gold was buried, and there the king pitched his camp, and he and his brothers, fasting, laid themselves down on beds of grass.

When the cloudless morning came, they worshiped Kúvera, the lord of treasures, with flowers and cakes; then, under Vyasa's direction, they caused the digging to begin. Countless vessels and seats and ornaments of varied and delightful shapes were dug out, thousands of jars of golden coins, finely wrought. Some of this wealth was carried on men's shoulders, on yokes of wood with baskets slung at either end; some was carried on the backs of camels and elephants and in carts drawn by mules. When it was loaded on all the carts, on thousands of animals, and on the shoulders of hundreds of men, the sons of Pandu set out for the city called after the elephant, making short marches, for the host was sorely burdened by so much treasure.

It was at this time, when the Pándavas were absent from the city, that Uttara, the daughter of King Virata and the wife of Abimanyu, gave birth to the son who alone could carry on the line of Pandu. Since all their sons had been slain in that awful battle, the hopes of all the Pándavas depended on this child. Kunti, Dráupadi, and Subadra, like shipwrecked people who finally reach the shore, were filled with joy when they saw the child in his mother's arms. Poets and musicians, astrologers and actors praised the young prince, and the citizens raised a shout of joy that seemed to fill the sky.

When the baby was a month old, the Pándavas came back to their capital, bringing the treasure with them. The citizens decked the city with garlands of flowers and bright flags and pennons. It was filled with the hum of thousands of voices that sounded like the distant roar of the ocean, and the sound of singing and of stringed instruments rose here and there. The officers of the government proclaimed that this was to be a day of rejoicing and went out to meet the king and to announce to him the happy news of the birth of Abimanyu's son. Then the Pándavas, with joyful hearts, entered the city.

After they had celebrated with due ceremony and festivity the birth of the young prince, Yudhistra said to Vyasa, "O wisest of men, I wish to devote this treasure that you have brought us to the celebration of the Horse Sacrifice. I pray you to initiate me when the time comes and to perform the sacrifice for us, for we depend on you for its success."

"You shall be initiated on the day of the next full moon," answered the sage, "and I shall perform the ceremony for you. Now let the Sutas who are expert in the knowledge of horses choose one that is worthy of your sacrifice. Then let the horse be loosed to wander over the earth freely, at its will, for a year, as the scriptures ordain, and let Arjuna follow it and protect it. He will, according to the holy ordinances, allow it to roam and graze as it will, but if the king of any country where it roams attempts to stop it, then Arjuna must challenge him to battle and make him acknowledge you as lord of the earth. When the horse returns and all the earth is subject to you, the sacrifice will be celebrated."

Therefore Yudhistra summoned Arjuna and said to him, "You alone, O sinless one, are able to follow the sacred steed and to protect it. If any kings come forward to challenge you, do not slay them! Ask them to come to this sacrifice of mine and make friends of them!"

Arjuna Follows the Horse

When the full moon came, the king was initiated and the year-long preparation for the sacrifice began. The beautiful black horse that the Sutas had selected was let loose and Arjuna, in his chariot with its white steeds, Gandíva in his hand, followed it. All the citizens and the children came out to behold him, and their voices rose all round him as they cried, "Behold the son of Kunti and the steed of blazing beauty! There is the famous Gandíva of terrible twang! Blessings go with you, O son of Pandu! Go safely and return to us and may all dangers fly from your path!" And the horse, feeling its freedom, shook its mane and trotted out of the city, Arjuna following it in his chariot.

The sacred and beautiful steed wandered first into the north and then turned eastward. It entered the kingdoms of many monarchs who were the sons or grandsons of kings who had been slain on the field of Kuru Kshetra, and many of them stopped it and challenged Arjuna to single combat, for their hearts were still sore from the loss of fathers and kinsmen. Arjuna defeated them but did not kill them; mindful of the words of Yudhistra, he said to them, "Rise up and return to your city, and when the full moon of the month of Chaitra comes, go to the great sacrifice of King Yudhistra in Hástina!"

They promised to do so and made offerings to the sacrificial steed, which now turned toward the south. It was received with honor there and passed through all the kingdoms, whose young rulers came out to pay homage to Arjuna. They begged him to enter their cities and to rest and refresh himself, but he answered, "You know that I am under a vow and cannot stay, but must follow the horse wherever it may go. Come to the sacrifice of King Yudhistra in the month of Chaitra!"

Then the horse turned westward and came into the land of Sind, whose king had been slain by Arjuna after he had caused the death of Abimanyu. There again the horse was stopped, for the men of Sind still had a bitter memory of that defeat, and could not bear the sight of the son of Pandu. They fought fiercely against him, and Arjuna tried hard not to kill them; he cut their weapons to pieces with his arrows before they reached him, and he disarmed them and stopped their chariots, but still they fought on, even though they knew well that no one could vanquish the wielder of Gandíva.

Now it happened that Kuru's only daughter had been married to the king of Sind; she was therefore Arjuna's cousin. She now came forth from the city with her grandson, a young child, in her arms and went to Arjuna, weeping, and said, "Behold this child, whose father and grandfather and kinsmen have all been slain! Even as the son of Abimanyu is the only

Arjuna follows the sacrificial horse.

one to carry on your line, so this child is our only hope. See, he bends his head before you and asks for peace!" Then she forbade the warriors to fight any longer, and Arjuna comforted her and promised her that there would be peace between their kingdoms.

He went further, following always the wandering of the horse, sometimes meeting enmity and sometimes friendship, until he came, last of all, to the kingdom of Gandhara, which Shákuni, that cheater at dice, had once ruled over. His son now ruled, and he had not forgiven the sons of Pandu for his father's death; therefore he stopped the horse and challenged Arjuna to battle, although that son of Kunti had met him with friendly words and did not wish to slay him. Though he was very young, he fought bravely and well, but his mother, with the ministers of state, came out of the gates of the city and bade him lay down his arms, while they offered food and gifts to Arjuna and water for his feet. Arjuna also did not forget that Gandhari was the sister of Shákuni; so he treated the young prince kindly and bade him come to the great sacrifice, and then went on his way, following the black steed.

When that beautiful horse had wandered over the earth for a whole year, it turned toward the road that led to Hástina. Yudhistra's messengers, who waited for Arjuna, hastened to the king to tell him that the horse had turned back and that Arjuna was well. His heart was filled with joy; he sent for his brothers and told Bhima to prepare a place for the sacrifice, since the time had come for its celebration.

Then Bhima summoned those men who knew the rules for laying out the sacrificial grounds and buildings. Under the direction of the sage Vyasa the earth was leveled and the altar erected; columns and wide triumphal arches brightly adorned with gold were raised and mansions were built for the many kings and their ladies and attendants who were expected to come from many and diverse lands. Stables were filled with grain and sugar cane for the animals that would come with the royal guests. Many great sages came from all sides of the earth to that sacrifice, and the foremost Brahmans with their disciples gathered there.

When all was ready, the invited kings arrived and Yudhistra took each of them to the pavilion that had been prepared for him, while the guests looked with wonder at the splendor of that sacrifice. It seemed that the whole population of the world had assembled there from all its realms and provinces. Thousands of men, adorned with garlands and golden earrings, offered food to the Brahmans and attended to the needs of all the guests.

Krishna came with many of the Yadu warriors and was joyfully received by the Pándavas. "A messenger of mine has told me that Arjuna is very near," he said. "He saw that hero and says that he is very thin and worn because of the many battles that he has fought."

"It pains my heart," Yudhistra answered, "that Arjuna always seems to bear the heaviest burden and hardly ever has any rest or comfort. Why should that be? His body bears every fortunate sign."

"I see nothing imperfect in him," said Krishna, "except, perhaps, that his cheekbones are a little high. Perhaps it is for this that he rests so little." When he said this, Dráupadi looked askance at him angrily, for she could not bear to hear a word against Arjuna, but Krishna smiled and was pleased at this sign of her love for his friend.

While they were talking, a messenger arrived who bowed before Yudhistra and told him that Arjuna was approaching. The whole city went to the gate to watch for him, and a great shout arose as the people saw him standing in his chariot in a haze of golden dust raised by the hoofs of the sacrificial horse and his own white steeds. He was welcomed joyfully by all his brothers and Krishna; after saluting them all, Arjuna entered his palace, where Dráupadi awaited him and where he took his rest, like a shipwrecked man who, after long wandering, reaches his home at last.

On the third day after his return the sacrifice began, for the full moon of the month of Chaitra was at hand. Vyasa said to Yudhistra, "Since you have such a wealth of gold, you may give away three times as much as is usually given, O son of Kunti. Thus you will have the reward of three Horse Sacrifices, which will free you of every sin."

The king agreed gladly. On the first day he was anointed, and made abundant gifts of food and other pleasant things to all who were assembled there. In the great enclosure the sacrificial stakes were driven into the ground; the priests moved about in all directions, performing every ceremony in the proper way, never swerving from the rules laid down in the Vedas. Vyasa was the high priest and directed the different acts of each day.

On the second day, Yudhistra, clad in armor and carrying his weapons, entered the enclosure in his chariot, drawn by the sacrificial steed and three others. He took his place on his throne, surrounded by his brothers and by all the kings of the earth, adorned in royal robes and flashing jewels. Animals and birds, both tame and wild, were tied to the stakes and assigned to all the gods, while the black steed that had roamed the earth was bound in the center. After the other animals had been sacrificed and their flesh cooked, that beautiful steed was slain and its body cut into pieces, as the scriptures demanded. The Brahmans took the marrow of its bones and cooked it; then they presented it to Yudhistra and his four brothers, who breathed deeply the smoke of that marrow, which cleanses one of every sin.

On the third day the ceremony was completed, and King Yudhistra took the bath of purification. He accepted the homage of all the kings and was acclaimed their head, the sole lord of the whole earth. Then he gave to the Brahmans hundreds of thousands of gold coins, and he gave to Vyasa the whole earth. The sinless Vyasa accepted the gift and said to him, "The earth that you have given to me I now return to you, O best of kings. Give me the price of it in gold, for Brahmans need wealth and have no use for the earth." Yudhistra and his brothers rejoiced and gave the holy one three times the wealth that should be given at a Horse Sacrifice. Vyasa took it and gave it to the sacrificial priests, who divided it among the Brahmans, giving to each all that he desired. The rest was given to the Kshatrias and Vaisyas and Shudras, and to the barbarian tribes; and the holy Vyasa gave his share, which was large, to Kunti.

There was none among the assembled guests who was unhappy or hungry or poor. The sons of Pandu gave to all the kings jewels and gems, elephants and horses and ornaments of gold; to the citizens of all castes food and clothing, gold and ornaments were given. There were food and drink and sweetmeats in abundance, and the spacious grounds echoed with the sound of drums and flutes and stringed instruments. The vast space was filled with happy men and women; people speak of that great sacrifice in all the different realms to this day.

And King Yudhistra, when he had given away that untold wealth and had dismissed the assembled kings with due honor, returned to his capital with his heart at peace, for he was cleansed of all his sins and the purpose of his life was fulfilled.

Listen now to a most wonderful thing that happened at the end of that great sacrifice.

The Mongoose's Story

After everyone had received abundant gifts and all were praising King Yudhistra, a blue-eyed mongoose, with his head and one half of his body turned to shining gold, came into the enclosure and spoke to the Brahmans in a human voice as deep as thunder.

"You holy ones," he said, "this sacrifice is not equal to one handful of powdered barley that was given away by a kind Brahman who lived at Kuru Kshetra."

The Brahmans were filled with wonder at these words and crowded round him, asking, "Whence do you come? What knowledge and power is yours that you thus belittle our sacrifice? Everything has been done here according to the scriptures; men and gods have been abundantly satisfied. Explain your words!"

"My words are true, O sinless ones," answered the mongoose, smiling, "and I have not spoken them out of pride. I say again that this sacrifice is not equal to a handful of powdered barley. Now listen to me as I tell you something that I saw with my own eyes and that turned half my body to gold.

"In that holy place that is called Kuru Kshetra, where many righteous people live, there was a Brahman who had taken a very hard vow. He ate only what he could pick up from the fields after the farmers had gathered the harvest. He and his wife, his son and his son's wife lived thus like birds and ate but once a day. They were pure-minded and had cast off all pride and anger. One time there was a dreadful famine in the land. The grain and the plants were all dried up, and that righteous Brahman and his family had nothing stored away, for they picked up their food day by day. They had nothing at all to eat and passed their days in great suffering.

"One day he succeeded in picking up about a quart of barley. He and his family powdered it, and after they had finished their daily worship and their silent meditation, they divided that little measure of grain among them so that each one had about a handful. Just as they were sitting down to eat, a guest came to their house. They welcomed him gladly and brought water to wash his feet, offering him a seat of clean grass. Then the Brahman gave the guest his share of the barley to eat. The guest ate it all but was still hungry, and the Brahman tried to think of something else that he could give him.

"His wife said, 'Give him my share of the barley.'

"But the Brahman, seeing how weak and thin she was from hunger, said to her, 'Even among animals and insects, O lovely one, wives are fed and protected by their husbands. If I fail to do this, I shall certainly never go to heaven.'

" 'All that I have is yours, O blessed one,' answered his wife, 'All my life you have taken care of me, and in return for that I pray you to take my share of the barley to give to our guest.' So he took her share and gave it to the stranger, who ate it and was still hungry.

"Then the Brahman's son said to him, 'Give my share of the barley to our guest, O best of men. It is the duty of a son to take care of his father when he is old. It is shameful to send a guest away hungry from one's door; therefore let me save you from that shame by giving him my share of the barley.' And the father took his son's share and gave it to the guest, who ate it but was not satisfied.

"His daughter-in-law brought her handful of powdered grain to him and said, 'Because you had a son, I have had a son, and through him I shall attain happiness in this world and the next. Take my share, therefore, and give it to the guest.' Her father-in-law accepted it and gave away the last bit of their food.

"Now that guest was no other than Dharma himself, the God of Righteousness, who now revealed himself to those four generous ones and said, 'O best of Brahmans, I am exceedingly pleased with this pure gift of yours. Truly the blessed ones in heaven are talking about it and flowers are falling thence upon the earth. The gods, the holy sages, and the heavenly messengers are all praising you, struck with wonder at this deed. For hunger destroys wisdom and courage; therefore he who can conquer hunger conquers heaven. You have overcome your love for wife and children and the craving of your own body for the sake of virtue and so have deserved to dwell in the region of the blessed.

" 'The door of heaven is hard to open,' said Dharma. 'Greed is the bar to that door, and it is fastened by desire. Those who conquer anger and greed, who give according to their ability, are able to open it. He who has a thousand and gives away a hundred, he who has a hundred and gives away ten, and he who has nothing and gives away a cupful of water, are equally rewarded. That king who gave away the flesh of his body to save a pigeon is rejoicing now in heaven. This gift of yours, O Brahman, is greater than those gifts that are made in many Rajasuya Sacrifices or many Horse Sacrifices. A heavenly chariot is here for you; mount upon it now with your wife, your son, and your daughter-in-law, and go to those regions where there is no hunger and no sorrow.'

"All this," said the mongoose, "I beheld and heard from

inside my hole. After that learned Brahman with all his family had gone away, I looked out of my hole, and the fragrance of that powdered barley and the celestial flowers that had fallen to the earth turned my head to gold. As I came farther out, half of this broad body of mine was turned to gold because of the gift of that Brahman who held fast to virtue. Ever since that time, O sinless ones, I have gone to the hermitages of holy sages and to the sacrifices of kings so that the rest of my body might also become golden. When I heard of this great sacrifice, I came hither with high hope, but behold, my body remains as it was. Therefore I said that this sacrifice cannot compare with that gift of powdered barley, and so I still believe." With these words the mongoose disappeared from the sight of those Brahmans.

This wonderful happening has been told so that no one may think too highly of sacrifices. Many a holy man has gone to heaven because of his good deeds alone. Indeed, if one hurts no living creature and is contented and true, self-controlled and generous, he has offered the highest sacrifice of all.

The Forest Dwellers

The Old People Go to the Woods

For many years the high-souled sons of Pandu ruled the earth justly and with great happiness. They gave the old king, Kuru, the place of honor and asked his advice about everything they did, going to him and sitting beside him after touching his feet. Kunti also obeyed Gandhari, her elder sister-in-law, and Dráupadi and Subadra behaved toward the old king and queen as they would have behaved toward their own parents. Fish, flesh, wines, honey, and many other kinds of delightful food, costly beds, robes, ánd ornaments were given to Kuru so that he might have everything that he had enjoyed in the days of his glory; for Yudhistra desired that his uncle, who had lost all his sons, might not die of grief or be unhappy in any way. Indeed, the father of Duryodha had never been so happy with his own children as he was with the Pándavas, and Gandhari, too, loved them as if they were her own sons.

There was one among the Pándavas, however, who did not follow the example of his older brother, and that was Bhima. He could not forget the gambling match to which Kuru had invited them and all that followed as a result of it; he did not enjoy the sight of his uncle, and although he honored him outwardly, he did so with a very unwilling heart. Secretly he did things that were disagreeable to the old king, and he bribed the servants to disobey his orders. One day, when he remembered with rage the unhappy days of the past, Bhima clapped his armpits and said loudly to some of his friends, in the hearing of his uncle and Gandhari, "All the sons of the blind king, though they were great warriors, were sent to Yama's realm by these powerful arms of mine."

These words and others like them pierced Kuru's heart as if they had been sharp arrows; after fifteen years, Bhima's unkindness and harsh words drove him to grief and despair. Yudhistra knew nothing of this, nor did Arjuna of the white steeds, nor Kunti, nor Dráupadi, nor the twin sons of Madri, who did everything to please the old king and never said anything that could displease him.

One day Kuru, with tears in his eyes, said to his friends, "You all know that the Bháratas were destroyed because of me. All wise men gave me the same advice, but I did not follow it, for I was blinded by my love for my eldest son, the evil-minded Duryodha. I made him king and followed his wicked counsels. I now repent bitterly, and I am trying to atone for my sins. Once a day I eat a little food, just to keep myself alive; I sleep on the ground and spend my time in silent prayers. Gandhari knows this and does as I do, but I have hidden it from everyone else for fear of Yudhistra, who would be deeply pained if he knew how I was living."

Shortly afterward he spoke to Yudhistra, saying, "May you

be blessed, O son of Kunti! I have lived these fifteen years very happily with you, for you are always devoted to virtue. Now, my son, with your permission I wish to retire into the woods with Gandhari, clad in the bark of trees and deerskins. It is right, when old age comes, to leave the throne to one's children and to live in the forest. I shall always bless you there, and you shall have a share in all the good acts that I may perform, for the king has a share of all the good and evil deeds that are done in his kingdom." Then he told Yudhistra of the penances that he had already performed.

"Alas," Yudhistra said, "my brothers and I did not know you were grieving so, fasting and sleeping on the ground. You are our father and our mother, the eldest of our line; how shall we live without you? You are the king and I depend on you; how can I give permission to one who is higher than myself? If you go to the woods, I will follow you, for this earth, with its belt of seas, so full of wealth, will give me no joy if I cannot share it with you."

"O delight of the Bháratas," answered his uncle, "my mind is set on retiring to the woods, and it is fitting that I should do so. Therefore give me your permission, my son."

When Kuru had spoken thus, he fell against the shoulder of Gandhari and looked like one dead, for he was faint with hunger. Yudhistra's heart was melted with pity as he looked at the old man and remembered him in the days of his might. He knelt before him and rubbed Kuru's feet between his strong hands and, when the old king came to his senses, begged him to eat some food. He could not make up his mind to grant his uncle's request, but as he knelt there, silent, the great sage Vyasa, who often visited them, said to him, "O Yudhistra, give without any doubt the permission that the king has asked of you. Let him follow the path of the great men of old; do not let him die an inglorious death at home. Kings should die either in battle or, when they are old, in the forest, according to the scriptures. Therefore do not stand in his way, O son of Kunti. The time has come for him to go."

And Yudhistra, bending humbly before his uncle, said to him gently, "So be it! What the holy Vyasa has said, what you yourself desire, shall be done. But first, I pray you, take some food."

When Kuru had eaten some food and rested, he summoned all the citizens to come to his palace. Brahmans and Kshatrias, Vaisyas and Shudras gathered together in the courtyard, and the king came out of the inner apartments and spoke to them thus: "We have lived together for many long years, each helping the other, wishing each other well. Now I have set my heart on retiring to the woods, and the son of Kunti has given me his permission. I pray you also for yours. Since Yudhistra has ruled the kingdom I have enjoyed great happiness, greater, I think, than I could have known if my own son Duryodha had been on the throne. Through the wicked deeds of that prince and his pride and my own foolishness as well, a great slaughter of warriors took place. Whether I acted rightly or wrongly, now with joined hands I pray you to erase that memory from your hearts. Say to yourselves, 'This one is old; he has lost all his children; he was once our king and is the descendant of former kings'—and try to forgive me.

"Yudhistra the son of Pandu, with his four mighty brothers, will rule you like one of the gods, and should be cherished by you all. I give him to you as a trust and I give you to him as a trust. I am worn out with the load of years on my head and thin with fasting. What other refuge have I save the woods? You blessed ones, grant me the permission that I ask of you."

When the blind monarch had spoken thus, the people said nothing, but only looked at one another, their eyes filled with tears. Then they began to talk to one another, each telling the other what he felt, and finally they asked a certain Brahman to answer the king for them.

"O King," the Brahman said, "I will voice the answer that this assembly has asked me to make, and do you listen to it. O foremost of men, follow the path that the Vedas have pointed out to you. If you leave us, we shall pass our days in sorrow, remembering your many virtues. We were well ruled and protected by King Duryodha, as we were by you and by Pandu, that lord of earth. Your son never did us any wrong. The slaughter that the Bháratas suffered was not brought about by you or by your son; destiny caused it, and nothing could have stopped it. Eighteen armies were brought together and in eighteen days they were destroyed. Who can think that this was not caused by destiny? Therefore, in your presence, we forgive you and your son Duryodha and give you our permission to leave us. Those mighty warriors, the sons of Pandu, will protect and cherish the people. Therefore, O King of kings, set your heart at rest and do as you desire."

Kuru, with joined palms, bowed down to that assembly of the people and returned to his palace with Gandhari.

The next morning Vídura came to Yudhistra and said to him, "The king will set out for the woods on the next day of the full moon. He asks you to give him some wealth, O lord of earth, so that he may perform a sacrifice for the souls of Bhishma and Drona and for all his sons."

Yudhistra and Arjuna were pleased to hear this, but Bhima grumbled, for he did not wish to give anything to his uncle or to help the souls of the cousins whom he had slain. Yudhistra, however, said to Vídura, "Say to the king that he may take from my palace anything that he wishes in any quantity. Whatever wealth is here belongs to him; let him spend it freely as he likes and pay the debt that he owes to his sons and to his friends."

Kuru was delighted when he received this message and ordered a great quantity of food and drink to be prepared and many chariots and robes, gold and jewels, elephants and horses richly decked to be gathered together. These he gave away in the name of the dead, calling upon Bhishma and Drona, Duryodha and his other sons in due order as the gifts were made. Scribes and tellers kept asking the old king, "What gifts, O monarch, do you wish to make? All things are ready to your hand." When the king spoke, they gave what he ordered, but if he said ten, they gave a hundred; if he said a hundred, they gave a thousand, for so Yudhistra had told them to do. At last, after ten days, when he became tired of giving so lavishly, Kuru brought his sacrifice to an end. Everyone ate and drank as much as he desired, while actors and dancers made merry to entertain the guests.

On the day of the full moon, he put off his royal robes and dressed himself in deerskins. He honored with lovely flowers the palace in which he had lived and gave rich presents to his servants. Then the sacrificial fire that he worshiped each day was taken up so that he might carry it with him, and he set out on his journey.

Kunti, also, wanted to go to the woods, to take care of the king and queen, for he was blind and Gandhari, all her life, had covered her eyes so that she might share all that her lord suffered. The sons of Kunti begged her to stay with them, for they could not bear to think of her living in the forest in her old age.

"Why do you wish to abandon us, O Mother?" asked Yudhistra. "Do you no longer care for us? Long ago when we were exiled, when we escaped from the blazing house, during all our misfortunes, it was you who gave us courage. Are you now going to turn away from those Kshatria duties which you taught us all our lives? Do not leave us now!" Kunti heard him with tears in her eyes, but was silent.

Then Bhima said, "When, after so much grief, the kingdom is ours at last, and you are free to enjoy all that your sons have won for you, why do you wish to live away from them? We were born in the forest; why did you bring us out of it when we were children if you desire to return and live there now that we have won the earth? Stay with us, O Mother! Behold, the sons of Madri are overwhelmed by sorrow! Do not leave us!"

"By the spell that a Brahman taught me in my girlhood I gave you gods for your fathers," she answered. "By that same spell these twins were born of Madri. I brought you out of the forest so that your fame should never die and that the line of Pandu might live forever. When you were unfortunate and had lost everything, I put courage and high thoughts into your minds so that you might not live watching the faces of others, dependent on them for your food. I put courage into your hearts so that you would regain your kingdom and that the wrongs of this dear daughter of mine, Dráupadi, might be avenged. But now that you have won wealth and happiness, I do not desire to enjoy them with you any longer; rather, by my own efforts, I wish to reach those regions of bliss where my husband, Pandu, dwells. Therefore do not entreat me, my sons. Be always devoted to righteousness and let your minds be always great."

Then the Pándavas were ashamed and tried no longer to hold her back. She walked ahead, bearing on her shoulder the hand of Gandhari, while Kuru walked trustingly behind his wife, his hand on her shoulder. Vídura and Sánjaya went with them, too. Yudhistra and his brothers, with all the ladies of the royal household, weeping and lamenting, walked with them out of the city, and all the citizens with their wives and children came out into the streets from every side. They were as much distressed by the old king's departure as they had been years before by the departure of the Pándavas after their defeat at dice. Ladies who had never seen the sun or the moon came out into the streets, and great was the grief and uproar as Kuru, trembling with weakness, walked with difficulty through the city and out of its gate. There he bade all those citizens to return to their homes and said farewell to the Pándavas. They walked around the king and queen and their mother, saluting them with devotion, and returned sorrowfully to the city.

On that day, Kuru and his companions reached a place outside the city on the bank of the Ganges and rested there for the night. Brahmans lit the sacred fires, poured libations upon them and worshiped the thousand-rayed sun as it was setting. Vídura and Sánjaya made a bed of grass for the king and near his bed another for Gandhari, while close to her the excellent Kunti laid herself happily down. Vídura and Sánjaya slept within hearing of those three; the Brahmans who had come with the king chanted many sacred hymns, while the holy fires blazed forth around them and the night seemed delightful to them all.

The next morning Kuru and those who had come with him continued their journey to Kuru Kshetra, to the hermitage of the holy Vyasa. There Kuru was initiated into the forest dweller's life and at once began to train his body and his mind, fasting and meditating, clad in bark and skins, with his hair unkempt. All that he did, Gandhari and Kunti did also, and Vídura and Sánjaya began to purify their hearts and minds of all sin.

The Dead Arise

After those blessed ones had left them, the five brothers were very sad and talked constantly about their elders, wondering how they were bearing the hard life of the forest when they were used to every comfort and pleasure; they were so anxious, indeed, that they took no delight in anything and did not even attend to their kingly duties. Finally they decided that they must go to the forest to see their mother and the king and queen; Dráupadi also longed to see Kunti once more. So Yudhistra commanded: "Let the elephants and chariots and horses be prepared to go forth to Kuru Kshetra! Let all the carriages and closed litters for the ladies be made ready, and carts to carry the food and clothing and treasure that we shall need! If any of the citizens wish to see King Kuru, let them come with us!"

He waited for five days for the citizens who wished to go with him and then set forth with all his household, followed by a great number of chariots and elephants and carts, while many people from the city and the neighboring towns followed on foot. Bhima, that son of the Wind-God, rode on an elephant as huge as a hill; the two sons of Madri rode on two swift steeds, and Arjuna went in his own chariot, drawn by his white horses.

They traveled slowly, resting by the banks of lakes and rivers, until they reached Kuru Kshetra, crossed the river Jumna, and saw in the distance the hermitage of Vyasa. They were filled with joy as they entered the forest, where they dismounted and went on foot to the hermitage, while the women and their attendants and the citizens followed them. The sages who lived there came out to meet them, and Yudhistra, bowing humbly, asked them, "Where is my sire, the eldest of the Bháratas?" They told him that the king had gone to the river to get water and flowers, and the Pándavas, walking quickly along the path that the sages showed them, saw the three old people coming toward them.

Sadeva ran to Kunti and fell at her feet, weeping, and she raised him up and embraced him, for he had always been her favorite; then she saw the others and hastened toward them, leading Gandhari, who led the king. The Pándavas knelt down before her, and the old king, knowing them by their voices and their touch, greeted them and comforted them. They rose and took the jars of water from their elders and walked back along the path with them. Then Dráupadi and the ladies of the court, followed by all the citizens, came forward to greet the king, and Yudhistra presented each one to his uncle, telling him the name and the family of every one. Surrounded by them all, the old monarch, with tears of joy in his eyes, felt that he was back in his own city, for the forest retreat was filled with crowds of men and women, all desiring to see him and to do him honor.

"Where is Vídura?" asked Yudhistra, "I do not see him here. I hope that he and Sánjaya are well and at peace."

"Vídura is well, my son," answered Kuru, "but he has taken hard vows and is living on air alone. He lives in the deep forest, but is sometimes seen by the Brahmans."

While the old king was speaking, Yudhistra saw Vídura at a distance, coming toward the hermitage; but when he saw so many people there, he turned and walked swiftly back into the deep forest. Yudhistra followed him, sometimes seeing him, then losing sight of him, calling to him, "Vídura, O Vídura! I am Yudhistra, your favorite!" At last with great difficulty he caught up with his uncle in a solitary spot in the forest. Vídura was leaning against a tree; he was exceedingly thin, his hair was unkempt, and his body hardly clothed. Yudhistra bowed before him and said again, "I am the eldest son of Kunti," but Vídura looked at him steadfastly and said nothing, for he was deep in meditation. Then Yudhistra saw that the life had fled out of his uncle's body, though it still leaned against the tree. At the same time he felt that a wonderful thing was happening within himself, for he was aware of new virtue and power, and he understood that his uncle's life had entered into him, because of Vídura's love for him and the power of his soul. He returned and told his brothers and the old king what had happened, and they were all filled with wonder. They talked long about Vídura, remembering his wisdom, his love for all his family, and his good counsel.

Then the Pándavas ate the fruits and the roots and drank the water that Kuru gave them, spread grass for their beds under a tree near their mother and lay down to sleep.

The five brothers, with Dráupadi and the other ladies of the royal household, spent about a month very happily in the forest. Toward the end of that time the holy Vyasa came back to the hermitage. He had been far distant, but he always watched over the Pándavas, and because he knew all things, he came to them when they needed him. They gathered about him, and there was excellent talk about things human and divine, for they always asked his counsel. When they had talked for a long time, he said to the blind king, "I know that you are burning with grief because of your children, O King of kings. I know the sorrow that dwells in the hearts of Gandhari and Dráupadi and the grief Subadra bears because of Abimanyu. I have come here to grant you any wish that you desire, for I have gained enough soul power to fulfill the dearest desires of your hearts."

"My mind," answered Kuru, after thinking for a while, "is always tortured by the memory of the wicked deeds of my son. Many high-souled kings followed him and were killed. What has been the fate, O sinless one, of those men who were killed for his sake? What has been the fate of my sons and my grandsons? This thought burns my heart day and night and gives me no peace."

Gandhari also, her eyes covered, joined her hands and said to the sage, "O holy one, we, too, the wives and mothers of those high-souled heroes, can have no peace. What has been their fate, O mighty seer? You alone can free us from our grief."

When Gandhari had spoken, Kunti thought of her secretly-born son, that child of Surya. Vyasa saw her sorrow and said to her, "Tell me, O blessed one, what is in your heart."

And she, bowing her head to the sage, said shyly, "O foremost of sages, I cast onto the water my infant son Karna, and I never said that he was mine, even though he knew me for his mother when he was grown. For this reason he met his death. I pray you to tell me the fate of this first-born son of mine."

"Cast off all your doubts," Vyasa answered. "You shall behold Karna, and you, O Gandhari, shall behold your sons and brothers and kinsmen this very night, like men risen from sleep. Dráupadi shall behold her five sons, her father, and her brothers, and Subadra shall see Abimanyu. Before you asked me, this thought was in my mind. Go to the Ganges, for there you shall see all who were slain on the field of battle."

Kuru with his companions and the Pándavas with all those who had come with them went to the bank of the Ganges, and the day seemed to them as long as a whole year, so greatly did they long for the night to come. When the sun set, they bathed in the sacred stream, and when they had finished their evening worship, they came to Vyasa. Kuru, with purified mind and heart, sat beside the sage with the Pándavas, while Gandhari, with Kunti and Dráupadi and the wives of Kuru's sons, sat in a more retired place, and all the people who had come from the city took their places according to their ages.

Then Vyasa entered the Ganges and with mighty soul power summoned all those dead warriors who had fought with the Pándavas and those who had fought with the Kúravas. At his word, a deafening uproar, like that which had been heard on the battlefield, arose from within the waters, and those kings, headed by Bhishma and Drona, with all their troops, rose by thousands from the waters of the sacred river. There were Virata and the king of Panchala, with their sons and their armies; there were Abimanyu and the sons of Dráupadi; there were Karna, Duryodha, and the other sons of Kuru, headed by Dushasa; there were the mighty Shákuni, the kings of Sind and Madra and many others, the list of whose names would be too long to tell, with their sons and their armies. All of them rose from the Ganges with shining bodies, each one equipped as he had been on the field of battle, each one with his standard, but now they were clothed in heavenly garments and all wore brilliant earrings and fresh garlands. They were free from all anger, pride, or jealousy, and Gandharvas sang their praises.

Through the power of his soul, Vyasa opened the eyes of Kuru for this night, and the old king beheld for the first time his children and was filled with joy. Gandhari then uncovered her eyes and saw her sons and kinsmen who had been slain. All that were assembled there beheld, with steadfast gaze and wondering hearts, that glorious spectacle.

Then those mighty men, free of anger and jealousy, met one another with happy hearts; sons met fathers and mothers; wives met husbands; friends met friends. It was like a high carnival, so great was the rejoicing. The Pándavas met Abimanyu and their sons by Dráupadi; with happy hearts they went to Karna and were reconciled with their brother. All those warriors forgot their quarrel and talked together in peace and friendship. The women who saw again their husbands and sons, their fathers and brothers, forgot their grief and were filled with delight. The whole night was spent thus in great happiness, as if the place were heaven itself, for there was no fear, no grief, and no reproach.

When the night had passed, those heroes and their wives, mothers, and sisters embraced and took their leave of one another, and the holy Vyasa dismissed that host that had risen from the water. In the twinkling of an eye they vanished in the sight of all those living people, plunging into the river with their chariots and their standards, their horses and all their followers, returning to their heavenly abodes. Some among them went to the highest region of heaven; some went to the regions of the gods who protect the earth. All had died in battle without turning their backs to the foe, and therefore had attained to regions of bliss.

After they had gone, the mighty Vyasa, who was still standing in the waters of the sacred river, spoke to those women whose husbands had been slain, saying, "Those among you who wish to share the blissful regions where your husbands dwell may now plunge into the Ganges!" And many of those women, trusting his words, plunged into the river, and then,

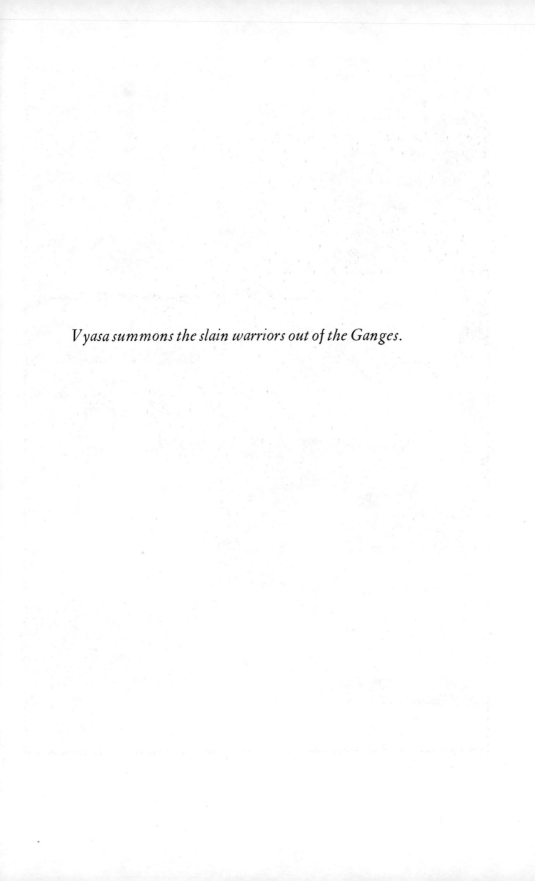

Vyasa summons the slain warriors out of the Ganges.

freed from their human bodies and clad in shining forms clothed in heavenly garments and adorned with jewels and garlands, they joined their husbands in the happy regions where they dwelt.

When Kuru had beheld that exceedingly wonderful sight, the reappearance of his children, his heart was free of all grief. He returned to the hermitage and shortly after summoned Yudhistra and said to him, "O sinless one, the purpose of my life has now been fulfilled. I shall take even harder vows and I shall not live long. You have served me in every way that a son can serve his father; therefore go now and do not tarry here any longer. The burdens of the Bhárata realm have fallen upon you, my son, and you know all the duties of a king. Depart now, either tomorrow or this very day, and my blessing go with you!"

Gandhari and Kunti spoke in the same way, and so the five brothers, with the permission and the blessing of their elders, took their leave of them. Bhima forgot his anger toward his uncle and showed his love and obedience to the old king, who comforted and embraced him. Then the shouts of charioteers were heard, the grunting of elephants and the neighing of horses, and King Yudhistra, with his followers and his animals, his litters and chariots, set out for Hástina, leaving the old people happy in the silence of the forest.

The Sacred Flame

Two years after the Pándavas had returned from the forest, Vyasa came again to Hástina. When he was rested and refreshed, he told the king that he had recently come from the Ganges, whereupon Yudhistra asked him eagerly, "Have you seen my royal sire there, O holy one? Are he and my mother,

are Gandhari and Sánjaya well and at peace? How goes it
with them?"

"Listen, O King, with calmness," answered Vyasa, "as I tell
you what I have heard about them. When you left them, the
king went deeper into the woods, with the two queens,
Sánjaya, and the two Brahmans who were with them. He took
hard vows; he fed on air alone and spoke to no one. In six
months nothing was left of him but skin and bones, and he
was greatly honored by all the others who dwelt in the forest.
Gandhari lived on water alone, while Kunti took a little food
once a month, and Sánjaya ate a little every sixth day. They had
no fixed dwelling, but wandered through the woods, Sánjaya
guiding them over the rough ground, Kunti leading Gandhari,
who led the king.

"One day they came to the bank of the Ganges, and the king
had his sacrificial fire duly lighted. When he had performed
his worship with it, the Brahmans cast the embers out into the
woods, and they then went on their way. The smoldering
embers set fire to the woods; a wind arose and fanned it into
mighty flames that burned the forest all around that place.
Animals and snakes hurried to the nearest marshes and rivers,
but the king, as he felt the fire coming nearer from all sides,
was unable to move, for he was weak from lack of food. He
said to Sánjaya, 'Go quickly where the flames cannot reach
you. As for us, we shall let our bodies be destroyed and our
souls shall be freed. Death by water, fire, wind, or starvation is
good for forest dwellers. Therefore leave us, good Sánjaya.'

"Then the king sat down, facing the east, and concentrated
his mind and all his senses; he sat like a post of wood and the
highly blessed Gandhari and Kunti, your mother, did likewise. They met their death thus, consumed by their own sacred
flame. Sánjaya left them and escaped; he came to our hermitage

and I heard from him all that I have told you. Shortly afterward he departed, going toward the Himalayas. No one in the hermitage grieved for the king and those two queens, for they met the fire of their own free wills and died with their souls at peace. O King of kings, you, too, must not grieve for them, but perform the needful rites in their honor, with your brothers."

Nevertheless, the sons of Pandu grieved deeply for their mother, for the blind king and the faultless Gandhari. They sent to the forest and gathered the ashes of their bodies, and the funeral ceremonies were duly performed, with perfumes and garlands and the giving of many gifts.

Even so did King Kuru leave this world, after spending fifteen years under the rule of Yudhistra and three years in the forest.

The Ascent to Heaven

Gandhari's Curse

After his uncle's death, Yudhistra sadly took up the burden of royalty and ruled justly over the earth for twenty years. In the twentieth year after Kuru's death, the thirty-sixth year after the great battle, that lord of men beheld many unusual omens. Hot strong winds blew from every direction and birds flew in circles; the horizon seemed always to be covered with fog, meteors fell on the earth, and there were fierce circles of light around the sun and the moon. These and many other omens foreboding evil and danger filled the hearts of men with fear and anxiety.

Shortly afterward, a messenger came from Dváraka, the city of Krishna, to say that all the Yadu warriors had slain one another and that Krishna himself was dead; none remained alive but the old king, his father. The curse of Gandhari, uttered on the field of Kuru Kshetra, had thus been fulfilled.

To the Pándavas, the death of Krishna was like the drying up of the ocean. They could scarcely believe it and were filled with sorrow and despair.

The messenger told them that Krishna, when his kinsmen had all been slain, summoned him and said, "Go to Hástina and tell Arjuna about this slaughter of the Yadus. Bid him come here quickly."

Then he said to his father, "Arjuna will come here soon; protect the women of our household until he arrives. He and I are but one person; he will do whatever is best for the women and the children and the citizens, and he will perform your funeral rites. After he has gone, this city, with all its palaces and walls, will be swallowed up by the ocean. As for myself, I shall go to some holy place and await my hour."

With these words, he touched his father's feet with his forehead and quickly left him. He then went to the forest, where he wandered about thoughtfully for a while and finally sat down in a solitary place. He knew that this calamity had come because of the curse of Gandhari, uttered so long ago, and that the hour of his own departure from the world was at hand, for he knew the destiny of all things; therefore he concentrated all his senses and his mind and lay down in deep meditation. A fierce hunter came through the forest, chasing deer. When he saw Krishna lying there clad in yellow robes, he mistook him for a deer and pierced his heel with an arrow; then running forward to seize his prey, he saw instead a man absorbed in meditation and was overcome by fear and remorse. Krishna comforted him and then cast off his body and rose into heaven, filling the sky with light.

When Arjuna received the message of Krishna, he set out at once for the city of Dváraka to see the old king, who was his uncle, the brother of Kunti. Dváraka, bereft of its princes and warriors, looked like a woman just widowed, like a lotus flower in winter, its beauty wilted. Arjuna went quickly into the palace and touched the feet of the king, who said to him, weeping, "Krishna told me that you would come, O son of Kunti. Do now all that he asked of you! This kingdom, with all its women and children and its wealth, is yours now. As for myself, I shall cast my life away, for it is no longer dear to me."

"O Uncle, I can no longer bear to look upon the earth when that hero of unfading glory has left it," Arjuna answered. "My brothers and Dráupadi feel as I do. The time for our departure from the world is also at hand, but I shall first take to Indra Prastha the women, the children, and the citizens of this town. On the seventh day from today, at sunrise, we shall set out." Then he ordered all the women of the palace and the people of the city to prepare themselves for the journey. He spent that night in the palace of Krishna, sorrowing for his friend, and at dawn he heard that the old king had given up his life.

After he had paid all due honor to the father of Krishna, Arjuna mounted his chariot on the seventh day and set out from the city, followed by the wives and children of the Yadu heroes, riding in litters and in carts drawn by mules and bullocks, while the citizens and the inhabitants of the country traveled on foot and on horseback, in chariots and carts, carrying with them all that they possessed. After they had left the city, the ocean poured into it; as they left each part of the land, the ocean immediately covered it with its salt waters. Beholding this, they hurried on, following Arjuna, who traveled by slow marches so that they could rest in pleasant woods and by the side of lakes and rivers.

When they came into the Land of the Five Rivers, he set up a camp, for the land abounded in grain and in cattle, and both the people and the animals were in need of food. A band of robbers saw those lordless ladies escorted only by Arjuna, and the sinful wretches said to one another, "Here is only one warrior with a crowd of women and children and unarmed men, carrying much wealth. They are easy prey."

Armed with clubs, they attacked the camp of the Yadus, frightening them with great shouts and slaying anyone who stood against them. Arjuna heard them, took up his mighty bow and went forth to meet them. He tried to string Gandíva, but was barely able to do it, for he was old, his strength had left him, and he had lived in peace for many years. He summoned the heavenly weapons that he had won from Indra, but they did not come to him, for it was long since he had used them. The citizens and attendants of the Yadus were fighting furiously against the robbers with any weapon they could find, and Arjuna, too, pierced them with his arrows, but these were soon used up, whereas formerly his quivers had been always full. He did his best to protect the people who were in his care, but he was not able to drive the robbers off, and he was deeply ashamed, feeling the loss of his power. The camp was large, the robbers attacked it in different places, and before his very eyes they carried off many of the women with all their wealth.

Filled with sorrow and sighing deeply, he went on with those who remained and with the wealth that the bandits had not been able to carry away. He settled some of the people in various cities and led the rest to Indra Prastha, where the Pándavas first had their kingdom. He gave that beautiful city to the great-grandson of Krishna and left there the last of the men and women who had come with him from Dváraka.

When he had taken care of them all, he went to the hermitage of Vyasa at Kuru Kshetra to see that holy sage who

always helped them when they were in need. He found the
island-born one seated in a solitary place and bowed before
him, saying, "I am Arjuna." The holy one welcomed him and
bade him be seated; then, seeing that he sighed so deeply and
was filled with despair, he asked Arjuna the cause of his
unhappiness.

"Alas," answered that son of Kunti, "my friend of im-
measurable soul, he who wielded the discus and the mace, who
was dark-skinned and dressed in yellow robes, whose eyes
were like lotus petals—he has cast off his body and risen to
heaven, while his kinsmen have slaughtered one another in
battle. Without him I no longer desire to live. But a still more
painful thing has happened, O best of men, which is breaking
my heart. Before my very eyes many of the Yadu women,
whom Krishna had entrusted to me, were carried off by
robbers in the Land of the Five Rivers. When I took up my
bow, I could hardly bend it; my weapons did not appear, and
my arrows were soon used up. The might of my arms has left
me. Tell me now, O sinless one, what I must do, for I wander
with an empty heart, having lost my friend, my kinsmen and
my power."

"Do not grieve for what has happened," Vyasa answered
him, "for it was ordained and could not have happened otherwise. You and your brothers have now fulfilled the purpose of
your lives and have been crowned with success. The time has
come for you to leave the world. Time brings everything to
birth and again time withdraws everything from life, at its
pleasure. One becomes mighty and then loses his power and
becomes weak. One becomes a master and rules others; then
he loses his mastery and serves others. Your weapons brought
you power and glory and then they returned to the gods who
gave them to you. Now you must leave your son's son on the

throne of the Bháratas, and with your brothers, seek the highest goal of life, the freedom of the soul. Leave your home and cast away your sacrificial fires, calling nothing your own, fixing your hearts on God, and follow that path from which there is no returning."

The Last Pilgrimage

Arjuna took his leave of the holy one and returned to Hástina, where he told Yudhistra all that had occurred. The just king answered, "Time cooks all creatures in his caldron; time brings all things to pass. Let us gladly follow Vyasa's counsel and leave the world!"

Bhima and the sons of Madri agreed wholeheartedly with the king's resolve, and they prepared for their journey, after providing for the welfare of the kingdom.

Yudhistra placed Abimanyu's son on the throne. He was thirty-six years old, as strong and beautiful as his father and his father's father, and the Pándavas had taught him all they knew of wisdom and duty and of skill in arms. The king said to Subadra, "This son of your son is now the king of the Bháratas. He will rule in Hástina, while the great-grandson of Krishna rules in Indra Prastha. Watch over them and counsel them to follow always the path of virtue."

Then he summoned all the people from the city and the leaders of all the castes from the provinces and told them what he desired to do, asking their permission, as Kuru had done many years before. They listened anxiously and said to him, "This must not happen." But he did not listen to them, for his heart was set on leaving the world, and at last he persuaded them to consent to it.

He cast off his royal robes and dressed in cloth made from

the bark of trees; his brothers and Dráupadi dressed themselves also in bark and skins, just as they had done when they went out of the city after their defeat at dice; but this time the Pándavas were happy to be starting on their journey. Yudhistra gave rich gifts of robes and jewels to the Brahmans in memory of Krishna and asked the blessings of the gods on their purpose. Then they cast their sacred fires into the water and took their leave of everyone in the palace.

The five brothers and Dráupadi walked out from the gate of the city named after the elephant, Yudhistra leading them. After him came Bhima, with Arjuna walking behind him, and then the twins in the order of their births; last of all came Dráupadi, the best of women, large-eyed and beautiful, and a dog followed them. The citizens and the royal household went with them for a distance, but no one dared to ask the king to stay. Then those high-souled ones, their minds fixed on God, turned their faces toward the east and began their pilgrimage.

They traversed many countries and rivers, as they had done during their exile in the forest, until they reached the sea. Arjuna was still carrying Gandíva and his two quivers, for he could not bear to part with them. Now, at the shore of the sea, the Pándavas beheld Agni, the smoke-bannered God of Fire, standing before them like a hill, blocking their way. The god said to them, "You heroic sons of Pandu, scorchers of your foes, listen to what I say. Let Arjuna now cast aside his great bow, for he has no longer any need of it. This Gandíva was given to me by Varuna, lord of waters, and I in turn gave it to Arjuna when the Kándava forest was burned. Let him now return it to Varuna."

And Arjuna hurled into the ocean the bow and the two quivers, and Agni disappeared from their sight.

At the seacoast they turned their faces toward the south, then the southwest and the west, for they wished to go round the whole earth. In the west they saw how the city of Dváraka had been covered by the ocean; thence they turned to the north. They controlled their senses and concentrated their minds, for they strove to purify and to free their souls so that they might enter the blissful regions of heaven. They beheld the mighty Himalayas and crossed them, as they had done before; they passed the Gandamádana, where they had met Arjuna and had been so happy. Then they came to Mount Meru, that highest of all peaks, which rises from the center of the earth and leads to heaven. Each rapt in his own thought, the Pándavas began to climb that heavenly peak; Dráupadi, as strong of soul as they, came after them, and the dog followed her.

When they had climbed a long way, Dráupadi weakened, fell down on the earth and died. Seeing her fall, Bhima said to Yudhistra, who walked before him, "O lord of earth, this princess never did any sinful deed. Why has she fallen down and died?"

Yudhistra said, "She always loved Arjuna better than the rest of us; because she was partial to him, she has fallen down now." And Yudhistra went on, his mind withdrawn into itself.

Then Sadeva, the learned one, fell dead upon the earth, and Bhima asked, "Alas, this son of Madri has served us all so faithfully and humbly; why has he fallen down?"

"He thought that no one was his equal in wisdom," Yudhistra answered. "For that fault he has now fallen on the earth." The king went on, leaving Sadeva there, and the others followed.

When Nákula saw that both Dráupadi and his brother had fallen, he himself fell down and died, for he loved them dearly. And Bhima said to the king, "This brother of ours was always righteous and obeyed us and was more beautiful than any other man; behold, Nákula, too, has fallen down and has died!"

"His soul was righteous and he was wise," answered Yudhistra, "but he believed that no one equaled him in beauty, and for this fault he has fallen." And he went on, followed by his two brothers and the dog.

That slayer of foes, Arjuna of the white steeds, beholding Dráupadi and the two sons of Madri dead, fell down in great grief of heart and died. When he who was the equal of Indra fell, Bhima said to the king, "I do not remember an untrue word ever spoken by this high-souled brother of ours; even in jest he never said anything that was false. Why then has he fallen on the earth?"

"He said that he would slay all our foes in a single day, and that he did not do," Yudhistra answered. "He was proud of his heroism and thought himself better than any bowman on earth. For this reason he has fallen." With these words the king went on.

Then Bhima fell. Lying on the earth, he cried to his brother, "Lo, I, whom you love best, have fallen! Why has this come to pass?"

"You were a great eater," Yudhistra said, "and you boasted of your strength. O Bhima, when you were eating, you did not care about other people's needs. For this fault you have fallen." And Yudhistra went on without looking back at his dead brother, with only the dog to follow him.

Then Indra, making the earth and sky tremble with his thunder, came to Yudhistra in his shining chariot and asked him to mount it. But Yudhistra said to that god of a thousand eyes, "My brothers have all fallen down upon this mountain; they must go with me. The delicate princess Dráupadi, who deserves every happiness, must also go with us, for we have never been separated from one another. I do not wish to go to heaven without them, O lord of all the gods."

"You shall behold your brothers in heaven," Indra said, "for they have cast off their human bodies and have reached it before you. You shall see them there with Dráupadi, in heavenly bodies and raiment. But it is ordained that you shall go there in this very body of yours."

"O lord of the past and present," Yudhistra said, "this dog is devoted to me, and my heart is full of pity for him. Let him go with me!"

"You have attained today the highest goal of life," Indra said to him, "eternal life and all the joys of heaven. There is no place in heaven for dogs; therefore leave him, O King!"

"It is a great sin," answered Yudhistra, "to abandon a devoted creature or one who seeks protection, one who is suffering or one who is afraid. Therefore, O mighty Indra, I shall not leave this dog for all the joys of heaven. I cannot give him up as long as my own life lasts."

"You abandoned your brothers and Dráupadi," said the lord of heaven. "You have given up everything. Why then can you not give up this dog?"

"Everyone knows that neither love nor hatred can touch the dead," Yudhistra said. "When my brothers and Dráupadi died, I left them because I could not bring them to life again, but I did not leave them while they were still alive. O god of a thousand eyes, the dog lives and I cannot leave him."

As he spoke these words, the dog vanished, and Dharma, the God of Justice, the father of the king, appeared in his place and said to his son, "I am well pleased with you, O King of kings, for you have compassion for all creatures. I tested you once in the forest by the lake where all your brothers seemed to have met their death. You chose that Nákula should be brought to life, so that he might carry on the line of his mother, Madri. Now you have given up the very hope of heaven for the sake of this dog, whose shape I took to test you. Truly, no one in heaven is your equal and infinite happiness awaits you."

Then Indra and Dharma, taking Yudhistra with them, went up into heaven from the mountain top, making the sky blaze with their glory. The other gods and the holy sages came out to meet them and all that concourse of gods welcomed the king and praised him.

Yudhistra Enters Heaven

When Yudhistra arrived in heaven, he beheld Duryodha seated on a throne, wearing all the glorious emblems that belong to heroes and shining like the sun. His anger blazed up and he turned away, saying loudly to his companions, "I do not wish to share eternal happiness with Duryodha, who was defiled by greed and jealousy. It was his fault that friends and kinsmen, over the whole earth, were slaughtered. You mighty ones, I do not even wish to see him! Wherever my brothers and Dráupadi are, there I want to be."

Indra said to him, smiling, "Do not speak so, O King of kings! In heaven all hatreds cease. Duryodha poured forth his life in the sacrifice of battle; he fulfilled the duties of his caste and was never afraid. Therefore he has earned the reward of heroes. You should not remember any longer the wrongs that he did you. Meet him courteously, O lord of men! This is heaven, and there is no hatred here."

But Yudhistra said, "If Duryodha, that sinful one for whose sake the whole earth was emptied of its warriors, who did us such wrong, dwells in these blissful regions, I wish to see the place where dwell those high-souled heroes, my brothers, who

Indra comes to take Yudhistra to heaven.

faithfully kept their promises, spoke the truth, and were so brave. I do not see here that son of Kunti, the noble Karna, or the king of Panchala or Virata, or the sons of Dráupadi, or Abimanyu, or all those other great warriors who also poured their lives as sacrifice on the fire of battle and met their deaths for my sake. I do not see them here, O lord of heaven! If they have not been worthy to dwell in this high place, then know that without these brothers and kinsmen of mine I will not dwell here either. I wish to see Bhima, who is dearer to me than my life, the godlike Arjuna and the twins, who were mighty in prowess; I wish to see the righteous princess of Panchala. You gods, heaven is where they are; to me no other place is heaven."

The gods said, "If you long to go there, then go without delay, O son of Kunti! For we wish to do whatever is pleasing to you." And they ordered a heavenly messenger to take Yudhistra where his friends and kinsmen were.

Then the messenger and the royal son of Kunti set forth, the messenger going first and the king following. They went along a steep and dangerous path through murky darkness; the ground was covered with moss and hair, and the path was slippery with blood and foul with the stench of rotting bodies. Beside it were trees whose leaves were sharp as swords, and crows and vultures with iron beaks sat on the branches. A river filled with boiling water ran beside the path; its sands were hot as embers, and its rocks were iron; thorn bushes grew beside it. Beholding all these frightful things, Yudhistra asked the messenger, "What place is this and how far must we go to reach the place where my brothers dwell?"

The heavenly messenger stopped and said, "The gods commanded me to bring you here, O King of kings, and then to return. If you are weary, you may turn back with me." Yudhis-

tra was dazed by the foul sights and smells and sorely grieved
at heart, so he turned back to retrace his steps, when he heard
pitiful voices all around him. "O son of Dharma, stay with us!
When you drew near, fragrant breezes blew upon us. Great joy
is ours at seeing you, O best of men. O stay but a few moments
more, that our joy may continue!"

These words, spoken with pain, made the king stand still,
for the voices seemed familiar to him, although he could not
say whose they might be. Therefore he asked, "Who are you?
Why are you here in this dreadful place?"

And they answered from all sides, "I am Karna!" "I am
Bhima!" "I am Arjuna!" "I am Nákula!" "I am Sadeva!" and
"I am Dráupadi!" "We are Dráupadi's sons!" Even so did those
voices speak in painful tones.

"What unjust fate is this?" Yudhistra asked himself. "What
sinful deeds were done by these virtuous ones that they should
dwell in this dark and frightful place, while Kuru's son is
enthroned in heaven? Am I asleep or awake? Is this a night-
mare of my disordered mind?"

Then he was filled with anger against the gods and against
the God of Justice himself, the mighty Dharma. He turned to
the celestial guide and said, "Go back to those whose messenger
you are and tell them that I shall not return, but shall stay here,
since my presence brings comfort to these suffering brothers
of mine." And the messenger went back and told Indra all
that the king had said.

A moment afterward, all the gods with Indra leading them
came to the place where Yudhistra stood. As they approached,
the darkness vanished; the boiling river and the iron rocks, the
thorn trees and the fearsome birds were there no longer, and a
cool, pure breeze brought the fragrance of blossoming boughs
and flowers.

Indra spoke comforting words to Yudhistra, saying, "Come, come, O chief of men, this delusion is ended. Hell should be beheld by every king, and I gave you a sight of it for your own good. On the battlefield, you deceived Drona, telling him that his son was dead; therefore you, too, have been deceived by this sight and by the voices of your brothers and kinsmen. They, too, have been shown this place of sinners, and all of them have been cleansed of any wrong they have done. They and all those kings who fought for you and were slain in battle have gone to heaven. Come and behold them, O chief of the Bháratas! Come and enjoy the reward of all your good deeds, your gifts and sacrifices and the labor of your soul. The place that you have won is far above that of kings; it is where Haris Chandra dwells with all the holy sages. There you will live in bliss. Behold this river, called the heavenly Ganges, which flows through the three worlds. Bathe in this, and your human form and nature will leave you. You will be free of grief and anger and ready to mount to the highest heaven."

Then Dharma, the God of Righteousness, also spoke to his son, "I am greatly pleased with you, O King! This is the third test that I have put you to and I find that you cannot be turned aside from the path of virtue. I examined you once, in the forest, in the form of a crane, and again when I took the shape of a dog. This has been your third test, when you chose to stay in hell for the sake of those you love. You are cleansed of all sin; be happy now!"

Yudhistra, led by Indra and Dharma and the other gods, bathed in the heavenly Ganges, where he cast off his earthly body. Free of grief and anger, he appeared in a shining form, clad in heavenly garments, and went with the gods to the place where his brothers and friends and kinsmen were. There he beheld Krishna, with his blazing celestial weapons, and beside him Arjuna, radiant and happy; there he saw Karna, as splendid as his father, Surya. Bhima stood beside the Wind-God, his father, and the Storm Gods stood near them. With the beautiful Gods of Twilight and Dawn he beheld Nákula and Sadeva, and there, too, was the beloved Dráupadi, adorned with garlands of lotuses. All of them welcomed him with love and joy.

Indra said, "Behold Kuru, your eldest uncle, and the renowned Gandhari, who have come to this place because of the power of the penances they performed in the forest. There is your father, that mighty bowman, Pandu, with his two wives, Kunti and Madri. He often comes to see me in his chariot. There is the royal Bhishma and there is Drona. The kings who fought for you and those who fought against you, O lord of earth, have slowly won their way to this happy place, for they have conquered heaven by the virtue of their thoughts, their words and deeds, and by the sacrifice of their lives in battle.

"All sin and grief is ended, O best of men, and everlasting happiness is yours!"

About the Author

Forty-five years ago, Elizabeth Seeger, then a teacher of history and literature at the Dalton School in New York City, introduced a year of Oriental history into the curriculum and a companion course in Oriental literature. Subsequently, she wrote *Pageant of Chinese History* because, she says, "there was not one in existence for children at the time." This book, along with her later *Pageant of Russian History* (both published by David McKay), still continues to be widely read.

Miss Seeger hopes that this book and her forthcoming version of the *Ramáyana* will contribute to our increasing knowledge of India and Indian culture.

Miss Seeger lives in Bridgewater, Connecticut, and when not writing she finds pleasure in drawing portraits.

About the Artist

Gordon Laite's magnificent illustrations for the *Mahabhárata* reflect his long interest in and regard for Oriental culture. He has been for many years a member of the Bahá'í Faith, which originated in Persia and whose main theme revolves around the oneness of man.

Mr. Laite has had a distinguished career as an artist. He has had numerous one-man shows of his work, has illustrated more than twenty books, and has appeared in many anthologies as well.

Mr. and Mrs. Laite have made many friends among the Navajo, Hopi and Zuni peoples in the area around Gallup, New Mexico, where they live. Mr. Laite is honored to have been named "Djahpah" by the Zunis and "Hasteen Ba'ha'jhoni" by the Navajos. Many of his paintings bear these signatures today.